MARIE VON CLAUSEWITZ

MARIE VON CLAUSEWITZ

THE WOMAN BEHIND THE MAKING OF *ON WAR*

VANYA EFTIMOVA BELLINGER

OXFORD
UNIVERSITY PRESS

OXFORD
UNIVERSITY PRESS

Oxford University Press is a department of the University of
Oxford. It furthers the University's objective of excellence in research,
scholarship, and education by publishing worldwide.

Oxford   New York
Auckland   Cape Town   Dar es Salaam   Hong Kong   Karachi
Kuala Lumpur   Madrid   Melbourne   Mexico City   Nairobi
New Delhi   Shanghai   Taipei   Toronto

With offices in
Argentina   Austria   Brazil   Chile   Czech Republic   France   Greece
Guatemala   Hungary   Italy   Japan   Poland   Portugal   Singapore
South Korea   Switzerland   Thailand   Turkey   Ukraine   Vietnam

Oxford is a registered trademark of Oxford University Press
in the UK and certain other countries.

Published in the United States of America by
Oxford University Press
198 Madison Avenue, New York, NY 10016

Library of Congress Cataloging-in-Publication Data
Bellinger, Vanya Eftimova.
Marie von Clausewitz : the woman behind the making of On War / Vanya Eftimova Bellinger.
pages cm
Includes bibliographical references and index.
ISBN 978–0–19–022543–8 (hardback : alkaline paper) —
ISBN 978–0–19–022544–5 — ISBN 978–0–19–022545–2
1. Clausewitz, Marie Sophie von Brühl von, 1779–1836.   2. Clausewitz, Marie Sophie von
Brühl von, 1779–1836—Marriage.   3. Clausewitz, Carl von, 1780–1831—Marriage.
4. Clausewitz, Carl von, 1780–1831. On War—Sources.   5. Clausewitz, Marie Sophie von Brühl
von, 1779–1836—Correspondence.   6. Clausewitz, Carl von, 1780–1831—Correspondence.
7. Generals' spouses—Germany—Biography.   8. Women editors—Germany—Biography.
I. Title.
CT1098.C53.B45 2015
943'.070922—dc23
[B]
2015010789

1 3 5 7 9 8 6 4 2
Printed in the United States of America
on acid-free paper

Contents

List of Illustrations

Figure 0.1. Carl von Clausewitz, after 1830, by Wilhelm Wach. *In Private Hands.*

Figure 0.2. Marie von Clausewitz, after 1810, by François-Josèphe Kinson. *In Private Hands.*

Acknowledgments

My most sincere and heartfelt thanks to my husband, Michael, my greatest supporter and unabashed cheerleader. This book would not have happened without you, babe.

My dad, Eftim, has given me the taste for great literature and powerful narratives. My mother, Penka, showed me long ago what it means to be a successful woman. From the very beginning, my mother and father in law, Kathy and Tom, have embraced me in their very American, unconditional and wholehearted, way. I will be forever grateful to Lili Berbenkova for helping me discover the beauty of the German language.

Throughout the years, an ever-widening circle of friends and associates have supported the research and the writing of this book. Johannes and Lori Allert never grew tired of listening to my litanies and reading my early drafts. Marinela and Martin and Iskra and Lutz offered me their unconditional friendship and guest rooms during my research trips to Berlin. Dr. Kat Cleland, with Virginia Surgery Associates, helped me investigate Marie von Clausewitz's cause of death. Dr. Christopher Bassford patiently read my scattered drafts and encouraged me to work on this project. Clausewitz scholars Peter Pater, Donald Stoker, Andreas Herberg-Rothe, and Paul Donker shared ideas and invaluable advice.

Throughout the years, the team of the Prussian Privy State Archives/ Prussian Cultural Heritage Foundation in Berlin did their outmost to accommodate my research. Indeed, just before Christmas 2012, its director, Dr. Ingeborg Schnelling-Reinicke, sent me an email with the incredible news that the complete correspondence between Marie and Carl von Clausewitz has been deposited at the institution. I will be forever grateful to Dr. Walrab von Buttlar and his wife Vita for deciding to open their family archive to the public.

Mere words cannot express my gratitude to Olaf Thiel and Bernd Domsgen from the Clausewitz society (*Freundeskreis Clausewitz*) in Burg bei Magdeburg. They shared with me their research and enormous collection of unpublished documents, and helped me understand better Carl and Marie von Clausewitz's lives. Thanks to Birgit Heitfeld-Rydzik's tireless work and passion, the Clausewitz papers at Münster University and State Library are finally rearranged and accessible to scholars.

Last but not least, I owe a great debt to my team at Oxford University Press–USA. The editor of this book, Keely Latcham, has been my true partner from day one, throughout the uneasy writing and the exhausting editing and revising. Executive editor Tim Bent supervised the process and saw this project through. Alyssa O'Connell is the best editorial assistant any author could ask for. The rest of the team has done their best so this book can happen. Thank you all!

Introduction

It is one of history's great ironies that the West's seminal treatise on war—an activity traditionally inseparable from constructions of masculinity—was edited and published by a woman. For the last two hundred years up to the present, the military realm, still blatantly dominated by men, has passionately debated Carl von Clausewitz's book *On War*. It remains perhaps the most influential study of the nature of organized violence ever written. Clausewitz's observations and precepts lie at the heart of modern military doctrine—indeed they form its foundation. Taken as the bible of warfare, *On War* has been translated into every major language (in Chinese alone there are over thirty different editions). It has been applied to virtually all conflicts since its publication nearly two centuries ago, including irregular conflicts and, most recently, to the asymmetrical violence known as global terrorism. Its most famous premise, that war is a continuation of politics with other means, has come to dominate the arenas of foreign policy and conflict resolution.

Among these various interpretations, the first and arguably most far-reaching was of Marie von Clausewitz, but her impact has been missing from the debate about *On War*, despite the fact that she was and remains a constant fixture in Carl's life and achievements. Scholars frequently cite the twenty-six letters Marie wrote to the famous military theorist and credit her with preserving his seminal work after his death and seeing it through to publication. Even the first biography—by Karl Schwartz and dating from 1878—bears the joint name *The Life of General Carl von Clausewitz and Madam Marie von Clausewitz*, born Countess von Brühl.[1] Yet at the same time Marie has remained virtually unknown, and her influence has been underappreciated and understudied. A long list of questions surrounds her personal life and her involvement with the writing of *On War*, and every new work about Clausewitz seems to add to these unanswered questions.

At the heart of the questions is Marie herself. Was she instrumental in the development of her husband's ideas, or just a sympathetic and passive listener? What part did the social divide between the countess and the young aspiring officer play in their marriage? Was Marie a fervent German nationalist, and did she also radicalize her beloved in 1808–1809? What prevented her from stopping Carl when, just a little over a year after their wedding, he decided to resign and transfer to the Russian service, a seemingly reckless act that irreversibly affected his military career? And perhaps most significantly, after his death, did Marie complicate the understanding of Clausewitz's seminal theory by mistakenly mixing the time sequence of his last notes?

Without even one lengthy published study devoted specifically to Marie's role, it is no wonder that her story contains numerous contradictions, speculations, and outright errors. Both objective and subjective factors have contributed to this. Carl von Clausewitz's biography has been mainly of interest to military historians, and this field lags considerably when it comes to studying women's roles and the homefront.[2] Then too, even when scholars have recognized the unusual nature of Carl and Marie's intellectual partnership, they based their understanding on only a few of her published letters and writings, sources that are far too insufficient for a detailed examination. Yet Marie was the one who posthumously preserved, edited, and published Clausewitz's lifework. The lack of scholarly attention to her involvement and the decisions she made after his death, therefore, have meant that the nature and magnitude of her part in editing and publishing *On War* have either been misconstrued or ignored. The conundrum has been widened by the fact that the manuscript for *On War* was an unfinished work and many of its original drafts were lost.

Fortunately, this gap in knowledge may finally be narrowed. In July 2012, the Prussian Privy State Archives/Prussian Cultural Heritage Foundation (Geheimes Staatsarchiv/Preußischer Kulturbesitz) in Berlin received as a deposit the archive of the very old and established aristocratic Buttlar family. Throughout the ages the Buttlars have produced soldiers and statesmen in almost equal numbers, although today many of them are long forgotten. Among the documents discovered by the archivists was the nearly complete correspondence between Marie and Carl von Clausewitz, including 283 of her letters that have never been published before. This significant discovery allows historians to examine, at last and in greater depth, Marie's influence on and contribution to her husband's writing and military career. It provides further insight into Carl's cultural and social surroundings, the political processes that shaped his ideas, and the theorist's writing routine, all of which are crucial for understanding an unfinished text such as *On War*. Most importantly, the newly discovered letters finally bring forth a much fuller understanding of Marie's life and legacy. Next to her contributions to Carl's seminal work, analysis of the correspondence illuminates such interesting but understudied issues as women's roles in the Napoleonic Wars, political processes in the nineteenth century, and the way ideas are born and developed.

The story of how this private correspondence remained unpublished for almost 200 years reveals much about the uncomplete state of Clausewitz scholarship. Since Carl and Marie remained childless, the majority of their estate went to Marie's brother, Friedrich (Fritz) von Brühl, and his wife Hedwig (the daughter of Clausewitz's close friend August Neidhardt von Gneisenau). According to archivists in the Prussian Privy State Archives, Fritz and Hedwig's youngest daughter, Franziska, was the first one to attempt at least partially to arrange the papers and leave notes on their protective jackets. Franziska married the owner of the Venedien Manor, Ludwig von Lücken, and after her death the correspondence and other personal belongings passed to their daughter Hedda. Hedda, for her part, happened to marry into the Buttlar family, and for over a century the Clausewitz correspondence remained in the family's possession. Honoring these connections, the archivists in Berlin now have named the literary estate "Buttlar-Venedien."

Karl Schwartz, the author of the first Clausewitz biography, included a significant part of the intimate correspondence between Carl and Marie in his work. His *The Life of General Carl von Clausewitz and Madam Marie von Clausewitz* was dedicated to Marie's sister-in-law, the then–still-living Hedwig von Brühl—strongly suggesting that she was the one who allowed him to look into the family archives.[3] Hence it remains unclear when exactly the Clausewitz correspondence went into the Buttlar family archives. Significantly, while Schwartz published almost all of Carl's letters in his 1878 biography, only twenty-six of Marie's letters to her husband became public. It remains an open question whether Schwartz himself was disinterested in the countess's views or if the family restrained access to the remaining 283 letters due to their often highly political nature, bold remarks about then–still–living members of Prussian high society, petty jealousies, and explicit references to intimacy. Later editions of Marie and

Carl's correspondence have simply reprinted the Schwartz book's tran-
scriptions.[4] The original letters were never lost, just thoroughly forgotten.

Now stored at the Prussian Privy State Archives, some of these letters
are in poor condition. In cases where parts of the letters are missing, this is
typically the result of Marie's habit of writing on the envelope, the part of
a letter that often is the first to disintegrate, get discarded, or become misplaced. Only in a handful of cases could one suspect that a family member
had destroyed pages intentionally. Tellingly, Carl meticulously kept most
of Marie's letters, though they amassed into a bulky baggage that he lugged
around during the ferocious Russian campaign and the Wars of German
Liberation.

This book is the first attempt to use the newly discovered correspondence to study Marie's life and her contributions to her husband's works.
This process has also led me to examine many of Carl's letters in their original form. The majority of his correspondence had been published but,
perhaps unsurprisingly, not in their full versions. Next to the understandable requirements of space and relevance, it appears that in his biography
Schwartz had also followed the nineteenth-century code of respectabil-
ity and omitted many remarks concerning Carl and Marie's relationship
that clearly revealed it to be more complex and egalitarian than the societal norms of the day. I have profited as well from new materials found
and reevaluated in various archives in the quarter-century since the
Reunification of Germany, including Marie's cousin Carl von Brühl's
exhaustive correspondence in the Saxon State and University Library
(Sächsische Staats- und Universitätsbibliothek) in Dresden. Some of Marie's
papers were made available to me, as were her diary from 1813 and her journal covering the years 1831–1836, both located at the University and State
Library in Münster. I am also in great debt to Bernd Domsgen and Olaf
Thiel, two historians from Clausewitz's home city Burg bei Magdeburg,
who have amassed an incredible collection of never-before-published family letters and documents.

The fact that Marie and Carl's partnership has not previously been studied in depth does not mean that it has remained uncommented upon, as
we've seen in Karl Schwartz's biography. Yet despite recognizing Marie's
momentous role, *The Life of General Carl von Clausewitz and Madam Marie
von Clausewitz* still described her in the conventional and acceptable terms
of an ever-faithful wife putting her husband's and the country's needs
ahead of her own. Just a few decades later, however, the published memoirs

of both Elise von Bernstorff and Caroline von Rochow, two of Marie's closest friends throughout the years, painted a more unsettling and singular picture of her character. From their pages she emerged as a restless spirit and a politically active woman who often challenged societal conventions, spoke her mind, and lived an industrious life often independent of her husband's.[5] The highly personal content of Ludwig von der Marwitz's letters to Marie, published in 1913, also introduced a fairly complex individual.[6] These peculiar traits, however, were never extensively studied but conveniently brushed aside.

Never was Marie's part more ignored than during the Third Reich. She was one of the central characters described in a book written by a journalist and glowing supporter of the Nazi Party, Liane von Gentzkow, that was devoted to the exemplary and laudable women who had supported famous German soldiers. Gentzkow's *Love and Courage* was so popular that by 1941 it was in its third edition.[7] Gentzkow never hid her ideological motivation for writing the book. Indeed, she summarized it on the paper jacket with a quote from Marie: "You act, I shall bear it." The message was clear—German women had to support their men in such an unconditional way and sacrifice for the war effort. Another romanticized biography of the Clausewitzes dating from 1940 perpetuated this stereotype as well, although in a less openly ideological manner. *Clausewitz and the Most Accomplished of All Women* by Alfred Rother-Carlowitz avoided explicit comparisons to contemporary politics and concentrated on the story in its own context.[8] Yet the image of Marie as a patriotic woman, ever waiting at home for her husband to return from war, selflessly supporting him, and never complaining or ceasing to believe in the German nationalistic cause, was almost identical to the Nazi ideal of womanhood. It should not come as a surprise that during World War II a home for war widows studying at the University of Marburg was named after Marie von Clausewitz.[9]

Carl von Clausewitz's biographers in the post–World War II years have emphasized Marie's independent and vivid nature and her strong art and literary interests, but seldom have they tried to analyze these aspects in the greater context of his lifework. Devoting his life to the search for and preservation of the military theorist's literary estate, Werner Hahlweg, in his preface to the jubilee edition of *On War* in 1980, was the first historian to draw attention to Marie's close involvement in the creation of the treatise, citing passages written in her own handwriting.[10] Of course, the spirited (and ongoing) debate about which of the notes left by Clausewitz regarding the state of his work should be considered his last—the one from July 10, 1827 or the one undated but later attributed to 1830—is intimately connected with Marie's role as editor of *On War*.[11] As distinguished Clausewitz scholar Azar Gat's (1989) argument goes, the undated note was written before the one from 1827, and by mixing the dates Marie complicated our understanding of the seminal theory.

Carl's death (in Marie's arms) in 1831 was untimely. He was only fifty-one. In an inconceivable turn of events after surviving the cholera epidemic in Posen and the painful demise of his closest friend August Neidhardt von Gneisenau, he fell sick in the relatively disease-free city of Breslau. Next to the terrible grief she felt, the death of her beloved husband of twenty-one years also presented Marie with an enormous challenge. She had to edit and publish Carl's seminal theory on war on her own, an especially arduous task because he had not had the chance to finish the manuscript before his sudden death.

During their two-decades-long marriage and the prolonged courtship preceding it, Carl and Marie had shared almost everything—ideas, political views, and experiences during the Napoleonic Wars. Still, Carl's decision to leave the manuscript with Marie constituted an unusual move. She had never served in uniform nor fought a battle; indeed Marie had personally seen a siege only once. Despite reading extensively, Marie was not even a writer in her own right—the few essays she composed were shared only with closest friends and family. Now she had to sift through a myriad of pages, enlist a small team of friends and scholars for proofreading, and publish a book that aimed at nothing less than an overhaul of all existing theory on war.

It remains unknown whether on his deathbed Carl gave his wife any last wishes or instructions on how to proceed with his lifework. Yet he must have had enough confidence in Marie's abilities to leave the manuscript in her hands—Carl had even openly declared that she should be the one to present it to the world. More tellingly, despite his persistent health problems, the military theorist never felt the urge to finish and publish *On War* prematurely. It would appear that, in case of sudden death, he was comfortable trusting his wife to see to its publication, confident in Marie's intelligence, broad knowledge, and skills through which she had supported his work for many years. Carl had few close friends and in 1831 lost the best of them, his commanding officer Gneisenau. Yet with none but Marie did he share everything. He wrote in her presence and occasionally used her help in research and writing. Even if Marie lacked specific knowledge and publishing experience, she was the only one he could confidently rely upon to make the work public in a manner closest to his own ideas. Revealingly, she too believed herself to be closely enough involved in Carl's work to take the lead in the process of editing and publishing *On War* instead of entrusting the manuscript to one of her numerous male relatives or friends. The latter was certainly the more logical and convenient step for a woman in the first part of the nineteenth century.

What was previously considered mere conjecture based on Carl's final act and Marie's own telling becomes a clear notion when one reads the newly discovered letters from the Buttlar-Venedien archive. Throughout their prolonged engagement and two decades of marriage Marie significantly broadened Carl's understanding of art and connected him to the cultural endeavors of the time. As a privileged daughter of German nobility Marie was unusually well educated, and she lived in period when intelligent women could rise to prominence and influence in Europe. Berlin's cultural revival and exciting new literary movements brought about popular salons where, for the first time, ladies could shine with knowledge and wit, and these gatherings lured distinguished and ambitious men. It was indeed this air of social prestige and sophistication that first drew Carl, an unknown junior officer from the provinces, to the formidable countess. From a modern perspective, it might seem that in the course of his career and work he took advantage of Marie's skills, qualities, and connections. But for Marie, unhappily restrained in the role of an early-nineteenth-century woman, his love, reliance, and ambitions became the long-sought central purpose in her own life.

In addition to shedding light on Carl's decision to leave his work in Marie's hands, the newly found correspondence also reveals many interesting details that deepen our understanding of Carl's life, personality, and times. Much of the information and ideas previously published in his letters came as answers to Marie's questions or musings. Her letters now provide the other side of the story, creating a richer and more comprehensive picture. Carl's decision to transfer to the Russian service in 1812, for instance, was not a provisional answer to Prussia's alliance with Napoleon, as previously thought, but a joint plan for prolonged if not even permanent emmigration to Russia. Only financial problems and the uncertainties of the new country stopped Marie from leaving with him. Additionally, in light of her letters throughout different periods, Friedrich Wilhelm III's hostility toward Carl, extensively discussed in previous biographies, appears less willful and less consequential for his later career. In fact, Marie did not consider the Prussian king's attitude against her husband to be based on deep personal animosity but rather saw it as the result of unfavorable circumstances. Similarly, our former perception of the years 1819–1830 in Berlin as a period when Carl lived a publicly inactive and secluded life, removed from politics, comes into question. The Clausewitz couple visited some of the most influential political and literary salons in the capital and, as the correspondence reveals, their connections with the royal family, especially the younger generation, grew stronger. The letters also create a more complex picture of the couple's attitudes toward various issues, some of which continue to reverberate today, like Jewish emancipation and social acceptance of minorities. Marie and Carl even openly debated problems that we tend to think of as relatively modern and a sign of our own changing times—such as the role of military families in standing armies.

But perhaps the most unusual discovery is how much time Marie spent in the military camp or close to it throughout the campaigns of 1813–1814 and 1815. During the prolonged maneuvers and pauses between battles and movements, Carl felt an overwhelming need to have her around. Although he sent his wife back to the safer areas well before any battle occurred, Marie's sheer presence in the military camp for extended periods of time still speaks volumes about their close and loving marriage. Indeed, from the very beginning of their romance, the couple determinedly defied the parochial attitudes of the time and strived to build a relationship if not equal in status, then at least equal in nature. As the correspondence and Marie's other writings lay bare, it was Carl's promise to treat her as an independent and free individual that made the formidable countess decide upon marriage with a man of lesser social standing. And he never wavered in this bond.

The correspondence also suggests the extent to which Clausewitz viewed women's roles in the broader political sphere. His chief premise in *On War* centers on war as an expression of politics, with rational and irrational forces shaping its conduct. Yet his understanding of politics has remained understudied. In the intimate correspondence with Marie, one can clearly appreciate how fully he grasped the complex ways that politics were conducted and the role women had started to play in these activities. Concerning this aspect, quite revealing is the fact that Carl never appeared unnerved by Marie's outspoken activism. On the contrary, he valued and relied on her insight into the informal side of government. This is rather remarkable at a time when many men openly expressed irritation or outright hostility toward the slowly but surely growing female participation in the public sphere. In an era that irreversibly connected citizenship and political rights with military service, thus overtly excluding women from politics, such progressivism was hardly a widespread position. This enlightened grasp of political realities, if not yet full anticipation of the sociopolitical processes about to reshape the world, would have lasting consequences for Clausewitz's theories about war. Clausewitz might not have foreseen the suffragette movement, women assuming governmental posts, or even women serving in the military, but he surely recognized that politics was not, has never been, and would never be a purely male domain. To the extent that Clausewitz never embraced the exaggerated perception of masculinity and chauvinistic attitudes toward politics, he also kept such language out of his writings. He even openly criticized the romanticized and heroic notion of war. Without a doubt, this is one of the reasons for the continuing relevance of *On War* in times when society, politics, and war do not look anything like their counterparts in the early-nineteenth-century West.

The newly discovered correspondence also brings out once more the extraordinary and far-reaching nature of the Revolutionary and Napoleonic eras. In 1789 the French Revolution created out of former subjects of the Crown new citizens bursting with vigor to defend a state they recognized as their own. Beyond the almost limitless resources and manpower the new armies enjoyed, the transformation of war from a king's business into the people's business also escalated passions and the chances of unrestrained violence. Clausewitz spent decades analyzing this transformation and eloquently described the many surrounding questions in *On War*. This is surely one of the reasons for the continuing relevance of his lifework because advanced technologies and the proliferation of democratic institutions in modern days have, if anything, magnified these challenges.

Marie and Carl's correspondence, in its crisp and straightforward manner of describing and debating their initial encounters with questions that today are long-standing, provides a better understanding of their roots and outgrowth. Next to the thorny issue of how demands for greater political participation for men turned into the ostracizing of women's public influence, we also find themes including the application of violence in the name of political and economic rights and the dangerous and unpredictable side of populism. For instance, read in the context of Marie's letters,

Carl's well-known hostility toward the Belgium Revolution and the Polish November Uprising in 1830–1831 displays much in complex reasoning. After more than two decades of almost constant war, the Clausewitz couple had grown wary of any attempt at achieving political rights through violent means. It made them also remorseless in their opposition to rightful Belgian and Polish demands for freedom and independence.

The most important among these complex issues, of course, is the German nationalism that first arose during the Napoleonic Wars but reverberated with tragic consequences throughout the first half of the twentieth century. This is especially true in the case of Clausewitz, as militarists both on the eve of World War I and again during the Nazi regime often used his name and distorted his ideas to promote their own agendas. Yet examined in full, Marie and Carl's patriotism appears anything but unabashed or straightforward. In the years of the Napoleonic Wars they strongly identified with the German nationalistic cause, grew ever more radical in the tumultuous years 1808–1809, and then advocated the idea of greater integration among the German states. But when in their disappointment over the lack of tangible political gains the younger generation of patriots turned violent in 1819, Clausewitz showed very little understanding for it. Indeed, the forces of militant nationalism shocked him so much as to bring about reservations about how a constitution and institutions of popular democracy would function in Prussia. When studied in its full extent and complex context, Marie and Carl's nationalism reveals quite a different vision for Germany than the later disastrous turn. But it also gives clues, striking in their insight, about the processes that shaped European history in the first part of the twentieth century.

In Marie, Carl found not only sympathetic companionship but also an intellectual partner. While her writings lacked his precision, she was still a worthy, passionate, critical, and self-confident interlocutor. Marie was the first to listen to or read his deliberations, indulged his need as a thinker to test his ideas, and often served as the catalyst for their further development. To write a comprehensive theory of war was a tremendous endeavor, and the military theorist wrote and rewrote the text over the course of a decade, always looking for greater precision and economy. It is in this context as well that his lack of urgency to finish and publish *On War* prematurely should be understood. In order to create a truly complex treatise, Carl wanted to think and write without time constraints or the pressure of public opinion. And the military theorist knew he could rely on Marie to see his lifework published.

Marie's letters undoubtedly depict Carl in a sympathetic light and in direct contradiction to the image of a cold misanthrope that was proliferated by outsiders and later applied by detractors when attacking his legacy. Yet because the correspondence was written mostly for his eyes only and was often candid about feelings, prejudices, and fears to the point of embarrassment, the emerging portrait should be accepted as closest to the man as he really was. To study Clausewitz's biography from Marie's perspective is also to put our own perceptions about his life and work to the test and to discover how many of these are rooted in either misunderstanding or in sheer ignorance of her writings. The most far-reaching and omnipresent example is Marie's letter to her friend Elise von Bernstorff in the immediate hours after Carl's death, widely quoted as evidence of his perpetual state of depression and despair due to lack of public recognition. Many biographers have already pointed out that no such desire for popular applause could be found in Carl's own writings, but only when put into the context of his wife's entire papers do the infamous lines reveal that it was she who truly begrudged the deficient acknowledgment. Later on, Marie carefully rectified the despairing image and clarified the circumstances of Carl's death almost immediately, yet these texts were never thoroughly studied.

After his demise, Marie assumed her most visible and, from a historical perspective, most significant role as the posthumous editor of *On War*. As the correspondence makes clear, her publication of the seminal work in 1832-1834 was not the only—or even the first time—that she made his writings public or served as an agent for his ideas. In the process of editing *On War*, having previously been engaged as an integral part of Carl's extended deliberations and writing process gave her authority to authenticate and apprehend revisions spread throughout different versions of the papers. It also left Marie with a deeply felt sense of regret that future readers would never have the chance to encounter the ideas he had developed but failed to write down. She understood the treatise as a work of genius that was also unfinished. Yet for Marie, the incomplete state of the work also reinforced Clausewitz's central premise that war theory should not be prescriptive. She even went a step further by welcoming the upcoming and inevitable debates over the work as a way to better comprehend both Clausewitz's ideas and the phenomenon of war. Unfortunately, her own unexpected death in 1836 robbed her of opportunities to continue publishing Clausewitz's texts, correcting some misunderstandings, and perhaps setting her own mark as an independent writer.

While this book brings to light unusual or understudied aspects of Carl von Clausewitz's character, life, and work, it certainly does not wholly revise the already existing narratives. Telling the story from Marie's perspective is not an attempt to diminish her husband's accomplishments but rather to create a better understanding about the cultural, social, and personal circumstances that shaped and nurtured them. Especially for modern readers, the greatest difficulty in understanding *On War* stems from scant knowledge about its context. In this regard, Marie's role and influence should serve as a vehicle of comprehension. Even had he not met and married her, Carl would have fought in the Napoleonic Wars, risen in the ranks of the Prussian military reformers, and probably distilled his experience into a complex theory about politics and war. Yet without Marie's critical insight and support, it seems doubtful *On War* would have become the enduring masterpiece it is today.

I

Two Worlds Apart (1779–1801)

When Carl von Clausewitz met Marie Countess von Brühl in 1803, nothing pointed to a possible future marriage. She was the offspring of one of the most ambitious German noble families, had grown up in the royal family's immediate vicinity, and had been carefully educated to become the wife of a man of stature. He was a penniless junior officer from the provinces with a dubious claim to nobility. But these circumstances were not as insuperable as they appeared. Marie had grown up at a time when women around Europe had began assuming more public roles and had gained some autonomy. Most of all, society and the wider world were about to change rapidly and unpredictably.

Just six months before Marie's birth, in June 1779, the overjoyed Louis XVI and Queen Marie Antoinette also celebrated the arrival of their first child, Marie Thérèse, in Versailles. The American Revolution was in its fourth year, and France, Spain, and the Dutch Republic were now actively aiding the colonists against George III. "Germany" was just a geographical term. It referred to over three hundred political entities loosely unified by the Holy Roman Empire, a medieval structure dating back to the time of Charlemagne. Shared language and culture made it possible for talented men to transfer and serve under different princes than the ones they were born under. Nobles sometimes owned estates in one German state while making an illustrious career in another. In Russia, Catherine the Great yearned to be recognized by the world as an enlightened ruler. Frederick II, now known as Frederick the Great, still ruled Prussia with an iron fist.

In 1779, the thirty-year-old Johann Wolfgang Goethe was a celebrated but still young writer, living in the duchy of Saxe-Weimar. Only five years previously, his novel *The Sorrows of Young Werther*, the most important work so far of the rebellious Sturm und Drang literary movement, had became an instant bestseller.[1] Friedrich Schiller, a student in

Stuttgart, was yet to make public that other famed text of the period, *The Robbers*. Despite such brazen challenges to rational congruity and the social order, the ideas of the Enlightenment continued to dominate the cultural outlook. Knowledge was seen as the foremost instrument for personal and social improvement, while passions had to be restrained and compelled to a humanistic ideal.

Marie was the oldest child of Carl Adolph von Brühl and his wife Sophie Gomm. Carl Adolph, called by the family with the French equivalent of his name, Charles, was born in 1742, at a time when his father, the Imperial Count Heinrich von Brühl, enjoyed the height of his power in Saxony and Poland. When two decades earlier the nineteen-year-old Heinrich had appeared at the court of Augustus II of Saxony as a page, whose main duties were to care for the royal silverware, none could have foreseen his later illustrious career. His family had exchanged their heavily encumbered Gangloffsömmern estate in Thuringia for life as courtiers in the tiny duchy of Saxe-Weißenfells, on the northern edge of Saxony. Later Heinrich investigated the family's origins and confirmed that the Brühls originally stemmed from the Baltic region of Livonia, moving to Thuringia in the fifteenth century. Finding that in these early days the Brühls were related through marriage to the Baranowni family, which had once ruled the Polish duchy of Oświęcim, from 1748 on Heinrich adopted the name Brühl-Oświęcino and became a recognized member of the Polish aristocracy, the *szlachta*.[2]

As the legend went, Augustus II, elector of Saxony and king of Poland, hated reading the lengthy documents piling up on his desk and ordered courtiers to summarize them in no more than ten sentences. Heinrich von Brühl once completed the assignment in only eight sentences. Impressed, the king gave him the task of supervising all reports. Soon the ambitious young nobleman became an indispensable member of the cabinet. In 1730, the aging Augustus tasked him with organizing the *Zeithainer Lager*, the month-long review of the 27,000-man Saxon army. The momentous event had the goal of both reorganizing the troops and impressing visiting foreign dignitaries. Brühl outdid himself with magnificent amenities like a luxurious temporary opera house, an observation terrace for 4,000 people, five hours of fireworks, and a closing lunch for 30,000 guests with a 1.8-ton pastry for dessert.

When Augustus II died in 1733 in Warsaw, Brühl did his utmost to secure the Polish throne for his son. In Poland, the aristocracy followed the unusual tradition of voting whom to give the crown to, and the ambitious Augustus II had held it twice (1697–1706 and 1709–1733). After the succession of his son, Friedrich August II, now known under his Polish royal name Augustus III, Brühl's career truly flourished, as he was the king's closest confidant. In 1737, in recognition of his considerable diplomatic skills, Brühl became an imperial count (*Reichsgraf*), a title given him directly by the Holy Roman Emperor. This granted his estate in Pförten independent status, a seat at the Imperial Diet, and recognition by all other German states. Starting in 1738, the diligent and determined administrator came to be in charge almost singlehandedly of Saxony-Poland's government and assumed the title of prime minister, now created especially for him. Just like his father before him, Augustus III had extravagant tastes, and Brühl saw his own task as being, first and foremost, as catering to it, no matter what the price.

In 1734 Brühl married Maria Anna Franziska von Kolowrat-Krakowsky, called Marianne by the family. The seventeen-year-old countess came from a prominent Bohemian-Austrian family and her mother, Anna Maria, served as *Oberhofmeisterin*, or chief lady-in-waiting, to Queen Maria Josepha. Marianne was a Catholic and the smitten groom a Lutheran, but the bishop of Krakow declared himself ready to wed them if their future children would be raised Catholic. The genuinely loving marriage of Heinrich and Marianne von Brühl produced a daughter, Maria Amalie, and four sons—Alois Friedrich, Carl Adolph (Charles), Albert Christian Heinrich, and Hans Moritz. Having lost his own mother at the age of two, the imperial count cherished his wife and, in a court notorious for its affairs, remained faithful to Marianne. This behavior turned out to be the prevailing pattern in the family. Even if the next generations continued the tradition of shrewd political intrigues, for the most part they built stable and happy homes.

Brühl and his family lived a lavish lifestyle, with palaces in Dresden and Warsaw, a manor in Nischwitz, and a château in Pförten. Brühl's own art gallery contained works of Rembrandt, Rubens, and Canaletto and his library totaled 62,000 books. The prime minister displayed the same lavishness and taste when it came to the policy of transforming Dresden into a leading European metropolis. The Italian architect Gaetano Chiaveri built the Catholic *Hofkirche,* Bernardo Bellotto, popularly called Canaletto, worked for over a decade in the city, and the court gallery acquired 4,000 new paintings. Among them were the masterpieces *The Tribute Money* by Titian, Jean-Étienne Liotard's *The Chocolate Girl,* and Dresden's most famous art treasure until this day, Raphael's *Sistine Madonna.*

Heinrich and Marianne von Brühl did not spare money, influence, or energy when it came to carefully educating and preparing their children to assume an important role in Saxon-Polish government. Together with the usual French lessons, the four boys and their sister learned Polish as well. Yet despite the prudence and care put into it, the Brühl offsprings' education lapsed in one important subject. Like most aristocratic German families of that time, parents and children communicated almost exclusively in French: apparently the imperial count and his wife saw very little use in studying their own native German extensively. Charles especially seemed to have had some troubles expressing himself eloquently in German, as his surviving letters to King Friedrich Wilhelm II bear witness.[3]

In her middle son Charles, Marianne von Brühl emphasized "prudence" as the most prevailing quality and described him as a young man of *franchise*

Figure 1.1. The Brühl Terrasse in Dresden. Nicknamed "The Balcony of Europe," it is where the Imperial Count Heinrich von Brühl's grand rococo palace used to stand. *Photo Vanya Eftimova Bellinger.*

et probité or "openness and integrity."[4] At the tender age of five he was already signed up in the cavalry and, thanks to his father's influence and political maneuverings rather than actual time served, became lieutenant colonel at sixteen, colonel at eighteen, and major general at twenty. In 1763, the year of the prime minister's resignation and death, came the last promotion when, at age twenty-one, he became a lieutenant general. As such, he received his own carabinier regiment with a steady income.[5] This pace was nothing unusual in the Brühl family—at eleven, the oldest son Alois Friedrich became a Starost (governor) of Warsaw, and the other brother Albert Christian Heinrich was officially assigned to the Saxon army at the even earlier age of three.

At the beginning of his reign, Frederick the Great sent a generous invitation to Brühl to transfer to Berlin and serve under him. Later, he ridiculed and passionately hated the prime minister as the mind and the heart behind

Figure 1.2. Frederick the Great, engraving made between 1786 and 1800. *Library of Congress Prints and Photographs Division, LC-DIG-pga-03428, Library of Congress, Washington, DC.*

the coalition, built between Austria, France, Russia, and Saxony-Poland, aimed at preventing Prussia's rise on the international stage. On August 29, 1756, before the coalition could gather military strength, Frederick started his preemptive strike against neighboring Saxony. This conflict would prolong into the Seven Years' War and come to include all the great European powers. It spread even to the American colonies where Britain, on one side, and France and France's native allies, on the other, fought in what is known today as the French and Indian War. While Heinrich von Brühl and Augustus III escaped to Warsaw, the sixteen-year-old Charles found a warm welcome in Paris and soon joined the Regiment Royal-Allemand, a unit composed of foreigners. If not for the strong disapproval of his parents, he might have enlisted permanently in the French army.[6]

The end of the Seven Years' War also spelled the end of Brühl's illustrious career and of his family fortunes. When in early 1763 peace finally came, Augustus III and his prime minister returned to a ravaged and impoverished Saxony. The year before, Brühl lost his beloved wife, and his own health was deteriorating. Prussian troops, under orders from Frederick the Great, had plundered his magnificent estates. In October, Augustus III unexpectedly died. Brühl resigned from all public offices and quickly followed his master into the grave. The new Saxon cabinet immediately used the situation to direct public anger about the lost war and Saxony's desolate economic state toward the deceased statesman, and sealed his papers pending investigation of his alleged improprieties and abuse of state finances. The case never made it to court, most likely because to indict the prime minister would have meant indicting the absolute monarchy that had created and allowed him to thrive. The accusations of corruption, as Brühl's biographer Walter Fellmann observed, were unsubstantiated, as Brühl's yearly salary of almost 90,000 thalers could easily have paid for his lavish lifestyle.[7]

After their father's death, the family kept Pförten and liquidated the other estates with little or no profit. The state had already sold the prime minister's marvelous art collection to Catherine the Great. The union between Poland and Saxony was over too, and the disgruntled *szlachta* took away all the state titles that the Brühl family had enjoyed in the country. The flamboyant oldest brother Alois Friedrich inherited the family estate at Pförten, but all of the siblings received annuities from it. Alois's rather mediocre management over the years would be a constant worry, but the passed-on annuity would also guarantee financial security later for Marie von Brühl.

All the Brühl siblings now moved to seek their fortunes outside of Saxony. Some years later, Charles served once more at the court of the embattled Polish king Stanisław II Poniatowski, hoping to recover some of the payments the state owed him from the time of his father's service. Yet these were some of the most tumultuous times in Poland's history, as Russia, Austria, and Prussia, capitalizing on Warsaw's weakness, made a deal among themselves to carve generous pieces out of its lands. Under the threat of facing its powerful neighbors' united armies—to be followed by greater losses of territories and lives—the Polish government was forced to accept a brazen agression, commonly known today as the First Partition of Poland, in 1772. Disheartened by the continuing disarray in Warsaw and

Figure 1.2a. A British cartoon showing the First Partition of Poland in 1772. Catherine II of Russia, the Holy Roman Emperor Leopold II, and Frederick the Great of Prussia are seated at a table on which rests a map of Poland. Standing behind them and looking over their shoulders are Louis XV of France and Charles III of Spain. George III of Great Britain is asleep on his throne and disinterested in the European affairs. On the left, with head bowed, wearing a broken crown, and with hands bound behind him, sits the King of Poland, Stanisław II Poniatowski. To his left in chains is Selim III, Sultan of the Turks, just defeated by the Russians. *Library of Congress Prints and Photographs Division, LC-USZ62-123023, Library of Congress, Washington, DC.*

eyeing a new patron, in 1778 Charles von Brühl appeared at the court of Catherine the Great.[8] Although the count's quest remained unsuccessful, it was in St. Petersburg that he met Miss Sophie Gomm.

Sophie was the youngest child of William Gomm Jr. and Marie Jeanne Poggenpohl. Gomm's father was a prosperous cabinetmaker in London whose rococo designs remain of interest to art historians to this day.[9] William Jr. was the second son, however, and stood to inherit little. In 1750 he left for Russia where, due to changes in custom fee payments, British businesses enjoyed significant commercial advantages. Gomm quickly rose to prominence in St. Petersburg, but risky ventures like the export of Ukrainian tobacco kept him constantly only a step away from insolvency. Luckily the merchant came under the patronage of the wealthy and well-connected Count Peter Shuvalov, and in 1754 obtained from him the timber export monopoly over the vast region around Archangelsk. Gomm now set in motion one of the largest commercial enterprises in Russia in the mid-eighteenth century by constructing and developing the port of Onega.[10] With the swift improvement of his finances, Gomm married Marie Jeanne, the daughter of his fellow contractor at the Russian court, Friedrich Wilhelm Poggenpohl.

In recent decades Gomm has enjoyed the interest of Russian history scholars, allegedly as one of the most notorious examples of a reckless foreign merchant. According to Sergei K. Lebedev, he became the first court banker in the Russian Empire, although that position involved different tasks than in Western Europe. Since exports were the major source of income for the Russian Crown, a court banker in St. Petersburg was expected to regulate international financial transactions and facilitate these exports.[11] By the mid-1760s, Gomm's large-scale timber enterprise was spread so thin that Catherine the Great ordered several investigations into his business. Fearing greater damage to the Russian economy, however, she bailed him out.[12] The business never recovered, but the family kept its social status and connections. The Gomms indeed came to believe that the Russian government's interference had destroyed William's fortune, and described him as a man larger than life. As one family document stated, he was "a gentleman of the most unimpeached [sic] integrity and the most amiable manners," so deeply religious and curious that at one point he even learned Greek and Hebrew in order to read the Bible in the original.[13]

In the 1780s, Gomm was hired as a member of the British embassy in St. Petersburg and later moved to be a secretary at the embassy in The Hague.

Over the years his patriotism as a British subject only grew, and his children came to share this pride. Gomm's oldest son, also named William, served as a lieutenant colonel in Great Britain's 55th Regiment during the French Revolutionary Wars and in the West Indies. He eventually became a baronet. Marie's first cousin, the celebrated British field marshal Sir William Maynard Gomm, married the granddaughter of Pennsylvania's founder William Penn. Jane, the oldest Gomm sister, served as governess to King George III's daughters.[14]

Sophie Gomm was the youngest child, well educated and attractive, so when the thirty-six-year-old Charles von Brühl appeared in St. Petersburg, he fell quickly in love with the girl despite her being two decades his junior. The count might have believed, too, that Sophie would bring a rich dowry. He learned soon enough that this would not be the case but, perhaps remembering his parents' happy marriage, Charles banked on love and wed Sophie in August 1778 in St. Petersburg. Their first child, named Maria Sophia but called by the family Marie, was born on June 3 the following year in Warsaw, where the family had stopped on their way to Saxony.

Marie remembered her own childhood as sheltered and comfortable. In the early years of her marriage she composed an essay about the most important events in her personal life that serves as a guide for period before her first acquaintance with Carl von Clausewitz in 1803.[15] Paradoxically, in these pages Marie never mentioned her famous grandfather Heinrich von Brühl, nor the influence that his stellar rise to power and later disgrace had over her life. Neither did she assess other seemingly significant issues such as the adventurous existence of her mother's family in Russia or even the French Revolution. The notes contained merely the facts of Marie's own life. Nevertheless, throughout the carefully crafted pages are slipped references to family tragedies, social contradictions, and rising economic tensions, revealing a complex image at the turn of the nineteenth century.

In the spring of 1780, after too many unsuccessful attempts for restitution, the Brühls moved back to Saxony. The climate in Dresden had changed, and although they were still the subject of many wild rumors, the former prime minister's family enjoyed once again its high social status. As Marie's notes about her youth recounted, they lived between Dresden and the small garrison town Pegau, where her father resumed his service as the commanding general of a carabinier regiment. The family spent the summers with the regiment and the winters in the Saxon capital in order to participate in various social happenings at the court. Charles and Sophie appeared to have been attentive and loving parents and never left their children behind when they went on vacations to Carlsbad (now Carlovy Vary). The governess, Madam Kahn, came into the family's service in 1781 and stayed many more decades, caring for several generations of Brühls.

Through her life, Marie remained especially close with two of her Brühl cousins—Therese, the oldest daughter of Alois Friedrich, and Carl, the only child of Hans Moritz. Therese was a great beauty, and after marrying into the Bohemian-Austrian noble family Thun und Hohenstein, she devoted her time to politics and intellectual endeavors. Carl von Brühl was an exceptionally talented child, nurtured by his French-born mother Christina, an author and one of the first female landscape architects in Europe. He became a personal friend of Goethe and Johann Gottfried Herder, and later in life served as attendant-general of the Prussian royal theaters.

Like most noblewomen in that era, Marie was educated at home and Charles was her first tutor. "My father himself taught me writing. The first letter that I wrote under his guidance was to my grandfather [Gomm]; I still have the answer that I received to it," the young countess remembered.[16] Charles almost certainly taught his daughter reading and writing in French, his preferred language of expression. Marie had so much confidence in her own command of that language that she even allowed herself unkind assessments about other people's poor skills.[17] Even at the height of German nationalistic sentiments, she liked to pepper her letters with French phrases and quotes. Charles also trained her in the kind of letter writing that was thought to be important for a lady of high society.

As the daughter of a cavalry officer, Marie naturally mastered horse riding as well. Together with her younger sister Fanny, Marie joined Charles on hikes in Saxony's picturesque mountain Geiersberg, and their father sought to instill a love for nature in his children.[18] His young wife Sophie, not even eighteen when Marie was born and hampered by six more pregnancies in the next eleven years, appears to have had little involvement in her daughter's early education.

As romantic and peaceful as the young countess's description of the Brühl family's life sounds, her notes also contain sorrowful lines about the deaths of her siblings. In 1781, a baby boy named Heinrich was buried only four weeks after his birth. Less than two years later followed the death of another brother named Karl, from smallpox. Marie's sister Pauline suffered from hydrocephalus, a lethal illness in that period, and expired at the age of three, just one day after her mother Sophie gave birth to her sixth child. Eight months later this baby girl, named Luise, died as well. Thus the toll of high infant mortality did not exempt even a noble family like the Brühls. As the oldest child, Marie vividly remembered most of these traumatic events and seems to have developed a sense of tenderness and protectiveness toward her siblings, especially Fanny, four years younger, who had survived the smallpox epidemic. Marie often referred to her as "my beloved sister" and years later would take care of Fanny's orphaned daughter.

The Brühl family's life changed when in 1787 Charles attained the position of governor of the Prussian crown prince, the future Friedrich Wilhelm III. In Marie's recollections, the circumstances surrounding her father's new post and the family's subsequent move to Berlin received rather scarce attention, mostly because they happened unexpectedly and with little effort on Brühl's part. Frederick the Great died in August 1786, and his successor Friedrich Wilhelm II promised to change Prussia. The firstborn son of the king's younger brother, Prince August Wilhelm, Friedrich Wilhelm II was carefully educated and prepared to be Prussia's ruler. Although the childless Frederick the Great personally designed his heir's schooling, empathy and understanding never existed between the two men. While Frederick was ascetic, Friedrich Wilhelm II was flamboyant and very much interested in the ladies. During the reign of Old Fritz, as Frederick the Great was known among his subjects, no real court existed in Berlin, as the king preferred to spend his time at his residence Sanssouci in Potsdam in the company of French philosophers or his hounds. In contrast, his successor was devoted to arts, theater, and social life, and preferred to use the German language. Friedrich Wilhelm II, a handsome, stoutly built, and physically impressive man, was widely welcomed after Old Fritz's last stagnant years. The king's residence was moved back to Berlin, German literature was heavily patronized, and in the Academy of Science German was again the official language.

Like many other prominent men at the end of the Enlightenment era, the new king was bedazzled by mysticism, and it led him to the Rosicrucian Order. This secret society, an outgrowth of Freemasonry, dabbed in occultism but also debated sociopolitical transformation. The Rosicrucian Order was popular among men of ideas looking for an audience and connections to carry out their bold plans. In particular, the circle around the former clergyman and later popular economist Johann Christoph Wöllner debated the need for government reforms and an end to serfdom. Right after his ascension, Friedrich Wilhelm II turned to prominent members of the Rosicrucian Order for counsel and support. Wöllner was appointed privy councilor for finance and ennobled. Major Hans Rudolf von Bischoffwerder, who had once instructed Friedrich Wilhelm in matters of Rosicrucianism, became a lieutenant colonel and subsequently adjutant general of the king.

Charles von Brühl was another Rosicrucian promptly appointed at the Prussian court as governor of the sixteen-year-old crown prince and his younger brother Ludwig. Just like many other members of the secret society, Brühl came in contact with Friedrich Wilhelm II through Bischoffwerder. The latter also happened to have been born into a noble family from Thuringia that had served in Saxony and exchanged frequent correspondence with the Brühl brothers. Bischoffwerder might have believed that an outsider from Saxony, installed in a high post in Prussia by his recommendation would always be grateful and dependent upon him. According to some historians of Rosicrucianism, Charles von Brühl instructed the Polish King Stanisław in matters of the order, and Rosicrucian leaders might therefore have hoped that he could influence the young crown prince too.[19]

For the count himself, the appointment was as much of a surprise as it was for the court in Berlin, and he actually wrote to the king questioning whether he would be the best man to educate Prussian princes. "Concerning your faith, everyone here is too enlightened to take offense," Friedrich Wilhelm II personally assured Brühl to ease his worry about being a Catholic governor at a Protestant court.[20] Confirmed in his good opinion by Charles's prudence and humility, the king invited Charles's younger brothers as well—Albert Christian Heinrich to serve as a Prussian diplomat and general and Hans Moritz to be in charge of state highways in the Mark and Pomerania (i.e., all highways in Prussia).[21] After two decades of insecurity, the siblings readily embraced the state that had once so mercilessly destroyed their family fortunes, but the irony of the situation did not escape them. "If our father could have been witness to the developing events, he would have been greatly amazed, but he could not experience better satisfaction than to see the offspring of his biggest enemy left in the hands of one of his sons," Charles wrote to Alois Friedrich.[22]

According to Marie's recollections, when the Brühls moved into the Berlin palace it was "the admission into a new world."[23] For the family, the next six years became a time of social and cultural elevation. They lived in an apartment one floor above the crown prince and his brother's apartments, and although the future Friedrich Wilhelm III never felt particularly close to Charles, the royal children did spend time in the governor's salon. Count von Brühl's generosity, knowledge, and friendly demeanor won him respect at the court. In his notes from 1800, Friedrich Delbrück, the governor for Friedrich Wilhelm III's own sons, wrote warmly about his predecessor as a man whose appointment initially stirred a lot of controversies—especially by his being a Catholic—but when Delbück came to know the count, he could see Brühl only as an "excellent" choice.[24]

The question of the governor's Catholicism and his inclination toward mysticism apparently both soon lost their poignancy. On the one hand, while suspicions still existed in Protestant Berlin, the Enlightenment's leading principle of religious tolerance, instilled by Frederick the Great, remained highly valued. On the other, Brühl himself practiced a liberal form of faith, and his protestant wife never converted. As was the tradition in many other interreligious marriages, the sons were baptized in their father's denomination and the daughters in their mother's. Hence Marie and her sister Fanny were Protestants, while their younger brother Friedrich was Catholic. Charles's enthusiasm for the Rosicrucian Order also seemed to have cooled down since he did not appear, contrary to his brother Hans Moritz, to have been a member of Friedrich Wilhelm's intimate circle of mystics.[25] Later in life, Marie would display the same enlightened attitude—praying, religious ceremonies, and questions of morality were important for her, and she would even attend Catholic as well as protestant services. But as the pietistic Elise Hensel, who nursed her on her deathbed, observed, Marie's religiousness was "too worldly."[26]

In 1788 the crown prince came of age and Charles's position changed to chamberlain. In 1791, when Sophie gave birth to Friedrich Wilhelm (called Fritz) and he survived infancy, thus securing continuation of the Brühl family name, their happiness seemed complete. Sophie von Brühl in particular made the most of her special standing at the court. Friedrich August Ludwig von der Marwitz, the man who later married her daughter Fanny, described Countess von Brühl's life from that period in especially flaunty terms: "Because of the position and seniority of her husband, she had almost the highest rank in Berlin. She was considered a model of strict, noble, and distinguished breeding and manners, and soon set the fashion in this regard in Berlin. If she criticized someone, the damage remained; anyone she accepted or even better praised was regarded as someone special;

and indeed her judgment could be trusted so long as her egotism did not interfere." Of course, due to this high position, Marwitz noted, "she also was greatly feared. She was proud of her position, proud of her husband's family, and even proud of the nobility as such." This pride struck some as infelicitous; at times, Marwitz recalled, "it was whispered behind her back that this was highly absurd, since she herself was not noble, indeed as the daughter of a merchant could never have appeared at court, if she hadn't suddenly emerged from Saxony and been installed in the palace, but none dared to say it openly."[27]

Under Frederick the Great Berlin had started to acquire a modern look and European prominence. His successor continued the ambitious building program, most famously commissioning the Brandenburg Gate to Carl Gotthard Langhans. The French writer and intellectual Germaine de Staël, who visited Germany in the first years of the nineteenth century, described Prussia's capital as an "entirely modern city," with beautiful brick residences and broad, straight streets, where not even one Gothic monument or antique relic interrupted the view. Berlin, she wrote, was the single-minded project of one man—Frederick the Great—and his idea of an enlightened kingdom.[28] At the beginning of the eighteenth century the capital had only 55,000 citizens, but a century later its population had reached almost 175,000. The booming city drew nobles from their provincial estates, an entrepreneurial middle class, writers and intellectuals, émigrés looking for a new life, and the urban poor, who searched for employment as servants. The revival of German culture under the Enlightenment's leading men Gotthold Ephraim Lessing, Moses Mendelssohn, and Christoph Nikolai, followed by the virulent eruption of Sturm und Drang, had created a passionate although still small circle of readers. The reign of the gregarious Friedrich Wilhelm II reinforced interest in art, theater, and literature.

Yet among the wider circles of society, Friedrich Wilhelm II never fulfilled the high hopes many had held for his reign. Salacious scandals, financial irresponsibility, and poorly enacted political initiatives plagued his eleven years on the throne. Under a talented king like Frederick the Great, enlightened despotism led to a strong, proactive government, but a mediocre ruler like Friedrich Wilhelm II struggled with the responsibilities and lost the reins of his kingdom. The eruption of the French Revolution in 1789 only highlighted Prussia's deepening social and political problems. Frederick believed in the principles of the Enlightenment, which posited that the state's well-being resided in its numerous population, and he did not only rely on the rapidly rising birth rate but also encouraged skilled immigration and pushed a strong internal colonization policy in the Eastern provinces. Where the government failed was in providing living standards for the growing number of people, and as a result, the measures threatened to backfire. Furthermore, the long wars fought by Old Fritz had come with a high economic and human cost and the country was recovering slowly. Prussia was an overregulated and overtaxed state without enough space for free enterprise and the creation of early capitalist institutions. Frederick sponsored local industry, but there were simply not enough consumers in Prussia for the Prussian-made porcelain and clocks. The solution should have been political as much as economic—loosening the grip of the state and giving economic means and freedom to broader sections of the population—but Frederick failed to see this.

It wasn't only economic setbacks that plagued the Prussian middle class. The Enlightenment had made Prussians believe in personal merit, but in reality one's social rise continued to depend on birth. Frederick the Great's reign and military victories had created a strong identification with the state among an ever-growing group of intellectuals and middle-class people. They were interested in politics and eager to participate, but could not find an outlet. Prussia was and remained a state built on an uneasy compromise between the ruling Hohenzollern family and the landed nobility, the Junkers. Throughout his reign, Frederick confirmed the nobility's preeminent place in the officer corps and bureaucracy. Yet even in his ban on the sale of manors to commoners, there was a strain of anxiousness that the middle class's rise might be inevitable.

For young, ambitious, and educated men without ranked ancestry, however, the change could not come fast enough. Sturm und Drang made bold and open mockery of aristocratic privileges and pretensions and found a passionate core of readers. In Prussia, no one bought positions in the officer corps and bureaucracy as in other countries, but the higher the rank, the higher was the percentage of nobles, and some positions remained closed altogether for commoners. The majority of these jobs paid modestly, if not outright poorly, but in a stagnant state without many opportunities they promised security and status.

Friedrich Wilhelm II might have listened to debates about the need for economic and social reforms, but when it came to action, the furthest he went was to make minor improvements in the tax code and to reduce custom dues. As a result, when the French Revolution guaranteed sweeping new rights to the Third Estate—the commoners—the reaction in Prussia was overwhelmingly positive. "I would hold the failure of this revolution as one of the worst disasters that have ever affected humanity," wrote the young Friedrich Gentz in 1790. "It is the hope and solace for so many old evils under which humanity moans.... I can vividly imagine how everywhere the silence of despair will concede—against all reason—that the people can only be happy as slaves."[29] Although only a few years later Gentz would become the leading German publicist opposing the French Revolution, in the early days he was one of many who saw it as a beacon of hope.

Paradoxically, Carl von Clausewitz's dubious claim to nobility and his rise in the Prussian army perfectly illustrated the inherent unfairness of the system. Carl Phillip Gottfried was born on July 1, 1780, a year after his future wife, in the small garrison town of Burg just outside of Magdeburg. It appears that Clausewitz himself believed he had been born a month earlier: June 1.[30] The alteration probably came in the process of Carl's enlistment in the army, which occurred on the eve of a great campaign. The elder Clausewitz was likely eager to see his son accepted before it, and may have altered the date accordingly. Carl's father, Friedrich Gabriel, had entered the Prussian army in 1759, during the period when Frederick the Great experienced his greatest defeats in the Seven Years' War. The need for men had forced the king to loosen the otherwise strict policy of commissioning only nobility. Friedrich Gabriel's initial rank was that of officer-cadet, and he left the army shortly after the Seven Years' War—when Frederick went back to the previous commissioning policy—as a lieutenant. Nonetheless, the elder Clausewitz saw himself as someone firmly belonging to the Prussian officer corps and therefore as gentry. He kept the lower noble title "von" in his name, and a family legend about descending from a Silesian family of nobility took root. Conveniently, the legend held that after Friedrich Gabriel's grandfather had entered a profession, the family lost the title according to the habit of the time.[31]

Despite the family legend, scholars have never been able to establish any connection between Clausewitz and the prominent Silesian family von Clausnitz, obviously the one in mind here.[32] Friedrich Gabriel's father was a professor of theology in Halle and his ancestors were Lutheran ministers in Silesia. Carl firmly believed in the family myth, although he candidly described to Marie relatively early in their relationship the challenges to his status that he experienced as an adolescent in the Prussian officer corps. Insults like "usurper," the constant pressure to prove his status, and enforced shame created an atmosphere hard to bear and, as Carl admitted, only his own and his older brother's eagerness to protect their honor "with the rapier" saved them from further humiliations.[33]

After the army, Friedrich Gabriel became a tax collector in the tiny Burg. A longstanding settlement between the rivers Elbe and Ihle, Burg's most notable features, as the name suggested, were its medieval walls and eerie towers. Throughout the ages, Burg had welcomed Palatine, Walloon, and Huguenot refugees of religious persecutions, and they, for their part, had brought new ideas and technologies into the provincial nest. In 1768 Friedrich Gabriel married Friederike Schmidt, whose father managed a royal domain outside the town. Compared to Carl's ambitious father, until now virtually nothing has been known about his mother's character or life. Luckily Marie's letters contain a short but quite revealing anecdote told by the Clausewitz family. As the story went, Friederike once helped star-crossed lovers marry by approaching and persuading their disapproving families. After her death the couple planted flowers on her grave.[34]

Figure 1.3. Carl von Clausewitz grew up on Schulstrasse in Burg bei Magdeburg. Today the street is almost unchanged. *Photo Vanya Eftimova Bellinger.*

Friederike appears to have been a popular and influential member of Burg society, an outgoing and proactive personality not unlike the woman Carl would fall in love with one day.

The couple had six children, including four sons of whom Carl was the youngest. As a tax collector, Friedrich Gabriel received no more than 300 thaler annually, as Marie reported in her essay for Leopold von Ranke's *Historisch-Politische Zeitschrift*.[35] From her point of view this was a meager income. Yet Clausewitz's home, still standing in Burg, tells a slightly different story. Friedrich Gabriel built a fairly spacious and comfortable house on the best street of the town, Schulstraße, and later even enlarged it. Despite a small official salary, with his position as tax collector and representative of the king, he belonged to the provincial elite and had easy access to credit.

While Frederick the Great was still alive and enforced strict regulations for proof of nobility, the elder Clausewitz could not achieve his greatest wish: to see his sons commissioned in the Prussian army. His firstborn son, Gustav Marquard, became a civil servant. Soon thereafter Frederick died, and after the coronation of the new king, Friedrich Gabriel tried once again to get his sons commissioned. This time, he succeeded. In addition to the new monarch, something else had changed too—the Clausewitz

Figure 1.4. The Clausewitz family home in Burg. *Photo Vanya Eftimova Bellinger.*

family now had an influential patron, Gustav Detlof von Hundt. A prominent noble who served at the prestigious 34th Infantry Regiment, Hundt had married Carl's widowed grandmother. Most likely due to his patronage, the questions about the family ancestry were forgone, and the three younger Clausewitz boys entered military service with the clear prospect of commission and a chance to embark on a promising career.

It was not completely impossible for a commoner to achieve a high rank—Clausewitz's later mentor Gerhard von Scharnhorst, for instance, was a farmer's son. Nonetheless Scharnhorst's ennoblement after his transfer to Prussian service in 1795 only confirmed the restrictions, since without the title he simply would not have been able to rise further in the hierarchy. Even with Friedrich Wilhelm II and Friedrich Wilhelm III's more liberal policy of allowing non-nobility into the corps, in 1806 only 659 of the 7,096 officers in the Prussian army were not noble. Of those, only 30 were staff officers; the majority—289—served in the artillery, traditionally dominated by the middle class.[36] Clausewitz was a talented man and even without the deception, he probably would have found his way in life. But it is doubtful that he would have risen so fast and so high.

On the other end of the social spectrum, the Brühls continued to enjoy their privileged position at the court of Friedrich Wilhelm II. With the double wedding of the crown prince Friedrich Wilhelm and his younger brother Ludwig to the duchesses of Mecklenburg-Strelitz Louise and Friederike in 1793, Marie's father lost his position as their chamberlain but remained an influential courtier. Charles's younger brother Albert Christian Heinrich had died a year earlier and his wife Laura was now appointed as *Oberhofmeisterin,* or chief lady-in-waiting, for Princess Friederike.[37] Brühl continued to supervise the education of the youngest royal sons, Heinrich and Wilhelm, and became a part of the king's entourage. According to Marie's account, he accompanied Friedrich Wilhelm II to the signing of the Reichenbach Convention of 1790 that signaled the end of the bitter Prussian-Austrian antagonism.[38]

Brühl was also with the king in Pillnitz in 1791 when the two powers issued a declaration in support of Louis XVI, now held under house arrest in the Tuileries. Brühl's old friend Bischoffwerder led the faction arguing for a war with Revolutionary France, and his diplomatic efforts laid the foundation for the alliance with Austria. Charles's presence at the two events indicated that he, too, was in the anti-Revolutionary camp. Whether Prussia and Austria really intended to actively intervene remains a subject of debate, but in Paris the National Assembly interpreted the Declaration of Pillnitz as a statement of war. What followed turned out to be almost twenty-three years of constant warfare that ravaged the continent.

Carl von Clausewitz was only twelve years old when, in the summer of 1792, Friedrich Gabriel traveled with him to Potsdam and introduced him to the commander of the 34th Infantry Regiment. Although painful, sending young boys into the army was nothing unusual—in Prussia, fathers eager to see their sons rise in rank did not shy away from enlisting them as early as possible. Carl assumed the rank of *Fahnenjunker* or flag officer, the boy carrying the small regimental standard during marches—a position intended to prepare him to later assume duties as an officer. Soon after his arrival, the 34th Infantry Regiment, under the command of the king's brother, Prince Ferdinand, left for France.

Charles von Brühl's participation in the Campaign in 1792, according to Marie's notes, was very short. In the first days of the invasion in France, an old foot wound opened dangerously. The count was forced to stay in the surrendered city of Verdun, while the Prussian army continued its march through Champagne. Thus, Charles was lucky enough to avoid the cannonade at Valmy on September 20, 1792, where the superb French artillery broke the Prussian spirits. This first victory encouraged the Revolutionary Army to chase the retreating enemy into Germany. On October 21, the French occupied Mainz and advanced as far as Frankfurt am Main before their counterinvasion was stopped. Still weakened by his wound, Charles von Brühl was allowed to leave the army and rejoin his family in Berlin.

For Carl, however, the military involvement was just beginning. The next spring in 1793, he marched with his regiment back westward for the siege of Mainz. Prussian and Austrian forces, as well as troops from various other German allies, closed in on the city, which was occupied by a 23,000-strong French garrison. Carl was a thirteen-year-old and just promoted to ensign.[39] He described himself later as "a son of the camp," but added that it was life far from the "poetical world" created by Friedrich Schiller in the drama *Wallenstein*.[40]

On July 17, the bombardment of Mainz started, and horror mixed with excitement of that moment became Carl's greatest memory from his first war. "When Mainz became prey to flames that we fanned, the cheer of the crude crowd of soldiers yielded too my childish voice," he wrote in 1807 in a letter to Marie.[41] She, on the other hand, remembered the festivities for the victory: "In Carlsbad, the capture of Mainz was celebrated with a big ball."[42] Despite the celebrations, with growing tensions in the anti-French coalition and exhausted finances and energy, Prussia was increasingly looking for a way to end the war. Secret talks between the two powers produced an agreement that France would return all the lands captured east of the Rhine, and Prussia would recognize French control west of the Rhine. The Peace of Basel, signed in the spring of 1795, started a decade of Prussian neutrality. Berlin observed the Reign of Terror sweeping France, and the subsequent rise of a Corsican officer named Napoleon Bonaparte, from a safe distance.

What preoccupied Friedrich Wilhelm II at that time were the Second and Third Partitions of Poland. The partitions came in reaction to attempts at reform and revival in Warsaw, which were not viewed by either Prussia or Russia as beneficial to their own ambitions. The two mighty neighbors quickly swallowed the remaining Polish lands, with the result that Prussia now grew in size by one-third.[43] One of the beneficiaries of Friedrich Wilhelm II's success was Charles von Brühl, who was finally compensated for his losses more than three decades previously. The awarded estates, however, turned out to be far from prosperous—possibly because the count, living far away in Berlin, was a poor landlord—so he sold most of them and bought a farm in Groß-Ziethen, south of Berlin. The management of this estate turned out to be just as challenging, and as a result brought neither financial security for the family nor the planned new manor house that was to be built on it.[44]

Despite these failings, Charles's privileged status at court was confirmed once again when he became a part of the Prussian delegation to the funeral of Catherine the Great and the coronation of the new Emperor Paul I in 1796 in Russia. Thus, when Friedrich Wilhelm II died in 1797, the Brühl family had every reason to mourn him. The event changed, as Marie put it, her father's "plans" and their "whole life."[45] The new king, Friedrich Wilhelm III, strived to distance himself from the shortcomings of his predecessor and especially the old guard. Charles was allowed to keep his position as educator for the youngest princes until they reached maturity in 1800.[46] His rank as a lieutenant general (although without a regiment) guaranteed a salary of 5,000 thaler for life, but his plans for further rise in Prussia were finished. His wife Sophie in particular appears to have taken this development with great displeasure. From that moment on, she spent all her energy and ambition on securing her three surviving children's future.

Figure 1.5a. Carl Adolph von Brühl, called Charles by the family. *By Anton Graff. In Private Hands.*

In practical terms that meant doubling her efforts at expanding Marie and Fanny's knowledge and social skills and placing Fritz in the vicinity of royal family members. In the diaries of Friedrich Delbrück, the educator of Friedrich Wilhelm III's sons, the Brühls appeared often between 1800–1802. Delbrück probably sought out the advice of his predecessor,

Figure 1.5b. The best-known image of Marie von Clausewitz. *Karl Schwartz,*
Das Leben des Generals Carl von Clausewitz und der Frau Marie von Clausewitz
geb. Gräfin von Brühl, in Briefen, Tagebüchern, Aufsätzen und anderen
Schriftstücken *(Berlin: F. Dümmler, 1878).*

and the family, for its part, saw an opportunity to forge a close relationship between Fritz and the young princes.[47] Despite these efforts, the Brühl
male heir and the royal offspring never grew particularly close. The sisters
Marie and Fanny, already "well-bred and demure as none else in Berlin,"

according to the latter's future husband Friedrich August Ludwig von der Marwitz, took lessons in painting, music, languages, and history.[48] Their mother taught them English with great persistence, and they spoke the language fluently. In later years, Marie herself taught the children of her friends English and pedantically corrected their pronunciation.

Marwitz also bore witness that both Brühl girls excelled in their studies of history. Marie indeed remained a passionate scholar of the past, to the point that later in her life friends like August Neidhardt von Gneisenau would acquire history books as presents for her.[49] She had artistic talent and knowledge in the visual arts, and whenever visiting extended family in Dresden, she spent her days strolling through galleries and befriending artists. The portrait of Gneisenau that Marie painted in 1816 suggests that she had a trained eye, skills, and experience although she clearly lacked academic schooling. Marwitz wrote that Sophie von Brühl wanted to create out of her daughters "true phenomena," and while impressed with the results, he had little understanding of this overly ambitious parenting style. In his memoir he referred to Sophie, rather bluntly, as a "pure ego-ist." Marie was, according to Marwitz, the more assiduous student, always striving to please her mother. He, however, seemed to take a certain pride in the fact that the four-years-younger Fanny remained rather indifferent to Sophie's wishes.[50]

While Marwitz considered Sophie von Brühl's ambitions for her daughters to be motivated solely by selfishness, this is not entirely fair. After all, the countess herself was an enlightened woman who married up partly thanks to her sophisticated upbringing. Her unusually cosmopolitan background—born in an English home, raised in St. Petersburg, and living for some time in Saxony's refined capital—had exposed the elder Countess von Brühl to a wide range of ideas and lifestyles. She also strived to cultivate friendships with some of the most progressive people of her time. Sophie became intimately associated with Baron vom Stein and his wife, and built a lifelong friendship with the highly intelligent and influential Princess Louisa Radziwiłł. Subsequently, the Brühl family actively supported Marie's proximity to important and educated ladies in Berlin. Where others keenly attempted to limit their daughters' or young wives' interaction with literary women—the most notorious case being Friedrich Wilhelm III's disapproval of his wife Louise's friendship with Caroline von Berg—the Brühls encouraged Marie's interaction with Madam von Berg and her daughter Luise.

Nor was Countess von Brühl completely unpractical in insisting that her children should be well equipped with skills and knowledge. The traditional hierarchy, in which count (Graf) and duke (Herzog) constituted the high titles, and baron (Freiherr) and all others with a "von" in their name made up the lower nobility, had started to lose its importance. Wealth and title ceased to be overlapping terms because their original base—the agricultural estates—had eroded or completely disappeared. Some dukes and counts relied mostly on the generosity of the ruling family, while newly ennobled enterprising families enjoyed comfortable lives. The Brühls themselves could hardly live comfortably on their estates—the combined annual income from Groß-Ziethen, the remaining Polish estates, and Charles's share from the ancestral manor at Pförten was only around 2,000 thaler far less than his income as a general of 5,000 thaler. Marwitz, who reported these numbers and as a son-in-law was intimately involved in the Brühls' family matters, seemed to believe that the problem lay only with the count's inability to manage his assets.[51] Even so, the situation unmistakably articulated the landed elites' growing desolation.

Sophie von Brühl read the signs better and evidently saw her children's future firmly in the service of the state. Hence she strived to equip them with the best skill-set available. As women, of course, Marie and Fanny, remained excluded from public office. But precisely because a bright wife with all the right skills and contacts could be a valuable asset for any man, Sophie believed they had a chance for good marriages.

In Countess von Brühl and Marwitz's indirect dispute, two different worldviews about the nobility's place and future in the state clashed. Later, Marwitz would become the leader of the Junkers' backlash against social reforms and would passionately oppose the creation of a more equal and a merit-based order. Ennobled by virtue of her marriage, Sophie von Brühl was less inclined to see the nobility's privileges as God-given. She too believed in the entrenched hierarchy, but sensed its shrinking limits.

One area in which Sophie had little control, and which may have shaped her approach to each of her daughter's futures, was that of their physical appearance. In Marwitz's memoir, he tactfully noted that Marie was not as beautiful as her younger sister. He added that, due to this circumstance, Sophie was particularly interested in Fanny and believed she had a brighter future than her other daughter.[52] Marwitz's decision to court the younger sister, whom he barely knew, leaves little doubt as to what he actually thought about Marie's looks. His sister Caroline von Rochow held similar views. After praising Marie's qualities in her memoir *From the Life at the Prussian Court, 1815–1852,* she added that the countess was "not exactly the most ideal creature."[53] Other contemporaries, generally thinking highly of the countess, left out of their accounts any information about her appearance. Marie herself suffered no illusions about her features. In one letter to Carl, she described herself as having a "moon face" and "a Kalmykian nose" (i.e., with pronounced nostrils), and wondered that he did not find her "as ugly as I think myself."[54]

The best-known image of Marie is a lithographic copy of a long-lost oil portrait. Her cousin Carl von Brühl commissioned the lithograph after her death, and copies were sent to fifty friends and patrons. Unfortunately he did not leave any other information about the painting except to note that, while it was well liked by her friends, he still was somewhat dissatisfied with how her eyes were painted.[55] The known lithographic image shows a serious woman with rather inconspicuous features. The most remarkable facet is her lively eyes, looking intensely into those of the observer. Indeed, Clausewitz later named her "lovely, friendly blue eyes" as his favorite feature.[56]

In a time when a woman's physical appearance greatly mattered for her acceptance in society, Marie described herself as "treated by the elegant world as a good natured but utterly negligible being," adding that she "could never force myself to solicit more flattering approval."[57] Instead, it would be her charm, broad knowledge, connections, and pleasant demeanor that would become her greatest advantages on the marriage market. She was, as Marwitz noted, "extremely well educated." Gneisenau later gushed about the "richness" of her spirit and contemplated what a pleasure it would be to travel together to Italy and Greece.[58]

While Marie was carefully prepared for her future role, Carl, in his own words, was educated by "impressions, troubles, occasionally by chance." Carl would later write with some bitterness that he was inferior to Marie, although by no fault of his own: she enjoyed "all the luck and all the protection" of her parents, while he could only say that his lot could have been worse.[59] Yet Carl may have exaggerated the unsystematic character of his education, because the archives in Burg hold an invitation for an event at the local French Hugenot school where his older brother, Wilhelm Benedict, merely a five-year-old boy, gave the opening speech in French in 1779.[60] Such an accomplishment would be hard to imagine in a home where parents did not value and support their children's education. Indeed,

Carl himself spoke excellent French. Whether this was the result of sys-tematic learning at school, or if he picked it up from the still-significant Huguenot population in Burg and his older brothers' studies, is difficult to determine. Rather than revealing the true state of his early education, Carl's lamentations therefore divulge his ambitious spirit, always striving for excellence.

Even if he enjoyed a more rigorous schooling in Burg than previously assumed, it still ended too soon with his enlistment in the army. With the armistice in 1795, Carl finally had the chance to continue his education in an informal manner. While waiting for the signing of the Peace of Basel, the 34th Regiment was stationed in the vicinity of Osnabrück. There Carl lived with a farm family, and during these long, dull days he borrowed books from the nearby city. Among them were pamphlets on human per-fectibility written by members of the Order of the Illuminati, a secret soci-ety founded in 1776 in Bavaria. While it would be almost impossible to reconstruct what exactly the fourteen-year-old boy read, he probably was impressed not by the Illuminati's utopian and mystic ideas but by the con-cept that reason and education gave freedom to the human spirit.

The same deep resentments about his youth colored his memories about the next six years, when he was permanently stationed at the garrison town of Neuruppin, an hour north of Berlin. Clausewitz scholar Peter Paret argues that this time was far from wasted and introduced the young man to new ideas, some of which would even be found later in the pages of *On War*.[61] Carl, after all, served in a prestigious regiment close to the capital, and Neuruppin itself had a library with 2,000 volumes, four reading clubs, and a couple of private circulating libraries to offer to a curious adoles-cent.[62] The military historian Donald Stoker points out that as a junior offi-cer, Carl also broke with the prevailing orthodoxy of the day and trained his men in new skirmish tactics.[63] It seems that Carl resented not so much Neuruppin itself as the dullness of a daily military schedule and the lack of rigorous intellectual stimulation.

At the turn of the nineteenth century, the Prussian army was also grow-ing old and rigid, a result of the policy of keeping it a primary domain for the nobility and avoiding personnel reform. On the eve of the Battle of Jena in 1806, for instance, 79 of 142 generals—more than half—were over sixty years old. The statistics for colonels leading a regiment were even more discouraging—only 38 out of 65 were under sixty, and of 281 majors only 85 were under fifty.[64] Having had the blossoming of their careers under Frederick the Great, few of these men took to heart lessons about the changing nature of warfare that the French Revolutionary army had aptly demonstrated in 1792.

It should therefore not come as a surprise that Carl felt, on one hand, burdened by his daily duties as a junior officer and, on the other, intellectually underwhelmed: "Caged in a small garrison, surrounded and influenced by blatantly prosaic events and personalities, my existence was distinguished in no way from that of the better sort of my comrades, that is to say from still very ordinary people, except by a somewhat stronger tendency toward thought, toward literature and by my military ambition," he wrote. Once encouraged by the ideas of human perfectibility to dream big, Carl saw his aspirations diminished upon clashing with the reality of garrison life. His interests and ambitions were now, he wrote of his time in Neuruppin, "the only relic of the previous impetus."[65] This was, of course, an exaggeration. Carl had not lost his élan. Indeed, when presented with the opportunity in 1801, he applied to the Institute in the Military Science for Young Infantry and Cavalry Officers. Later known as the *Kriegsakademie* or War College, it was a newly founded institution by the great military reformer of the time, Gerhard von Scharnhorst.

In his disappointment with his early years in the military, Carl failed to see that such a bleak intellectual existence was the norm rather than the exception when it came to traditional Prussian institutions. Although more comfortable, Marie's life was also far from satisfying. Shortly after having been formally introduced at the court in January 1798, the eighteen-year-old Marie became a lady-in-waiting for Friederike Luise. The unhappy widow of Friedrich Wilhelm II played an insignificant role at court but was widely known for her eccentricities, like staging theater plays and telling stories of ghosts' appearances around the palace.[66] As a true courtier, Marie never spoke a word on the subject despite her seven years of service under Friederike Louise. However, Louisa Catherine Adams, the wife of then American ambassador in Berlin and later president of the United States John Quincy Adams, was less discreet and wrote in her memoirs with both bewilderment and amusement about her first audience with the dowager queen in 1798. Madam Adams could barely keep her face straight seeing the queen dressed "a la crazy Jane"—while still in widow's garb, Friederike Luise's hair was hauled up in elaborate rococo style and festooned with a string of diamonds; the whole bizarre structure was then covered down to her feet with a veil.[67]

As lady-in-waiting, Marie's duties included attending to the dowa-ger queen's needs, upholding the stiff social protocol, and participating in various events at the court. Thereby the young countess built upon her acquaintance with the Hohenzollern and became a shrewd courtier. Marie's brother Fritz wrote in jest about her ability, learned and perfected at the court, to compliment people in "the finest and most elaborated way."[68] Carl von Clausewitz marveled at his wife's ability to keep a "beautiful composure" no matter what surprising or hostile circumstances she faced.[69] Despite the portraits Marie painted of many of their contemporaries in her letters, often less than charitable, none of them answered with similar lines about her in their memoirs, a circumstance suggesting that, even when critical, she did not alienate people.

With the loss of their former illustrious position, the Brühl family found more pleasure in the company of British and American officials living in Berlin. Proud of her English origins (although there is no evidence that she ever visited the country), Sophie von Brühl and her family became popular members of this small but tight circle. "A most social and agreeable intercourse existed between us and the Families of Count [Charles von] Brühl, Dr. Brown, and Count Neale; and we met almost constantly with-out form or ceremony," Louisa Catherine Adams wrote in her memoirs about their tenure in Berlin (1797–1801). In her own notes, Marie named Brown's intelligent and highly educated daughters Margaret, Isabella, and Fanny as her best friends in that period. An extremely wealthy physician in the service of the royal family, Dr. Brown opened his house, as Mrs. Adams further elaborated, for "all English foreigners of distinction," and an atmo-sphere of "playful simplicity" free of "all the etiquettes of idle pageantry" prevailed.[70]

In 1799, Charles von Brühl and his family took the Adams couple on a trip to Saxony and proudly showed them Dresden, the city Heinrich von Brühl had made into a modern European metropolis.[71] Yet in her recol-lections, Louisa Catherine never explicitly named Marie, and curiously enough, the young countess also failed to highlight in her notes and cor-respondence these relationships. Still Marie must have interacted fairly often with the Americans, because Thomas Boylston Adams, the younger brother of John Quincy who served as his secretary, briefly recorded several encounters with her in his diary.[72] Whether the time in the company of the highly patriotic Adams family confronted Marie with the possibility of a more liberal and democratic society, one can only speculate.

Figure 1.6. Louisa Catherine Adams, painted by C. R. Leslie; engraved by G. F. Storm. *Library of Congress Prints and Photographs Division, LC-USZ62-14438, Library of Congress, Washington, DC.*

At the dawn of a new century, the places where new ideas emerged and interesting events occurred happened to be outside the long-serving institutions of the Prussian state. Both Carl and Marie found a way into these realms at almost the same time, and the experiences crucially influenced their lives and worldview. While for him this was his attendance at the newly founded War College, hers would turn out to be the informal world of literary gatherings where new ideas and texts were debated. In many ways, Carl's and Marie's different paths mirrored the gender separation of the times—the young officer with insufficient education now entered an institution of knowledge, while the countess, carefully schooled in her early life, had to rely on informal structures for deepening her interests.

When Carl was accepted at the War College in 1801, "the direction" of his life, as he wrote, "at once was in accord with my deeds and hopes."[73] Its founder Gerhard von Scharnhorst, a Hanoverian newly transferred to service under Friedrich Wilhelm III, had much bigger ambitions for sweeping reforms in the Prussian army. Despite his high opinion of the artillery officer's qualities, the king offered Scharnhorst only the role of educating its brightest young officers. Scharnhorst took this task to heart but also never entirely gave up on his vision of reform.

For Carl, despite his great dreams, his first year at the academy was anything but smooth. "In the beginning, it was very hard for him to follow the lectures because of his lack of essential knowledge. He was close to despair, and probably would have given up on the hard endeavor, if it wasn't [for] Scharnhorst, who encouraged him with his unique kindness and benevolence and at the same time through his enlightened teaching woke up and developed all the seeds of his mental resources," wrote Marie in her essay of 1832.[74] The older officer probably felt particular sympathy for the younger man, who, just like him, was an outsider with humble origins. For Carl, Scharnhorst replaced the distant Friedrich Gabriel, who died in 1802, and he later famously called Scharnhorst "the father and friend of my spirit."[75] The young officer spent so much time around his mentor that in 1815 Marie concluded that, after her, Scharnhorst's daughter Julie was the one who knew him best.[76]

At the War College, Carl came in touch with the ideas of the great Enlightenment philosophers Montesquieu and Kant. Scharnhorst probably introduced his pupil to the former's writings, and later Clausewitz admitted trying to emulate Montesquieu in the earliest version of On War.[77] In all probability, the young man never read Kant's treatises, but came into contact with them through the lectures of Johann Gottfried Kiesewetter, a prominent intellectual and popularizer of Kant. Clausewitz's tendency to use definitions and abstract notions in particular seems to correspond to the great philosopher's emulation of the method of the sciences in philosophy. Scholars have already pointed out how Kiesewetter, in the words of Paret, "not a profound thinker" but had an "exceptionally clear" mind, built upon Clausewitz's interest in philosophy and taught him structured thinking in Kant's manner.[78]

In her correspondence, Marie suggested that during this time at the War College instructor and pupil also grew closer on a personal level. Despite his humble background, Kiesewetter was a widely respected and beloved member of Berlin high society, and Marie visited his house often in 1807–1810. Although their "philosophies" differed, she wrote to Carl in 1807, she had "developed a real intimacy" with the intellectual, "as

I have come to know him as a very judicious man." Because of Kiesewetter and Clausewitz's friendship, Marie felt that she could also easily talk with Kiesewetter about her beloved.[79]

The young countess's own process of edification was rather typical for the way women acquired knowledge—and often recognition—in the late eighteenth and early nineteenth centuries. The first exposure to the literary texts that played such an important role in her life can be traced to an almost exact date. In her notes about her early life, she put May 1, 1802, as the day of departure for the summer retreat in Giewitz (now Groß-Gievitz), where, in her words, she came across her favorite works by German writers. The "discovery" should be understood here mostly metaphorically, because it would be improbable that a twenty-three-year-old high society lady living in the capital had never before heard about the much-discussed books of the time. Nonetheless, in Giewitz Countess von Brühl became a part of the literary women's circle and passionately embraced German literature.

The May 1802 date also coincided with the dissolution of the small, merry circle of English and American expatriates—Ambassador Adams and his family had left Berlin the previous year, followed in 1802 by Dr. Brown. Although Marie remained in close contact with the Brown sisters until her death, she would never again associate herself with any other culture but German: "In Giewitz, a new world opened to me; I first got to know all of the better German writers and found in them that I had searched in vain until this point."[80]

In the idyllic atmosphere of the Mecklenburg Lake District, Marie's friend Luise, now the married Countess von Voß, invited friends to her husband's beautiful family estate. The two young women were only a few months apart in age and, despite Luise's early marriage in 1800, had remained close. Thus, after the particularly sickly winter of 1801–1802 Marie accompanied Luise to the family's summer retreat in Giewitz. Luise's mother, the infamous Caroline von Berg, also drew a crowd of poets and passionate literati dilettantes, making the sojourn a truly cultural event. A highly educated woman, Berg grew up in Weimar and enjoyed the friendships of Goethe and especially Johann Gottfried von Herder. After her marriage dissolved, she assumed the position of lady-in-waiting to the young Queen Louise, and soon after rose to be her best friend and de facto mentor in German literature.

Berg actively functioned as the mediator between the literary world and the court, and her house in Tiergarten became one of the centers of Berlin's cultural life where members of the nobility, urban intelligentsia, and writers met. Among the famous guests were Johann Gottlieb Fichte, Jean Paul, Wilhelm von Humboldt, and Germaine de Staël when she visited Prussia. In 1807, Marie described Berg as "rather scattered, disproportionate (namely in her appearance because in her heart she is the most dear and dependable friend); hence one should get used to before one could feel comfortable with her."[81] Just like Berg, the young Countess von Brühl became a passionate reader of Goethe's mature prose and would later introduce Carl to it.

Restless ladies and their activities were far from widely accepted, but appreciating poetry and prose became a uniquely female way of broadening knowledge and becoming an accomplished individual. Thanks to the previous generation of socially and intellectually ambitious women, Berlin now boasted its own popular salons. With their emphasis on emotions, intuition, and fantasy, all traits perceived as primarily female, the literary movements Sturm und Drang, Weimarer Classicism, and Romanticism gave women a chance to grow into an active and integral part of the literary society. Marcus Herz, the husband of the first Berlin salon hostess Henriette Herz, famously said once when asked about a poem from Goethe, "Go to my wife; she knows the art of how to explain nonsense!"[82]

The reach of the avant-garde should not be overestimated, as in Berlin at the turn of the century the Enlightenment was still in its zenith. Yet these parallel movements created exciting social and cultural opportunities. In their early 1800s versions, the literary gatherings contrasted so sharply with convention that they had an almost revolutionary character and thus attracted significant attention. The salons gave the ladies a chance, either as hostesses or as guests, to play a role in the cultural debates of the time. During her stay in Berlin, Madame de Staël gushed that although in Prussia many groups lived separate lives—nobility and commoners, Jews and Christians, scholars and courtiers, women and men—in these gatherings they mingled together.[83] For that reason, the daughters of rich Jewish families, like Henriette Herz and Rahel Levin, became especially overrepresented in the group of salonieres since they enjoyed wealth but suffered under a severely restricted social status.

The gatherings at Berg's house summoned interesting guests, but they were not regular meetings as were the classical salons. The retreats in Giewitz, on the other hand, seem to have been organized as an annual cultural event where the visitors spent their time occupied by literature and art. "You have to admit, dear countess, that you have never known such a homely bliss," wrote another guest from 1802, Karl Gustaf von Brinckmann, Swedish envoy to Prussia and an amateur poet, to Marie. "All in all, the readings and the debating of the readings never end, and in doing so the spirit lives so well, just like the body by the marvelous meals that never end too."[84] These witty conversations in pleasant ambiance were probably what Marie meant about coming to know German literature first in 1802. The young woman not only read Goethe's mature texts but also started to understand them; she not merely grasped their ideas but articulated and discerned their meaning in a debate with other literati.

As it happened, in 1803 another popular fixture of Berlin high society, Prince August, received his infantry battalion and, with it, a brand new adjutant—Carl von Clausewitz. The young no-name lieutenant from the provinces had become a passionate reader of Schiller's fiery poetry and admired literary ladies from afar. It was only a matter of time before he met—and fell head over heels in love with—the formidable Countess von Brühl.

2

Falling in Love
(1802–June 1806)

From the very beginning, Marie and Carl's relationship was unusual. Many have contemplated how a poor, obscure young lieutenant with a questionable nobility claim could have even dreamed of courting, let alone marrying, the daughter of an imperial count and herself an intimate of the royal family. Peter Paret suggests that Clausewitz's pursuit of the clearly socially superior Marie underscores his audacity and strong character.[1] Almost a century earlier, Karl Schwartz, bluntly referring to Clausewitz as a *Subalternoffizier* (junior officer) with no means, concludes that the only explanation for their successful relationship was the strength and determination of their love.[2] This may be true, but the question remains: How, and why, did a countess raised in the highest social circles ever allow herself to consider marrying a man with conspicuously less social standing?

It is this issue that touches the core of Marie and Carl's relationship and the interplay between their strong characters. Her decision (and it really was mostly hers) to elevate the casual liaison to courtship, with marriage as its final goal, set a pattern that prevailed throughout their life together. Carl was audacious, romantic, and unyielding; yet he clearly had a tendency to strain at social limits. He gave Marie a clearer purpose and more direct goals for her—and their—life, and she provided him with comfort, confirmed his dreams, and strived to keep his aspirations in line with their goals for success. It was this productive interchange of personalities that made their relationship so loving and effective and, by extension, created the conditions from which *On War* emerged.

From early on, Marie recognized that she and Carl had a particularly unusual story, and she decided to put it in writing long before their partnership started to bear intellectual fruits. Just like the first undated notes about her family and early life, Marie left additional ones about her and Carl's first rendezvous and subsequent encounters between 1802 and the spring of 1806.[3] Although written at the same time, Marie separated the narrative of her adolescence and early twenties from the three years of initial courtship with Carl because she obviously thought of them as a new phase in her life. In writing the notes, Marie clearly had posterity in mind: "Here I will put some effort to be fairly correct in identifying the particular dates and events, and one day you could give the raw material I am gathering in this way a poetic, more worthy appeal," she wrote to Carl.[4] Her depiction of their courtship, and especially of her beloved, is unabashedly favorable: "I read your journal notes with the greatest interest," commented Carl after receiving them in the spring of 1813, "and I found it even facetious, not without the vain pleasure, to see myself referred to and examined as a real romantic hero."[5]

In her account, Marie concentrated on her thoughts and feelings, while describing the actual circumstances rather sparsely. Careful comparison with the elaborate account of Fanny's husband Friedrich August Ludwig von der Marwitz creates a more comprehensive notion of these years. Marwitz, who fell deeply in love with Fanny—and then was heartbroken when the marriage was cut too short—was meticulous in his extensive recording of the details of their courtship and her family life.

Figure 2.1. Marie's sister Caroline Franziska von Brühl, called by the family Fanny. *Friedrich August Ludwig von der Marwitz*, Ein märkischer Edelmann im Zeitalter der Befreiungskriege, Gesammelte Schriften, *ed. Dr. Meusel (Berlin: Ernst Siegfried Mittler und Sohn, 1908).*

Figure 2.2. Friedrich August Ludwig von der Marwitz. *Friedrich August Ludwig von der Marwitz*, Ein märkischer Edelmann im Zeitalter der Befreiungskriege, Gesammelte Schriften, *ed. Dr. Meusel (Berlin: Ernst Siegfried Mittler und Sohn, 1908).*

Figure 2.3. Caroline von Rochow, born von der Marwitz. *Caroline Louise Albertine von Rochow, Marie de La Motte-Fouqué, Vom Leben am preussischen Hofe, 1815–1852, ed. Luise v.d. Marwitz (Berlin: Ernst Siegfried Mittler und Sohn, 1908).*

When Marie met Carl, her heart was ready to be given. The previous two years had been particularly hard for her, filled with family tragedies and personal blows. First in 1802 Marie could not avoid suffering pangs of jealousy and rejection when the smitten Marwitz offered marriage to the "very charming" Fanny, whom he hardly knew. The Brühls, especially Sophie, were pleased to ally with one of the oldest noble families in Prussia.[6] The fact that her younger sister's great beauty could compensate for a meager dowry simply could not have escaped Marie.

Then a second and much more devastating blow came when in July 1802 Charles von Brühl died after suffering from complications of liver disease. His adoring family was devastated, and in particular his children felt lost without their caring and wise father. Marie, Fanny, and Fritz also had to endure their mother's severe mood swings. As Marwitz reported, the sudden death of the beloved head of the family led to many "ghastly" scenes that regularly occurred for at least the next six months.[7]

Sophie von Brühl not only lost the husband she loved. She also depended on Charles for her wealth and standing at the court. Marwitz knew that he could not expect his future wife to bring a substantial dowry—Count von Brühl made that clear early on, and the suitor himself described his future wife as "poor." But their father's unexpected death left the family in a desolate state. Of course, one should note that the financial need in this case was clearly a question of perception. As Marwitz explained in the same text, to him a meager dowry meant income enough for his future wife's "personal expenses, clothing, and servants."[8] Nonetheless, for the family's social standing their financial trouble was very great. These problems increased further when, after Charles von Brühl's death, instead of granting his widow the general's pay of 5,000 thaler as a pension to the end of her days, the king offered Sophie only 2,000 thaler. Despite the Brühls' many attempts to secure their standing at the court, Friedrich Wilhelm III felt less generous toward his former governor's family. "It was thus that cheerfulness was banished from this house for a long time," commented Marwitz.[9]

Charles von Brühl's death and the family's increasing economic insecurity also had particularly unfortunate consequences for his older daughter. While she was smart and popular in the Prussian court, the lack of a large dowry limited Marie's marriage prospects. In her later correspondence with Carl, she described in dreadful detail how in that time well-wishers attempted to marry her off as well: "I told you once that a couple of years ago the society came up with an old, half-crippled . . . but very rich man." Marie's refusal to wed him, as she explained, led people to have "doubt about my sanity."[10] Berlin society could not have made more clear how bleak they judged her future.

At the house in Groß-Ziethen, sharing her mother's voluntary isolation, Marie sank further into depression, wondering what the purpose of her life could be. She agonized whether anyone would fall in love with her and would she ever be happy: "I have always thought that only love could make me happy and through the death of my beloved father, I felt to have become completely superfluous and that my life had ended before it actually had began." Yet as lady-in-waiting Marie had little control over her time and she was recalled back to the court, while Sophie von Brühl decided to continue her voluntary withdrawal from the world. Back in Berlin, the young woman felt lonely and abandoned—"twofold orphaned," as she put it.[11]

It was in this dark time when Carl entered Marie's life. According to her notes, the first time they laid eyes on each other was on a day of roller-coaster emotions. Unfortunately, she could not remember the exact date, just the circumstances (although her notes point to a date in December 1803).[12] Still grieving and depressed, the countess attended a public event for the first time since coming back to court, a supper in Prince Ferdinand's chambers. The king's uncle and commander of Carl's former unit during the Campaign of 1792 had developed a particular fondness for the Brühls and they appeared, as Marie's writings bore witness, often in his Bellevue Palace (today known as the residence of the German president). By the early 1800s, also frequently visiting the palace were Ferdinand's younger daughter Princess Louise and her Polish-born husband Prince Antoni Radziwiłł, whom both Marie and Carl would count among their closest friends throughout their lives. When Marie entered the chambers, upon seeing her, Ferdinand's wife Elisabeth Louise warmly offered condolences. Unable to stop the tears, the young woman moved to the window to calm her emotions. When Marie turned around, she saw an unknown young officer walking into the room. It was the first sighting of her future husband.

Carl participated in the supper in his role as the adjutant of Prince Ferdinand's youngest son August, and at the time he was in fact living with the family in Bellevue Palace. A few minutes after entering the room, the lieutenant introduced himself to the countess, but she, still shaken, was unable to make small talk. In her later correspondence, Marie would share with pride remarks of friends and family describing Carl as a good-looking man with a "pleasant and distinctive voice," who could be very congenial when given a chance.[13] But on that first meeting, she noticed little of this.

Their second encounter did not go much better. Carl again accompanied Prince August during his visit to the dowager queen at her residence, Monbijou Palace, in the heart of Berlin. The young officer conversed for some time with Marie's cousin Carl von Brühl, who at that time served as Friederike Luise's chamberlain. Clausewitz made a superb impression on the knowledgeable courtier, and Marie remembered that he praised the adjutant afterward as "a very fine young man."[14] Carl von Brühl indeed

Figure 2.4. Bellevue Palace in Berlin. The former residence of Prince Ferdinand is nowadays the seat of the German president. *Photo Vanya Eftimova Bellinger.*

remained a trusted supporter and confidant when in later years Sophie von Brühl disapproved of Marie's relationship. On their third encounter, again at Bellevue, the countess took the initiative to chat with the young lieutenant. The ice between the two was finally broken.

In a letter written in 1807, Carl admitted to Marie that he had felt drawn to her from the very first time he saw her. By the time of their initial encounters, feeling lost and lonely at the court in Berlin, the twenty-two-year-old lieutenant was looking for a friend. In a rather clumsy word choice, Carl explained that he had always had certain preferences for characteristics and facial features and that Marie seemed to have met that type. Instantly he imagined being friends and then confessed that an association with a "bright [*gehaltreich*] woman" had a certain allure for him. But already by their third encounter, as the young lieutenant admitted, he was deeply in love. Even in his most sentimental moments, Carl could not repress his rational side. As he later concluded, the constant obstacles that frustrated his wish to see Marie transformed the longing for friendship into a desire for love.[15]

In the following weeks, the festivities surrounding the wedding of the king's younger brother Prince Wilhelm with Princess Marianne of Hesse-Homburg gave Carl and Marie opportunities to spend more time together. At balls, formal dinners, and the opera, it seemed that, while remaining coy, the young officer always tried to be around the smart lady-in-waiting. Marie likewise also enjoyed Carl's company, and thoughts of him occupied her mind, as she grew accustomed to seeking him out at events. Curiously, the two read each other's feelings inaccurately, and later these early encounters became a great source of debate between them. After being socially marginalized, Marie still could not believe that the young officer had fallen for her.[16] Carl, for his part, suspected her feelings were rooted in the pity and sympathy a sophisticated lady like her could feel toward a lonely, penniless lieutenant.[17]

Unfortunately, before they could spend more time together, tragic circumstances intervened. In March 1804, Marie's sister Fanny died from complications after giving birth to a baby girl. This sudden and terrible event kept Marie away from the court for months. Devastated and unable to care for his newborn daughter—also named Caroline Franziska and called Fanny, after his wife—Marwitz left her with the grieving grandmother and aunt. Marie's notes indicate that during this time, she shouldered the burden of taking care of her shattered family because Sophie was in a desolate psychological state and her brother was still a minor. Marwitz wrote his recommendations for Fanny's education straight to Marie ("give her heart, she will have her own head"). He also referred, in jest, to Marie's younger brother as "your child" (Deinem Kinde), and indeed her own correspondence with Carl indicates that Marie often treated Fritz more like a son.[18]

According to Marwitz, two years after Charles's death the Brühls sold the site of a house the king had once granted the family for 20,000 thaler. The property in Groß-Ziethen was put up for sale too and received the same price at which it was once bought by the late count—60,000 thaler.[19] Marwitz did not mention Marie as the executor of these transactions. More logically, one of the Brühls' numerous male friends or relatives would have arranged the sales. Yet with a despondent mother, it remains rather plausible that Marie as the oldest sibling was the one seeking advice, getting familiarized with the options, and overseeing the consolidation of family assets.

While not insignificant, the sums from these sales did not noticeably change the Brühls' financial situation.[20] It is likely that the family used the money to pay outstanding debt, arrange a new house, secure the standing of Fritz as the lone male heir, and guarantee Marie and her mother a decent living for the decades to come. Without their own estate and no older male son to obtain a lucrative state post, the Brühls now lived in rather humble conditions by the standards of the highest social circles. It did not help that as members of the Prussian upper class they also had to keep up a certain appearance in order to be allowed at the court. In later correspondence, for instance, Marie calculated an annual expense of 450 thaler for her clothing as the barest minimum, while her highly skilled maid cost her only 100 thaler per year;[21] and the whole Clausewitz family lived with just 300 thaler in Burg. Sophie von Brühl also insisted on keeping a spacious house with numerous servants, grandiose enough that even members of the royal family could visit, and this pressure to keep up pretenses brought a constant string of financial troubles.

Until the end of 1804, Marie and Carl's rendezvous remained infrequent. The dowager queen was ill, and her ladies-in-waiting seldom participated in social events. When Prince August came to see his aunt, Clausewitz had to stay outside of the chambers. The death of Friederike Luise in February 1805 terminated Marie's position at the court, after which she and Carl saw each other even more irregularly. Hankering for his company, she meticulously remembered every short moment they happened to spend together—at balls and suppers, riding horses in Tiergarten, and at Lustgarten, the park opposite from the Hollenzollern Palace, where Carl drilled Prince August's battalion. She noted that her friend Charlotte von Moltke wondered why the young officer did not declare his feelings more openly. Marie recorded one meeting at which, because of her excitement and haste, she broke the etiquette and greeted him first. Growing impatient to see the young officer more often, she began to realize that this might be more than a flirtation.

In October 1805, while watching the parade for the visit of the Russian Tsar Alexander from the palace, Marie put her hand on the window and then Carl his. They touched suddenly, but that was all. The same evening, Carl finally dared to help Marie wrap her shawl around her shoulders. In the early nineteenth century, when women wore dresses revealing the bosom and back, this was one of the most intimate gestures in public because if anyone helped the lady with the outer garment, he might touch her bare skin.

Talking about literature appeared to be the only way for Carl and Marie to overcome their shyness. "Do you still remember, my dear Carl, that by our first conversations you expressed your enthusiastic admiration of *Werther*?" Marie wrote in 1807.[22] She filled her notes, just like their letters later, with references to literature and literary chats: Goethe's *The Sorrows of Young Werther*, Schiller's *The Maid of Orleans*, and Adam Müller's *Lectures on German Science and Literature*. Held in Dresden, Müller's *Lectures* were an early example of the rising German Romanticism and nationalism. As a sign of how invested the countess was in the new ideas of the day, she sent them right away to Carl. The references about popular texts in Marie's writings are particularly interesting because at that point of his life, the young officer remained reluctant to publicly debate them. Carl read extensively but, even by 1807, he confided to Marie about feeling "not up to the task" to debate French literature with the sophisticated Prince August.[23] With the countess, it appeared, Carl did not experience such troubles. It was indeed her "quiet, peaceful soul," as he confessed, that led him to fall in love with her.[24] As the scholar Maria Hartl points out, throughout their lives Marie made Carl feel that his way of thinking about the world was natural and acceptable.[25]

This liaison of literary chats and elusive gestures might have unfolded indefinitely or even died down due to lack of tangible progress if the world around Carl and Marie had not started to tremble. The War of the Third Coalition was in the making, and the sense of urgency accelerated both the public's feelings and Marie and Carl's very personal ones. In the fall of 1805, Tsar Alexander I arrived in Berlin to pressure Friedrich Wilhelm to finally take a side against Napoleon. In the face of France's growing power, Britain and Russia had overcome their differences and in April 1805 signed a treaty of alliance against the emperor. Sweden joined the coalition by allowing Britain to use its territories as a military base. Then in May Napoleon assumed the Crown of Italy as well, leading Austria, who saw its traditional sphere of influence on the Apennine Peninsula fractured, to join the alliance.

Friedrich Wilhelm wanted to continue steering Prussia away from the impending bloodshed. However, in October, the French corps trespassed the Principality of Ansbach on their march to face the Russian and Austrian armies. As it belonged to Prussia's ruling dynasty, the king was forced to act upon the challenge to his authority.

On November 3, Friedrich Wilhelm, at last, joined the coalition, although with one condition: his army would enter the war only if France refused to make a peace on the basis of the Austrian-French treaty of Luneville of 1801 (meaning that Napoleon would surrender the Crown of Italy) within four weeks of the departure of the Prussian envoy from Berlin. With some hesitation and delay, the Foreign Minister Christian Count von Haugwitz left for the French headquarters. The situation in Central Europe, however, demanded bold actions. Napoleon recognized the dispersed forces across the continent as the main weakness of the Third Coalition. With a swift move, he crushed the Austrian army in Ulm on October 16–19 before the Russian troops could link up with it. Nothing now stood between Napoleon and Vienna, and the capital was occupied on November 13. Yet the French troops found themselves among a hostile population, far away from their lines of communication, and threatened by the greater force of the Austrian and Russian armies, which had finally united. Friedrich Wilhelm thus had a reason to believe that in this moment, with the growing danger of Prussian involvement as well, Napoleon might be ready for peace. Cleverly, the emperor would prevent Haugwitz from issuing his demands until the situation had changed dramatically.

In Berlin, everyone talked about war and mobilization of the troops. The urgency now forced Marie to look fervently for ways to hint to the young lieutenant her deep affection. "It was for me an awful thought to let him go on in uncertainty about my disposition," she wrote in her notes. Marie even shared that, in these nerve-wracking days, had a chance for a private meeting occurred, she would have broken all conventions and confessed her feelings to Carl.[26] But for weeks, while the situation in Europe grew more belligerent, and Friedrich Wilhelm ordered mobilization of the Prussian army, the opportunity never presented itself. Finally, on December 3, (she even recorded the time—between 11 and 12 at noon), they got their chance. Marie knew that Carl's battalion—which was ordered to deploy— would parade through the city streets, and she used her little niece Fanny as an excuse to be in the vicinity since the toddler needed new leather boots. Unfortunately, when Marie, the niece, the governess Madam Kahn, and the nanny finally arrived downtown, the parade was almost over. "Brokenhearted and hopeless," in her own words, the countess walked into the leather shop nearby—only to be pleasantly surprised when Carl entered the venue too.

While the nanny and Madam Kahn were busy helping the niece and other customers occupied the store owner's attention, Marie and Carl stowed away in a quiet corner. She said that she hoped he would not forget his friends back home. He answered that whoever saw her once could never forget her. They held one another's eyes silently for a moment and touched their hands. "We would have sunk into each other's arms if we were alone, and we would have been one lovely memory richer, but even so, this moment belongs to the most beautiful and important ones in our life," Marie wrote. She added: "We understood each other and the union of our souls was silently formed." Marie was happy as never before. Carl left but could not stop turning around. Excited and lost in thought, he entered the palace on his horse through the low-ceilinged pedestrian gate. Until the end of her days, Marie confided, every time she saw the gate she thought about their first declaration of love.[27]

As it turned out, the War of the Third Coalition was already over before the Prussian army even left Berlin. The decisive Battle of Austerlitz had taken place on December 2, and the Treaty of Pressburg between France and Austria was signed twenty days later, but news traveled slowly. Instead of pressuring the emperor for peace, Friedrich Wilhelm's envoy Haugwitz was now presented with a humiliating offer, or more accurately a dictate, for French-Prussian alliance. Austria's defeat and Russia's withdrawal of its army in Poland left Prussia exposed and threatened by Napoleon's superior army. Friedrich Wilhelm had no other choice but to accept the French alliance, the so-called Treaty of Schönbrunn, on December 15, 1805. The treaty's clauses effectively isolated Prussia from its natural allies Russia and Britain. It forfeited the Potsdam Alliance Convention of 1805 between Prussia and Russia, and Friedrich Wilhelm relinquished the principalities Neuchâtel, Ansbach, and Kleve to Napoleon. Prussia agreed to close its ports for British commerce, and in return France handed over control of the Electorate of Hanover, the ancestral home of the British ruling dynasty and its prized possession on the continent, which was seized by the French troops in 1803. In February 1806, the Prussian army came back from the border.

Now Berlin was in even greater shock and disarray. For Marie and Carl, the romantic sentiments and exalted thoughts that had broken societal conventions disappeared as well. Seeing Clausewitz back so early after their emotional goodbye confused the countess—she had revealed to him her passionate and sensual side—and made her now turn cold to him. Marie analyzed the situation acutely: "Now however everything went back too fast to ordinary prosaic existence to not wake me too from my sweet poetical dreams and to bring me back to a serious examination of my situation. I had come to the point where my relationship with C. would either be an indelible one or would go back to being simply comradely."[28]

Marie was almost twenty-seven years old, well past high society's usual marriage age. Even so, she still felt that simply saying "yes" to the only man who courted her was not an option. As Marie wrote, particularly because she was not "in first youth," she had to consider all circumstances surrounding the relationship. So instead of resuming the relationship, Marie withdrew to reconsider the situation. Despite more than two years' acquaintance, numerous meetings, and long talks about literature, Marie and Carl did not really know each other. The burst of romantic feelings before his departure in December 1805 made questions about their future more pressing when he came back in early 1806.

Marie wrote that she took her "errant coldness" far and avoided being alone with him, so the shy Carl had no other choice but to allude to others of the hopes he had boasted on the deployment day but had now lost. She pretended not to understand. It must have been a double disappointment for the young officer coming back from a humiliating campaign only to see his hopes for love shattered as well. Later Carl candidly described his feelings of these sad days: "Oh my wonderful, dear Marie! How much I love you, how happy I am to be loved by you! A couple of months ago this word could not go over my lips and only fearfully, not without anxiety to be humiliated, my eyes uttered it."[29] While Marie still struggled to make up her mind, Carl remained patient. One of the remarkable features that he continuously displayed—and it impressed Marie immensely—was his unwavering affection. While she remained uncertain for a long time, Carl seemed unyielding in his commitment: "I knew him indeed for three years; he remained in that time always consistent and his whole being should have inspired just as much respect and trust as love."[30] Needing some space, Marie decided to travel and spent March and early April 1806 in Dresden.

This description of her qualms rebuffs the prevailing notion among Clausewitz scholars that the disapproval of her mother was the main and only reason for the prolonged courtship. This narrative, if not entirely inaccurate, is still incomplete. Marie herself hesitated for some time to commit to the relationship. To be sure, her mother's hostility toward possible marriage with a young officer from an unknown family certainly played an important role in Marie's reservation. Her notes revealed that she anticipated Sophie's rejection early on: "In any case, the most fierce opposition from my mother's side was not in doubt."[31] Compared to Brühl's first son-in-law, Friedrich August von der Marwitz, Clausewitz, as Peter Paret writes, had little to show at that point of his life.[32] The young lieutenant realized the gulf between them as well, because in a later letter he disclosed to Marie the distress the questions about his family's status caused him in these early days. Carl even debated whether to ask the king about confirmation of his claim to nobility: "From the moment when our relationship allowed me to think about the possibility of having you, this matter became again dear to me."[33]

Even if Sophie von Brühl and Berlin's high society did not question his claim of a noble title, the Clausewitz family would have belonged to the provincial gentry—not only without a prosperous manor but also, in reality, with no estate at all. It is unsurprising, then, that observant readers of the relationship never failed to be astounded by Clausewitz's enormous boldness to imagine himself next to this daughter of court aristocracy. Curiously enough, Carl's ambition for societal rise was the one quality that Marie failed to discuss in her notes and letters. Yet in the early 1800s Carl went to a great length to acquire a pedigree. In the later correspondence with his own nephew Carl Leopold, for instance, he extensively described how one should study letter writing, thus revealing how much practice he had put to achieve his remarkable style and to compensate for his humble origins.[34] In the beginning of their correspondence, Marie, a high-society lady trained in the same discipline by her father, the royal educator himself, was amazed by the young officer's skills. None could accuse Carl of less than sincere intentions toward her; from all accounts, he felt in love deeply and genuinely. Nonetheless, Carl's choice of object for his affection was remarkably savvy—Marie had the brains, the connections, and the background to enable a splendid career for her future husband.

A more interesting question, perhaps, than how Carl found the determination to pursue Marie is whether his murky claims to nobility did really matter to his future wife. Just like her mother, the countess was proud of her family's history and standing, and after more than two decades of marriage she still signed the foreword of On War with her maiden name as well as her married one. In correspondence throughout her life Marie was also addressed as "Madam/or Madam General von Clausewitz, born Countess von Brühl," even by Carl, as a sign of her higher birth. Yet the Brühls themselves were social climbers, who had risen from the Thuringian province into the European elite. As mentioned, William Gomm Jr., Marie's maternal grandfather, was an even more glaring example of a man with dubious origins but ceaseless ambition.

Probably well aware of the prejudices against her own ennoblement by marriage, Sophie could hardly allow herself a more inclusive view. Marie, however, had already met distinguished persons like John Quincy, Louisa Catherine, and Thomas Boylston Adams, none of whom of course carried noble titles. She also grew up during the reign of Friedrich Wilhelm II, a monarch who prolifically bestowed titles upon distinguished citizens and soldiers. He ennobled five times more than his predecessor Frederick the Great.[35] This would have affected Marie's view of nobility as well. In 1813, for instance, she wrote to Carl, at that time in Chemnitz, to seek out the old regimental doctor Buttrich who had inoculated her against smallpox as a child, convinced by that time he had surely been awarded a noble title.[36] All this would suggest that Marie, born into privilege and assured of her courtly status, did not appear to share her mother's anxieties but had embraced a more liberal and inclusive view.

Nevertheless, the young countess never put on paper what she actually knew or thought about Carl's origins. The only vague remark found in her correspondence concerning his family's status came after she met and spent an extensive amount of time with his siblings in 1813. They were "so good and warm," Marie wrote to Carl, that "although we might be different as well in some things, I still prefer their company to anyone else."[37] Despite her deep interest in every aspect of her beloved's life, there is also no evidence that she ever visited his family house in Burg. Carl, for his part, was thankful for her trust in his personal qualities and silence on the subject of the unequal social status. Years later when his nephew Carl Leopold decided to divorce his wife, also noble, Clausewitz composed an unusually open and heartfelt letter. "Your wife gave you her hand when you had nothing else to offer but your personality," he wrote, without a doubt having his own fate in mind as well. "No wealth, no sure position, and a calf-love that guarantees so little. It was only boundless trust in your character."[38]

Even if Marie avoided the subject, she clearly realized that Carl's "circumstances," as she put it in her notes, cast a shadow over their love. Remarkably, up to this point, despite his declarations of love and persistence, the young officer had never even hinted at the question of marriage, something that Marie had not fail to notice.[39] With no inheritance and relying only on his lieutenant's pay, he could hardly afford to provide for a family, let alone a comfortable life to which a lady from high society was accustomed. In November 1805, Carl was promoted to a brevet captain, but that did not come with a significant pay increase. He received only a meager 20 thaler.[40] Since the majority of the officer corps came from the nobility, it was expected that initially their family estates would support them. The hard times would pay off eventually once they rose in rank and received their own company to lead and manage its finances. A company commander received a lump sum to use as pay for the soldiers, their equipment, and clothing, and the eventual savings went into his pocket. Even after the Seven Years' War, when Frederick the Great sharply reduced the company budgets, this bargain still appeared desirable in a stagnant state like Prussia. The low income of young officers meant that the majority married late and only after achieving a senior position. Often the only possible reason for breaking the tradition was an engagement with a wealthy woman.[41] For Carl and Marie, of course, that was not the case.

Although not rich, on paper she still enjoyed a greater financial security than her beloved, who had just started rising within the ranks. The countess had her own independent income: she held a 10,000 thaler stake in the Pförten estate that she could not withdraw or sell but received 5 percent interest annually on it. Marie also had a 12,000 thaler dowry, and until her marriage she was to receive an annual interest from it. Altogether this made approximately 1,100 thaler in annual income.[42] In reality, because of failed crops, draught, and a drop in commodity prices, the income of the agricultural estate was less secure. In her later correspondence, Marie often complained about delayed, partial, or missing payments. The countess still lived with her mother and this brought significant savings, but as the above mentioned expenses for courtly clothing (almost half of her yearly income) revealed, she hardly enjoyed a financially carefree life. Marie had to foot some of Sophie von Brühl's ever-piling bills as well.

What probably also gave her pause when considering a possible marriage with Carl was the fact that she belonged to the very small group of unmarried women in those times able to acquire status and income on their own. As a lady-in-waiting for the dowager queen, Marie held a highly respected and paid occupation at the court. Although the yearly income was no more than 300 thaler, she enjoyed comfortable quarters and food for free and benefited from allowances for wood and candles. Marie could also rise to become an *Oberhofmeisterin* or chief lady-in-waiting, a position that brought more than 1,000 thaler in annual income with additional benefits.[43] While the countess had not received a new position after the death of Friederike Luise, her intimate connections with the royals surely promised another opportunity in the future. After taking care of her shattered family, and with her significant experience as lady-in-waiting, Marie had little doubt that she would be able to make it in the world on her own, as an unmarried woman.

And there was one more aspect of her hesitation, something she enigmatically referred to twice as the fear of losing her "inner freedom." Remarkably, Carl understood what was troubling her. In a letter from 1806, he confessed enjoying enormously every sign of interest and affection she had ever granted him. But Marie herself, Carl commented, never noticed his delight because "the fear of losing your precious freedom, the continuous battle in your soul[,] did not allow this." He recalled her inner qualms further in language of deep personal conflict and surrender: "where I gathered the most beautiful fruits, you sacrificed."[44] Describing Marie's love as a form of self-giving and self-abandonment was not a sheer reference to the societal downsides of a liaison with a man with lesser standing; the poetic language used by both Marie and Carl forbade such a narrow reading. It was rather an expression of one of the great questions of early-nineteenth-century self-conception that the two reshaped in the language of their own particular situation.

The emerging autonomous self and its interactions with the world outside fascinated poets and philosophers but also mesmerized observers of the French Revolution's ambiguous fate. The notion of inner freedom that Marie valued so highly echoed one of the main themes of Schiller's drama *The Maid of Orleans* from 1801, a play she recorded having seen in Berlin in the company of Carl and other members of the court followed by a lively discussion afterward. In Schiller's interpretation of Joan of Arc's fate, the young woman suffers under the dichotomy of higher calling and personal desire, between greatness and the all-too-human need for love. This message seems to have resonated with Marie, who longed for love but was afraid that a commitment, or a marriage, would curtail her personal freedom. The young lieutenant, who courted her, understood this deep-seated ambiguity.

The questions about individual freedom and interaction with the outside world gained ever greater potency, in part because the Reign of Terror that followed the French Revolution shattered the most quixotic beliefs of the era. The mass executions of political enemies or people who simply failed to show the utmost fervent support for the Revolution in 1793–1794 in France shocked the world and demonstrated the destructiveness of unrestrained self-righteousness, paranoia, and hatred. Once the literary heroes of Sturm und Drang were vexatious personalities preoccupied with boundless passions; they rebelled against the world but ultimately were crushed by it. Now Goethe's *Wilhelm Meister* longed to learn the art of life and become master of his own path. Horrified by the Reign of Terror, Schiller wanted to bring the individual to a new level of being through his *Letters Upon the Aesthetic Education of Man*. In this new literary movement, Weimar Classicism, Goethe and Schiller turned to ancient Greek and Roman models as a way to convey aesthetic concepts and social values, emphasizing that the autonomous individual needed to find a way to live in harmony with the outside world.

Almost simultaneously, poets and philosophers of the Early Romantic period started exploring the wounds of the soul and searched for lost worlds in folk songs and the mystics of the Middle Ages. The Enlightenment's emphasis on reason had defined the individual, and then Sturm und Drang's rebellion against the constrains showed its weaknesses. Now the individual sought to band together mind and soul, reason and passion, freedom and love in a new, harmonious way. In the coming of age of Marie, Carl, and their generation, these great cultural processes were replicated on a smaller scale. They had grown up and been educated in an environment dominated by the Enlightenment, then riveted by Sturm und Drang's pure and overpowering emotions, only to find themselves asking how they, as feeling and autonomous individuals, would find their place in a broader societal puzzle.

Marie was not the only one pondering the great questions of the day. Military historians suggest that around that time Carl began too to depart from the ideas of his mentor, Scharnhorst. In the essay "Strategy" from 1804, Clausewitz established his belief in the power and abilities of a strong personality to change the circumstances around him. A general, he wrote, needed less of a detailed and abstract knowledge and more of a "strong, ambitious spirit."[45] Whether, as Paret asserts, this idea was born more out of the growing unhappiness with the Prussian state's ineptitude in the face of the threat from Napoleon or, as Azar Gat argues, it arose directly from the new individualistic cultural outlook, it nonetheless posed a challenge to the traditional Enlightenment military school.[46] Scharnhorst, after all, believed that the change would be institutional. Clausewitz put equal emphasis on the individual character.

Looking back just over a year later, Marie sarcastically called the early months of 1806 "an era of awkwardness."[47] In the notes of 1812, however, she described the circumstances of the long courtship as inevitable and necessary, because they set the stage for the extraordinary partnership that came to determine their life. Close to the events, she could not grasp why it had taken her so long to decide to commit to Carl, but from the hindsight of later years came understanding of how extraordinary the commitment was. Her choice of husband—a poor junior officer, at that a year younger than her—was profoundly different from the marriage of her sister Fanny and so many other young women in her social circle. It also required Marie to take an active, equal role in the relationship in order to help her husband rise in the ranks and secure their future together. This was also her practical answer to the dilemma of how to preserve her "inner freedom" in a patriarchal world where women had to assume a restricted role in marriage. Marie would become Carl's intellectual partner and, if not equal in status, then at least equal in ambition.

Of course her decision to marry him included a healthy portion of bravado and wishful thinking. In early 1806, Marie could not have foreseen how far Carl would rise in the ranks; how unprecedented events would give him a chance to play a historic role; and how being his partner and lover would grant her satisfaction in life. In those days, she could trust only her love and instincts that this young officer was destined for greatness; that he valued her as a woman and an individual; and that he would welcome her partnership and not try to subdue her.

On May 25, 1806 they met at the theater and watched together with friends once again *The Maid of Orleans*. Afterwards, Carl forced her hand with a simple question: "Do you love me, Marie?" A couple of days later, the countess finally made up her mind and in a straightforward manner on his birthday, June 1, asked for "a conversation." "I want to tell you so much more about this day, about this first kiss that I was so little prepared for, that it <u>scared</u> me as much it bestowed happiness upon me and made me lose the little composure and resolve which I had managed to gather with lots of effort," she described the scene later.[48] They still had to wait on marriage but, from the summer of 1806, Marie and Carl became a couple, best friends, and intellectual partners.

3

Disaster and Separation
(July 1806–October 1807)

During the same period, while Marie sorted through her very personal quandaries, the ruling class in Berlin underwent an even greater crisis. Friedrich Wilhelm and his cabinet struggled to compile an answer to the new political and military realities after Napoleon's victory in Austerlitz in December 1805. This indecisiveness would mark the lives of both Marie and Carl as it shaped the course of Carl's career, fostered their growing radicalism, and finally spurred his later advocacy for proactive political leadership throughout the pages of *On War*.

Despite the alliance signed with Napoleon in 1805, dissent against the French was rapidly growing in Berlin, especially in the faction gathering around the outgoing and energetic Queen Louise. The trespassing of the French corps through the Principality of Ansbach had not been forgotten, but Napoleon's formation in July 1806 of the Confederation of the Rhine out of various German states westward had even more profound consequences. Unable to resist Napoleon's pressure, Francis II of Austria, who also held the title to and reins of the Holy Roman Empire, abdicated from this position in August 1806. Thus the complex political structure that had unified and regulated numerous German territories since the tenth century ceased to exist. Coinciding with the creation of the client Confederation of the Rhine, the prosaic end of the Holy Roman Empire heightened suspicions that Napoleon was preparing to swallow German lands one by one.

"As a specimen of the public mind in Berlin, it was necessary that the Government should send military patrols through the streets when [the French Ambassador] Laforet gave his fete on the 15th [of July], to prevent the populace from breaking his windows," reported Sir Francis James Jackson, the British ambassador in Berlin.[1] The most radical group among

Figure 3.1. *Queen Louise of Prussia* by Gustav Richter. *Library of Congress Prints and Photographs Division, LC-D429-35003, Library of Congress, Washington, DC.*

the proponents of open hostility, Clausewitz wrote later, were members of high society along with many young officers and some senior ones who feared that the French desire for domination—"universal monarchy," as Clausewitz termed it—would spell the end of Prussia's independence and identity.[2] Caroline von Rochow observed in her memoirs that "everyone, who was even half-way young, was full of fervor and enthusiasm."[3] The better part of the military, together with the cabinet, did not trust Napoleon either. Yet at the same time they feared being entangled in a prolonged conflict that would drain the resources of the state. Sir Francis James Jackson, an expert on the matter of Prussian politics, concluded that despite the growing tensions, he rather expected that the crisis would "result in peace."[4]

Clausewitz later described the tumultuous first half of 1806 as marked by the urge to evade "danger by any means possible, even if it seemed increasingly unlikely that open conflict would be avoided."[5] For him, the events only demonstrated the ineptitude of the Prussian state, which would

Figure 3.2. *Friedrich Wilhelm III in 1814.* Engraving by Blood in the *European Magazine*, from an original painting by Ir Bolt. *Library of Congress Prints and Photographs Division, LC-USZ62-89453, Library of Congress, Washington, DC.*

later be mirrored in *On War*'s argument that lack of political vision always results in military disaster. Composing his essay about 1806 almost two decades later, he concluded somberly that even if Friedrich Wilhelm and his cabinet had managed to establish a better and more proactive policy, the nation still would have suffered defeat; such was the overwhelming force of Napoleon and the weakness of the other major players. Nonetheless, he suggested, with better governance and leadership Prussia would have been able to avoid the crushing defeat that was to come, and would have found itself afterward in a better position to rebuild its strength.[6] In other words, in 1806 Friedrich Wilhelm's cabinet not only lacked political vision and will but also did not know how to use the instruments of the military and war to maneuver the state into a more beneficial position.

Needless to say, in 1806 Carl was in the camp of those demanding daring actions in the face of an inevitable clash. In his position as the adjutant of Prince August, Clausewitz observed closely the hawkish faction's most potent voices and their debates in the immediate vicinity. He especially admired the prince's oldest brother, Louis Ferdinand, a "first-born son of Mars" in his words.[7] Louis Ferdinand had boldly fought in the French Revolutionary Wars, and like Clausewitz most of the young officers saw this reckless but charismatic figure as a counterbalance to the inactive Friedrich Wilhelm. The faction met in the homes of two other prominent members of Berlin high society—Caroline von Berg and Prince Antoni Radziwiłł.

As vocal opponents of Napoleon, Marie and her mother also visited these gatherings. Caroline von Rochow wrote that the older countess had at last broken the voluntary seclusion from society after her husband's death and was "reinvigorated from all the hatred against Napoleon, widespread among the English people of that time. She and her daughter Marie Brühl . . . lived only in the fervor of politics and the hatred against the French."[8]

It was one of the paradoxes of 1805–1806 that the most progressive circles of Prussian society turned against France, the very same country that had aroused daring hopes for social and political overhaul just a little over a decade previously. In 1789, the Revolution in Paris had wakened people's political energies in various German territories. Napoleon's aggressive expansionism did not thwart their aspirations but, on the contrary, galvanized them. Ironically, the dismay and disgust felt against the French attempts to subdue Europe became the nurturing grounds for a growing German nationalism. Once enthusiastically welcoming the French Revolution, intellectuals like Friedrich Gentz now became Napoleon's bitterest enemies. Even more tellingly, the poet Heinrich von Kleist, who in 1803 had even tried to join the French army, in subsequent years would embrace German nationalism and in the process bring the German language to a spectacular height.

Despite French victories on the continent, almost immediately after the horrid end of the Third Coalition in 1805, the Fourth Coalition against Napoleon started to take shape. The emperor tried to preempt its actions and sought peace with his greatest enemy, Britain. The leaked news of his secret offer to return the Electorate of Hanover to London tipped the balance in Berlin, which had just received Hanover as part of its own alliance with the French. Now Prussia joined Britain, Russia, Saxony, and Sweden in their quest against Napoleon.

Yet Friedrich Wilhelm's actions were, again, anything but resolute. He mobilized only the troops stationed in Prussia's west and center. Napoleon concentrated his own corps on the border south of Saxony. As a countermeasure, in early September Prussian troops entered the territory of its only active ally at the moment, the Electorate of Saxony. France followed with full mobilization, eager to force a decisive battle before Russia's Tsar Alexander with his vast army came to help Friedrich Wilhelm. At this point, Prussia was going to war against a vastly superior force and with almost no powerful allies ready to support it militarily.

In July 1806, Marie left Berlin for another sojourn in the province. In August Carl was mobilized and had to leave for the canton headquarters in Schönbeck, north of Berlin, where troops gathered to be outfitted prior to the march. On their way south, the Prussian troops marched through the capital, and this time Marie and Carl sought each other out for a brief moment together. He walked twice around her house, looking at her window and hoping to meet her. The second time Carl finally had his chance and, as he wrote, this meeting left "such a blissful sensation" in his heart.[9] As a token of her love, Marie gave Carl a ring.[10]

Clausewitz had known war since he was a twelve-year-old boy, but now he had a loving soul waiting for him. He poured his emotions out in long letters to Marie, and no matter the long marches, always found the time to write. Despite the confirmation of their love, in the fall of 1806 Marie and Carl were still early in their relationship and somewhat formal with each other. When addressing her in his letters, he continued using the respectful form of the personal pronouns *Sie* (You) and *Ihre* (Your) instead of the intimate *du* (you) and *deine* (your).

In the bustle of war preparations, Marie and Carl did not have time to set up proper channels for their correspondence. Marie's friend Friederike von Moltke, who served as lady-in-waiting for Elisabeth Louise, the mother of Prince August, was hastily enlisted as the mail courier since the adjutant's letters could be discreetly slipped next to those written by the prince to his parents. While only one of Marie's letters from the war of 1806 is preserved, Carl's letter from September 29 indicates that she answered him at least once more. In that long-lost piece of correspondence, the countess obviously informed him that her fifteen-year-old brother Fritz had been sent to the front too. Serving in a different corps, the chance the two would meet was slight to none. At that time only a few of their friends knew about Marie and Carl's relationship, and no one from her family was aware of it. Nevertheless Clausewitz promised, if the encounter happened, he would meet Fritz with a "friendly disposition," even though he was anxious about accidental disclosure of his feelings toward Marie.[11]

Carl left for war full of dreams about fame and military promotion that would lead straight to a marriage with Marie. He truly carried a marshal's baton in his backpack, as Napoleon's famous saying went. At the time, Marie wrote later, the "fulfillment" of their "wishes" appeared so close.[12] Hence in one of his letters from the fall of 1806, Carl made a curious analogy between the upcoming battle and their nuptials: "I myself look forward to this day with joy as I would to my own wedding day . . . I hope for victory."[13] The reality turned out to be grim and discouraging, and even if Carl at first cautiously shared his doubts, he could not conceal his concerns for very long. On August 30, at the beginning of the campaign, Carl wrote to Marie that although he was not "faintheartedly despaired," Prussia's future seemed to him "cataclysmic."[14] On September 11, he noted skeptically that "all our political hopes are fading."[15] On September 20, walking around Friedrich the Great's former headquarters in Roßbach, the young officer wrote that he wished the daring spirit of the old Fritz—"a desperate gambler" in the face of numerically superior enemy forces—could grip once again the nation's statesmen.[16] Despite the bad omens, the young officer still tried to sound hopeful in his letters to his beloved, writing that a victory would be snatched in some miraculous way at the very last moment: "When I draw an outcome from all observations that I am prone to speculate upon, still for me the possibility remains that in the next big battle we will be the victors; no matter how small the weight of reasoning for hope could be, it is enough to cheer me and you."[17]

The Prussian army was divided into three field corps: one commanded by the Duke of Brunswick (accompanied by Friedrich Wilhelm), the second under General von Rüchel, and the third under the Prince of Hohenlohe. This decision to segment the army opened the door to division and competition among the commanders, and in the end it fatally delayed the battle plan. Clausewitz became particularly bitter that the ideas of the man who grasped the situation better than anyone, his mentor Gerhard von Scharnhorst, now serving as chief-of-staff for Brunswick's army, were constantly questioned or rebuffed during the tedious planning sessions on the field. "How much must the effectiveness of a gifted man be reduced when he is confronted by so many obstacles of convenience, when he is paralyzed by constant friction with the opinions of the others. It is clear that an unfortunate outcome, if it should strike us, would be the result solely of these petty regards for convenience," he wrote to Marie.[18] It was, in fact, in this letter that Clausewitz used his famous term "friction" for the first time. Later it would come to describe circumstances that could afflict the conduct of real war contrary to one analyzed on paper.[19]

The first clashes with the Grande Armée in Saalfeld spelled a very bad omen for the Prussian camp. On the morning of October 10 Hohenlohe's vanguard, under the command of Prince Louis Ferdinand, clashed with the advancing French column of Marshal Lanne's VI Corps. The prince should have retreated, but months of idleness and frustration had made him reckless, and he decided to attack. What Louis Ferdinand did not realize was that the scattered French troops emerging behind the hill were part of the advancing and significantly larger corps. Leading a hopeless cavalry charge, he was killed by a French hussar. "The death of the prince brought the whole army to tears," Carl wrote to Marie two days later, giving an idea of the mood in the Prussian camp.[20]

In these days full of anxiety and confusion, Carl felt again the need to send Marie one last letter. On October 12 he wrote: "The day after tomorrow or in two to three days, there will be a great battle, for which the whole army is longing." The prolonged march and the unending barrage of bad news had created an atmosphere of almost unbearable anxiety. Now it seemed that the soldiers simply wanted to get over it. Carl could not hold his fears or feelings at bay as he continued. The distanced pronoun *Sie* in the beginning of the letter became the intimate *Du* by the end: "Good-bye, my beloved Marie, in this moment, like never before, I have felt so close to you, worthy of you. Good-bye until a happy reunion here or in another world." He followed simply with "Forever yours, Carl."[21]

On the same day, October 12, the Prussian ineptitude and lack of strategy was put on display once again. Afraid that the fast-moving French army would cut their way back to Berlin, Friedrich Wilhelm and his commanders now decided to retreat north with a part of Hohenlohe and Rüchel's troops delaying the enemy just outside the city of Jena. When French troops discovered the units in the vicinity of Jena, Napoleon believed he was facing the Prusso-Saxon main body. He took the initiative, captured the city, and prepared for decisive battle. Inexplicably these movements remained concealed from the Prussian and Saxon troops, and on October 14 the French attack came as a complete surprise. In the fierce clash that followed, Napoleon crushed the flanks and forced the Prussians and Saxons into retreat. At the same, time fifteen miles north in Auerstedt, Marshal Davout's III Corps, originally sent to encircle the enemy, stumbled upon the main retreating body of the army. Despite its numerical superiority of

Figure 3.3. *Emperor Napoleon Bonaparte during the Battle of Jena on 14 October 1806.*
Artist in all probability Jules Jacquet. *Library of Congress Prints and Photographs
Division, LC-DIG-pga-01688, Library of Congress, Washington, DC.*

63,000 men against only 28,000 French soldiers, the Prussian army col-
lapsed under Marshal Davout's fierce assault. Soldiers deserted by the thousands and officers quit the battlefield and their commands.

As a member of Prince August's grenadier battalion, Clausewitz took
part in the battle by Auerstedt. His unit was one of the few to put up a real
fight against the French. On the right flank, as a result of the leadership collapse, Prince August had to assume command of three more grenadier bat-
talions in addition to his own. One of them was handed over to Clausewitz,
and as Peter Paret points out, this was the largest command he would ever
lead into combat.[22] Clausewitz led his men into skirmishes and later covered the withdrawals of the Prussian army. "I thought, among all the other
urges of the moment, unstoppably about you, because what was decided on
that Auerstedt's field appeared to decide also about my fate and about the
possibility to have you," he remembered in a letter to Marie.[23]

Pursued relentlessly by the Grande Armée, the defeated Prussian troops
retreated north. Some units tried to block the French march to Berlin, others attempted to reach strongholds, but many fortresses capitulated without

even putting up a fight. King Friedrich Wilhelm III, Queen Louise, and their children escaped to East Prussia.

In Berlin, where Marie and her mother stayed, the reports about the defeat in Jena-Auerstedt came after days of anxious waiting. Prince Louis Ferdinand's death in Saalfeld was the first piece of bad news that reached the capital, but the Prussians still believed in victory.[24] Only on October 17, when the twin battles in Jena-Auerstedt had been lost for three days, and the Grande Armée was advancing quickly to the capital, did the news about the defeat come to Berlin. Many did not want to believe it, and in his memoirs Karl August Varnhagen von Ense remembered that "people ran on the street without direction, gathered in front of the houses where senior state officials lived . . . made their way in, insisted on information."[25]

Fortunately, on the following day, Marie learned that Carl had survived the battle—he had sent a letter to calm the parents of his patron, Prince August, and Friederike forwarded the information to her. "You can imagine how much it put my mind at ease, after the rumors spreading yesterday let me reckon the most horrible thing," she wrote back on October 18. Like many other prominent members of Prussian society known for their virulent anti-Napoleonic views, the Brühls decided to leave Berlin. Before heading to Voß's estate in Mecklenburg, Marie sent a short note to her beloved. Just like Carl in his letter on the eve of the Battle of Jena-Auerstedt, she too bounced between addressing him with the distant *Sie* and the informal *du*, only to finish on a most intimate note: "Live long my Carl, my most beloved—may the Lord watch over you, forever, forever yours Marie."[26]

Meanwhile the Prussian government was falling apart. On October 21, the governor of Berlin, General von Schulenburg, made public his notorious announcement: "The king lost a battle. The first duty of the citizens is to be quiet. This duty I charge the citizens of Berlin to perform. The king and his brothers are alive!" Despite this warning, many young Berliners insisted on bold actions and active preparations for the defense of the capital. But Schulenburg and his administration had lost their nerve and shortly after his appeal for keeping quiet, the governor turned over his powers to his son-in-law, Prince von Haßfeldt, and left Berlin for Königsberg.[27] Ten days after the disaster in Jena-Auerstedt, the French troops were standing outside of the capital.

"By the 25th [of October], we were on the heights around Berlin, having marched by stages without meeting a single enemy soldier," remembered the French soldier Charles Parquin. "What had become of the fine Prussian army which had but a short while previously waited so proudly for us at Jena? What had become of this army in which even the most modest officer thought that he was another Frederick [the Great]?"[28]

Seeing the Grande Armée for the very first time, the citizens of Berlin were even more perplexed. "As the soldiers followed, barging without marching through the gate, the hats on every which way ... the people started whispering into each other's ears wondering how it was possible that those hungry, small men could have overcome our proud warriors," wrote one witness.[29] Still living in a prenational state, the Prussians could not understand the vital energy and enthusiasm that the French Revolution had released in its citizen-soldiers or, most of all, how this new spirit of self-confidence made these men capable of overcoming even the best-drilled professional army. "Suddenly war again became the business of the people—a people of thirty million, all of whom considered themselves to be citizens," Clausewitz would later explain the origins of the French prowess on the battlefield. "The people became a participant in war; instead of governments and armies as heretofore, the full weight of the nation was thrown into the balance.... Nothing now impeded the vigor with which war could be waged, and consequently the opponents of France faced the utmost peril."[30]

Napoleon arrived in Berlin on October 27 and triumphantly marched once again the next day through the Brandenburg Gate. He then ordered the Quadriga on its top to be taken as a spoil of war to Paris. Caroline von Rochow and her mother watched the parade from a palace window, an act that promptly led to Marie and Sophie von Brühl's deep disapproval.[31]

While the citizens of Berlin experienced no real harm, Carl as an officer of the retreating Prussian army became the subject of relentless pursuit. After days on the run, hungry, tired, and disheartened, on October 28 Prince August, Clausewitz, and 240 remaining grenadiers—serving as the rearguard of Hohenlohe's army on its march toward safer grounds behind the Oder River—met the French one last time near the town of Prenzlau. On the road to the fortress, realizing that the French cavalry was furiously attacking the column in front of them and too tired to withstand a major assault, the prince and his troops decided to escape through the fields. The enemy, however, soon discovered them and launched a pursuit. After a fierce resistance, attacked by artillery and cavalry, moving along an unforgiving terrain, Prince August and Clausewitz finally surrendered together with around 100 surviving soldiers.[32]

A few weeks later, Carl described in a letter to Marie his own performance in the Campaign of 1806 as "without abundance of great deeds but also without any burden of guilt." Prenzlau was just sixty miles east from Giewitz, where Marie stayed. "I knew the place of your stay and—think about my feelings—some miles away from it, we, abandoned by the fate, had thrown ourselves in the arms of despair and played with its loaded dice," Carl wrote later to her. There would not be another day, he added, when he felt her closer than that October 28.[33]

After their surrender, Prince August and Clausewitz as his adjutant were sent immediately to Berlin to meet Napoleon. "The prince was admitted at once by the emperor, while [I] had to linger in a completely ruined uniform among all the brilliant, almost disdainfully elegant, uniforms of the imperial adjutants," he later bitterly wrote in *Nachrichten*.[34] Clausewitz was now a prisoner of war, waiting for the enemy to decide his fate. For the immediate time being, Carl had to stay in Neuruppin, the garrison town where he had spent much of his adolescence.

In his letters over the next couple of weeks Carl revealed the everyday life of a prisoner of war, the uncertainty of future and fate, and the dull days, full of inactivity and meaningless tasks, while elsewhere others continued to fight. He, of course, enjoyed captivity with fairly comfortable conditions, without forced labor or even real prison walls for that matter. Once the combat had ceased and the soldiers surrendered, the Napoleonic army turned back to the civilities. While conditions varied, as prisoners of war officers usually were subject to particularly loose restrictions. They benefited from a certain freedom of movement around the area of their confinement and even received small payments from the French government for lodging and necessities. The only requirements were to sign regularly with the authorities and to not attempt escape. Men of rank and stature expected to be exchanged fast or paroled.[35]

Since Clausewitz's fate as a prisoner of war was closely tied to that of his superior, a prince of royal blood, his treatment was even more preferential and a subject of careful design. Being a man of reason, Carl decided to use the time in Neuruppin to study while he was still waiting to hear where in France they would be sent. He reported to Marie that "the feeling of unhappiness" occupied his mind less when he devoted his time to studying mathematics. Fearing that the French occupiers might read his letters, Carl used the metaphor of a "sick person" (*der Kranke*) when discussing Prussia's fate. *Der Kranke*, he wrote to Marie, was not incurable as so many others thought, but rather, despite suffering terribly, was on his way to healing. Clausewitz then suggested that the desire for revenge sparked by defeat and resentments against the foreign power, had become the greatest advantage Prussia now enjoyed.[36]

After the quick exile in Giewitz, Marie and her mother were back in occupied but peaceful Berlin. Marie and Carl met probably twice before he left with Prince August for their captivity in France. In a set of notes composed in early 1813, Marie described the couple's goodbye when, on the eve of his departure on December 30, Carl came to the prince's family residence in Bellevue, and she used again her friend Friederike as an excuse to visit the palace. "This reunion made me unspeakably happy. The danger banished every trace of anxious or prideful reservation from my heart and let me feel in full what C. meant to me; with deepest love and utmost devotion I took him to my heart."[37] Then he was gone, and neither knew how long it would be before their next reunion.

From then on, Carl and Marie's fate became intimately connected with that of the Prussian state. For the near future, he was a prisoner of war in France waiting to be either exchanged or freed after a peace treaty. Carl's subsequent career in the military, and by extension his prospective marriage to Marie, depended on the ability of the king and the cabinet to find a path forward for the morally and materially bankrupt state. The two lovers had to wake up, as Marie wrote a couple of months later, from "a sweet dream" that a life together would come easily, and nothing had prepared them for this revelation.[38] Before 1806 Carl and Marie had shared interests in the political and cultural endeavors of the time, but after Jena-Auerstedt they invested all their energies in understanding the roots of the crisis and to push for reforms.

During his time as prisoner of war, the two had to carefully curtail the debates about political realities, mostly because of fear that their correspondence might be read. Marie could not write to Carl about the French occupation in Berlin either, although this surely must have been a heated topic among citizens of the capital. The cities burdened by the care for the French troops, and especially Berlin where 10,000 men were billeted throughout the winter of 1806–1807, faced incredible financial liabilities. Already a state in debt before the catastrophe in Jena-Auerstedt, Prussia now underwent a severe economic crisis. Prussian economist Heinrich von Buguelin, who would later become part of the reformers trying to bring the country back from collapse, described the situation: "The owners of

estates were exhausted through contributions, [war] supply, and billet-
ing. For house owners it was the same, but [on top of this] their properties
lost half of their value and only with effort they could rent a part of them
for half of the price. . . . The factory owner saw himself forced by the lack
of demand to fire his workers. The shop owner sold nothing or only on
credit."[39] The economic crisis also affected the Brühls, since Sophie von
Brühl's widow's pension represented a significant portion of their income.
In the political vacuum none knew when and from where the next payment
would come. Now they lived, Marie wrote to Carl, in "strict economy."[40]

Despite her complaints that the lack of carriages and horses in occupied
Berlin forced her to walk on foot, Marie's letters indicate that she continued her active social life.[41] The countess visited houses and gatherings
where the French occupation and the future of the state were discussed,
although she could write very little and mostly in code about it to Carl.
Marie cleverly continued to use the metaphor of *der Kranke* when discussing Prussia and even went further, writing as if the "sick man" was indeed
a close friend of theirs.

Notwithstanding the disaster in Jena-Auerstedt and the occupation
of Berlin, the king, the Prussian government, and parts of the Prussian
army had escaped the French, and the war continued. Now sheltered in the
remotest corner of his state, East Prussia, and encouraged by the Russian
Tsar Alexander's resolve to fight Napoleon, Friedrich Wilhelm sided with
the minority in his cabinet advocating continuation of the struggle. On
January 10, 1807, after the news of the beginning of the Russian offensive
toward Poland and East Prussia reached Berlin, Marie wrote to Carl that *der
Kranke* had made "great strives toward his healing."[42] Then came the Battle
of Eylau (February 7–8) where, despite the enormous losses the French suffered, the outcome remained unclear. Still Marie euphorically concluded
that simply by shattering Napoleon's relentless advance, the result was good
for Prussia. She also added, referring to the Prussian cabinet: "I have to
tell you that [*der Kranke's*] family had lost its head by the slightest sign of
relapse."[43]

On March 11, Marie commented that their "sick friend" was feeling better than ever and his healing process exceeded all expectations.[44]
Facing harsh winter terrain and tremendous loss of life, Napoleon offered
peace terms by which Prussia had to merely give up its West Elbian
territories—but Friedrich Wilhelm had renewed hope in the offensive. In
Silesia, however, the French continued to capture Prussian fortresses, and

the Russian army failed to capitalize on the momentum gained in Eylau. Nonetheless even after Danzig was captured by the French on May 24, Marie and the patriotic circles in Berlin continued to believe in possible victory in the East: "One could almost believe that this last bankruptcy would not have such a dangerous influence over him as we feared in the beginning."[45]

Under the command of Major August Neidhardt von Gneisenau, Kolberg, the only remaining Prussian fortress in Pomerania, heroically defied the French. The use of new tactics and the ability of Gneisenau to inspire the defenders aroused hopes of an honorable end of the war for Prussia. Yet on June 18 after the Russian defeat in Friedland, Marie wrote somberly that the patriotic circles swung now between "fake hopes" and "unnecessary worries" about the health of the "sick man."[46]

While the fighting in the East continued, Carl harbored hope to be exchanged for a captured French officer and to receive once more a chance to distinguish himself on the battlefield. Thoroughly involved in this plan, Marie had the specific task to keep reminding friends about the young officer's faith. In the winter and spring of 1807, she repeatedly wrote to her friend Charlotte von Moltke, who as Queen Louise's lady-in-waiting was with the court in Königsberg, asking her to invoke Clausewitz's name in front of Scharnhorst, by that time chief-of-staff for the army in East Prussia.[47] Yet Marie soon found out that the biggest obstacle for the exchange was Prince August's parents, all too happy to see their favorite son, and by extent his adjutant, living safely and comfortably in the French heartland.[48]

Carl now decided to write directly to Scharnhorst. He slipped the note between the pages he sent to Marie and asked her to forward it to Charlotte. Since the French could have considered Marie's and Charlotte's involvement as an act of espionage, Carl let the two ladies decide whether they were willing to engage in the secret delivery of a message to a senior officer on the enemy side. "How could you consider even for a moment that one of us would shy away from this task," Marie scolded him later.[49] Just a couple of weeks after this, the decisive French victory in Friedland put an end to the Russian offensive—and to Clausewitz's personal hopes of being part of the campaign in the East.

Unable to talk openly about politics, the two lovers used the time and their letters to share their most intimate memories, dreams, and wishes and to reveal to one another their aspirations. Marie never made a secret of her intentions to play an active role in Carl's life, and more than once openly wrote that she no longer had "any other satisfaction than to love you, to live for you, to have influence over your happiness."[50] Around her a cohort of spirited ladies might have enjoyed social prominence, but the countess never harbored any illusions about the limitations of a woman's role. Especially in 1806–1807, Marie came to resent how little influence she had over her own life and the fact that she could do almost nothing for the marriage to happen: "I have practiced [resignation] already often and it probably belongs to the peculiarities of my character."[51] Hence she pragmatically turned her attention toward Carl's qualities: "None observes you with more interest than me and none else could be so deeply preoccupied with your merits. It's certainly no flattery but my most intimate conviction when I say that I do believe you are capable of the greatest things."[52]

Ever striving for self-improvement, Carl eagerly welcomed Marie's ambitions and declared that whatever quality or skill she deemed necessary, he would "acquire it soon in your proximity and under the influence of your whole noble being."[53] She embraced the task with a fervor and diligence that took the young officer aback. Prince August and Carl were not bound by the usual restrictions for prisoners of war but were received in the highest circles of French society and enjoyed freedom of movement. In March and April 1807 the two men went to Paris. On the eve of this trip, Marie urged Carl to visit museums and demanded a detailed report about his impressions of artworks, especially her favorite, Raphael. Through the philosophy lectures at the War College, Clausewitz must have been already aware of Immanuel Kant's theory on aesthetic judgment. His answer to Marie, however, revealed how little by that point *Critique of Judgment* had penetrated his mind and understanding of art. Raphael's paintings might have been best situated in church, he analyzed, and then added casual gossip about their price. The response was a long lecture from Marie informing him that he ought not to superficially prattle about the great masterpieces but try to grasp their ideas. In his next letter, Carl, half joking, wrote that he felt like a general who, despite all his cautiousness, had been lured into enemy territory only to discover that "a hostile army was at his rear."[54] Yet despite the initial difficulties, Clausewitz persisted in aesthetic studies and until the end of his days he remained interested in the inner mechanisms of creation and perception.

Marie's tedious lectures might have soured the mood if she had not hesitated to reveal in the letters her own insecurities as well.

A passionate reader of Goethe, the countess judged her own abilities to express in writing the complexity of what was going through her heart and mind as deficient ("all words cold and weak compared to the intimacy of my feelings").[55] She also revealed the much greater insecurity about the marks that time was leaving on her body, at one point asking wryly, "And would you still love your old Marie, wouldn't you my dear Carl?" The countess was almost twenty-eight years old, and the occasional gray streaks in her hair brought her to despair.[56] For her displays of trust and openness, Marie demanded the same from her beloved: "Let your letters always be the true picture of your feelings, my dear Carl, and do not hesitate to sadden me with grievances."[57]

On June 28, Tsar Alexander and Emperor Napoleon met to negotiate peace on a raft in the middle of the Niemen River, near the town of Tilsit. Friedrich Wilhelm was also there but had to wait outside while the two emperors negotiated. Indeed, it was only because of the tsar's insistence that Prussia continued to exist as a country. Even so, it lost about half of its territory, had to reduce its army to 40,000 men, and was forced to pay a tribute of 154.5 million French Francs. Later the sum was cut to 120 million Francs, still a colossal amount, and until it was paid 10,000 French troops would occupy the Oder fortresses. "I myself do believe that our fate's horrible tragedy is not yet at its end," Marie wrote to Carl on July 24. Forgetting all caution she added, "The only consolation is this that at least concerning the last events, the shame was not on our side. . . . We have been betrayed in the most cruel way."[58] Like many others in Prussia, she bitterly decried the Russian tsar's decision to give up the offensive in the East and to sue for peace after the defeat in Friedland.

Despite the end of the hostility, by August Carl and the prince were only allowed to travel to Geneva (a French possession at the time) and stay in the nearby house of Madame de Staël while waiting for their passes to Prussia. In Berlin, Marie never lost sight of their plans for the future. The army's sharp reduction meant that many officers would lose their positions, and she followed the events closely. From Königsberg, Charlotte von Moltke informed Marie of the creation of the Military Reorganization Commission, led by Carl's old mentor, Scharnhorst, and stated that in all probability Clausewitz would be among the persons to receive an "agreeable position."[59]

Yet in the summer of 1807, the Prussian state appeared so degraded and distraught that the otherwise politically savvy countess, in a moment of despair, suggested to Carl that they should give up their dreams, withdraw from public life, marry, and use her small inheritance to buy an estate to live in the deep province: "Homely happiness is after all the only thing left on earth," she wrote.[60]

From the house of Madame de Staël in Coppet on Geneva Lake, where throughout September he and the prince continued to wait for their passes, Carl wrote back to Marie. He did not completely dismiss the idea of life as a provincial esquire devoting his time to history and war studies, but made clear that he would not accept her inheritance. And despite her suggestion of forgoing military life, he then asked Marie to pass another letter to Scharnhorst. Although his position as princely adjutant was safe, Carl still hoped that the reshufflings in the army would bring him in close proximity to his mentor.[61]

Soon after, the long wait for passes was over. In mid-October Prince August and Clausewitz finally made their way to Berlin.

4

The Long Engagement
(November 1807–November 1809)

When Carl and Marie met again in November 1807, both the country and their own lives were about to undergo wide-ranging transformations. The Prussian government had just introduced groundbreaking reforms to bring the country's social order and economy into modernity. Gerhard von Scharnhorst was taking the first steps toward reorganization of the army. In this short but turbulent period, Carl gained invaluable insight into military reformation and started to develop his mature ideas. Marie, meanwhile, found herself in the midst of the most radical patriotic wing.

In their epistolary debates during 1808–1809, the couple searched for context, underlying causes, and likely consequences of the events overwhelming their lives. Marie's and Carl's letters shared passion and candidness, and each tried to outdo the other in describing most comprehensively the transformation of their world. Quite revealingly, the only known letters of Marie's prior to the discovery of the Buttlar-Venedien archive are from 1808–1809, a period the Brühl family and Karl Schwartz must have believed showed her personality and ideas at their best.

In the months after Carl's return from France, he and Marie met each other almost every day.[1] She gradually divulged the secret of their relationship to a small circle of friends and used them often as couriers and alibis—Friederike and Charlotte von Moltke, Luise von Voß, her mother Caroline von Berg, and Marie's cousin Carl von Brühl. In March and April 1808, Prince August and Clausewitz visited the court in Königsberg. This time Marie revealed her secret to her longtime friend and politician Johann

August Sack. Probably the most energetic member of the reform circle, Sack worked for the government in Königsberg and while there, he agreed to serve as courier for the couple.[2]

In August, Carl had to leave Berlin once again in his role as Prince August's adjutant. The prince had been promoted to commanding officer of the artillery, and his new position required a permanent move to the city of Königsberg in East Prussia where the government and the royal family continued to reside. In these tumultuous times, Friedrich Wilhelm found the smaller, more frugal court in the province easier to manage and was not in a hurry to return to the capital. Before Carl's departure, he and Marie took the fateful step of revealing to Sophie von Brühl their feelings and plans for the future.

Neither Marie nor Carl directly described in the correspondence the scene that followed. However, their brief remarks left little doubt about the elder countess's fierce reaction. Sophie apparently accused Clausewitz of "exaltation" and her own daughter's feelings "as something out of a novel." "As though I were a vagrant fortune hunter," was Carl's short but bitter comment about the offensive qualifications. From the beginning, the two held no illusion about the reasons behind the disapproval: "Name, status, wealth are the real concerns, whether she would like to admit it or not," Carl told his future wife.[3]

The situation was complicated because Marie's high rank as *Reichsgräfin* clearly qualified an eventual marriage as unequal. Historically, the imperial counts had been independent rulers of their domains. Hence many families required the offspring to marry only within their own class (the so-called principle of *Ebenbürtigkeit*). Luckily for Marie, her grandfather Heinrich von Brühl had never included such a clause in his testament.[4] Even so, in Prussia until 1868 parents had to consent to the union of their children, and this remained one of the effective mechanisms by which the nobility controlled their future relations despite the growing societal liberalization.[5] To marry without Sophie von Brühl's blessing would have been not only legally impossible but also, even if the lovers took the desperate step to escape and wed abroad, they would have found themselves social outcasts with their ambitions terminated.

Before revealing their love to Marie's mother, neither Carl nor Marie harbored any illusion that the union would happen right away since his rank was too low and underpaid to allow for a family. The elder countess's fierce denial, however, meant that they could not even formally exchange vows and become engaged publicly. Nonetheless, Carl and Marie appear to have viewed the revelation in front of Sophie von Brühl as an informal engagement. When Sophie responded by proceeding to search for other suitors for her daughter, their reaction was one of outrage and disgust.

With no support from Marie's mother, their best hope for marriage became Carl's close relationship with the leader of the Prussian army's reforms, Scharnhorst, which opened the possibility of quick promotion. When Marie and Carl said their goodbyes before his departure for Königsberg, they believed in a relatively short reunion. Instead, the events would force upon them an almost eighteen-month-long separation. Soon after arriving, Carl realized that his chance of becoming a part of Scharnhorst's inner circle depended on the course of the reforms. To leave his position as adjutant without alienating as important a man as Prince August required, in Carl's words, a "small intrigue."[6] Only as part of an overhaul of the system and subsequent reshuffling of positions could Scharnhorst acquire a promotion and a new job for his protégé.[7] A couple of months later, when the general indeed followed through with the plan and requested permission from Friedrich Wilhelm for Clausewitz's transition, the king's initial answer was far from encouraging. As Carl reported to Marie: "He asked why I did not want to stay, I had it so good where I was, what one should do about me, what was this all about?"[8]

The brevet captain had to remain in his old adjutant position, but in the fall he also assumed part-time responsibilities in Scharnhorst's office. There the general discussed with his former pupil the events of the day. With pride, Carl wrote back to Marie that, "for the first time in my life, with my strength of mind I have stepped out of the influence circle of one narrow private life."[9] Under Scharnhorst's guidance, Clausewitz wrote newspaper articles and analyses propagating the military reforms.

In Berlin, Marie had to follow the uneven pace of progress in fear that the will for reforms would come soon to a complete stop. The disaster of Jena-Auerstedt opened the door for long-debated changes to happen and pushed the unhappy Friedrich Wilhelm to face reality. Marie, who had grown up in the king's vicinity, praised his "moral dignity" in the dark days of Tilsit but believed that the times overwhelmed the monarch's intellectual abilities and "great decisions do not live in his soul."[10] Yet for all his weaknesses, Friedrich Wilhelm gathered enough will to appoint a circle of talented bureaucrats and officers with bold ideas and, while far from

Figure 4.1. Gerhard von Scharnhorst. *Library of Congress Prints and Photographs Division, LC-USZ62-58870, Washington, DC.*

resolute or consistent at all times, followed the course that eventually led Prussia to victory just seven years later.

The reformers themselves were a group of colorful, ambitious, and uneasy characters, whose political views differed widely and often led them to openly defy each other. Equally striking were their backgrounds, with very few actually coming from Prussia. Heinrich Friedrich Karl vom und zum Stein, commonly known as Baron vom Stein, belonged to a family that independently ruled a tiny but ancient domain in the southwest near Nassau. Karl August von Hardenberg was a talented bureaucrat from Hanover. Scharnhorst was also from Hanover but, as mentioned, his father was a farmer. August Neidhardt von Gneisenau came from Saxony and had dubious claims to noble origins. The two central figures, Stein and Hardenberg, represented almost opposite ideologies—the former was a traditionalist, sympathetic to the needs of the old estates, and suspicious of central government; the latter was a proponent of strong bureaucracy and a centralized state. Yet the need for reforms was so great that in 1807–1808 they found themselves in the same faction, one pushing Prussia toward modernization. "If our misfortune was not so great and our future so unsure," wrote Marie, "one could find a solace in the notion that through this complete overthrow of all old relations, the merit of some excellent personalities has received more recognition and attained greater sphere of influence."[11]

Marie belonged to Stein's closest circle of friends, and he described her as "a lovely person . . . pleasant, talented, calm, and sensitive."[12] The baron's admiration, Marie wrote in jest, even led some members of Berlin society to seek out her friendship in those days.[13] In all probability she knew of Stein's reform ideas before Jena-Auerstedt. Therefore she described his recall by the king as a "glimpse of hope" in times when none expected anything good.[14] With a reputation for flamboyance and outspokenness, the baron had already served as financial and economy minister in Berlin. Stein had indeed approached Queen Louise with suggestions for reform in the days before the disaster of 1806. She, however, decided not to pass them on to the king. In the fall of 1807, Friedrich Wilhelm appointed Stein once again as minister with wide powers, and already in October the state had started to adopt the first measures.

The most famous act of the reform era, the *Oktoberedikt*, aimed at overhauling the ineffective and backward Prussian agrarian system and releasing the economic and patriotic energies of its subjects. Essentially it consisted of three measures: abandoning all restrictions on the purchase of nobles' land in order to free the land market; opening all occupations to persons of all classes, in effect ending the closed guilds and thus creating a competitive labor market; and abolishing hereditary servitude in the form of serfdom. From now on, the reformers believed, all Prussians would be elevated from subjects to citizens, equal before the law, and could come to identify themselves with the state and its fate.

Scharnhorst, who according to Clausewitz had been the first to recognize that the political revolution of 1789 underpinned the French army's nearly unlimited prowess, now rushed to capitalize on the newly minted citizens' will to defend the country.[15] On August 6, 1808, the Military Reorganization Commission headed by Scharnhorst announced sweeping measures as well: universal military service; appointments based on meritocracy and a phasing-out of the nobility's privileged access over the officers' corps; a new emphasis on education and training; abandonment of the most severe corporal punishments; an end to the hiring of foreign mercenaries; and ending the practice of giving company commanders and senior officers autonomous control over budgets for supply and equipment of their troops. Scharnhorst also managed to consolidate the military structures, dominated up to this point by cabinet councilors and the king's arbitrariness, and bring them toward a unified professionalized center—the future war ministry.

"Finally the whole supreme military council [*Oberkriegskollegium*] and with it, a whole shipload of invalid generals, have been sent into retirement," Carl wrote mercilessly to Marie after the reforms had been passed.[16] Assessing the events from a modern point of view, the historian Christopher Clark calls it "an unprecedented purge of the Prussian military leadership."[17] The Military Reorganization Commission relieved from duty 208 officers; out of 142 generals, 17 were dismissed and 86 honorably dismissed. Paradoxically, the overhaul made Carl's release from his dead-end duties as adjutant much harder, particularly because Scharnhorst could not bypass the new equalized and bureaucraterized rules for promotion he sought to install, even when it came to relocating his most talented disciple to his office. "Not that it would be impossible to achieve it but because an appointment for personal reasons only, without the needs of the state to have given a cause for it, would be completely against the principles that my friend is preaching," Carl explained the complexities of his situation to Marie.[18]

For all the passion the couple put into supporting the reform measures, the two debated strikingly little of their actual content. Courtiers, officers, and intellectuals had pondered for years, if not decades, over Prussia's desolate and unsustainable state of affairs but there was never enough political will to take action. Friedrich Wilhelm had considered abandoning serfdom even at the beginning of his reign; the corporal punishments had been in review since the time of his father; and for ten years, Scharnhorst had been continuously developing and discussing his ideas.[19] Hence while in 1808–1809 Marie and Carl remained preoccupied with the pace of the reforms and their opposition, they never questioned the need for overhaul. The countess in particular had only scorn for the concerns and angst surrounding the modernization of the state, believing them a product of ignorance, irrationality, or ill-defined self-interest. The state before 1806, in Marie's words, suffered from "the old soulless *Schlendrian*," a popular term from the late eighteenth century describing an ineffective and parochial approach, and it forced many talents to "idleness." Although an "unexpected destruction" had forced it quickly and mercilessly upon Prussia, the radical overthrow had been inevitable.[20] The more opposition the reforms faced and the more their pace slowed down, the greater the bitterness in Marie's language when describing the events and their instigators: "follies," "new level of stupidity," "imprudence," "cabals," and "ignobility" became her choice words.[21] Indeed, she and Carl both agreed that the reformers' greatest problem was their softness and hesitation to carry out bolder moves.[22]

For Marie, the processes had not only political but also deeply personal implications. Carl's promotion depended on the continuation of the military overhaul, and in even more immediate terms, the state's bankrupt budget directly dictated her and her mother's life and finances in 1808–1809. In all probability, Sophie von Brühl's widow's pension had been cut. While Marie avoided writing on the subject, the loss of income must have been considerable because in the fall of 1808 the two women had to give up their home. Sympathetic members of the royal family offered Marie and Sophie a place to stay at the now-empty palace (Marie cheerfully wrote that she moved into Prince Wilhelm's childhood room).[23] The young countess's finances were in such a desolate state that she could not even afford to buy a nice present for her brother Fritz's eighteenth birthday.[24] This most personal experience reminded Marie on a daily basis that passivity was not an option. Only modernized institutions and released economic energies could bring Prussia, and her own life, back from the spiraling downfall.

Nor was she encouraged by the ideas and personalities within the building antireform faction. In 1808 the opposition was still scattered and far from well organized, but Marie's brother-in-law Friedrich August Ludwig von der Marwitz had emerged as one of its vocal leaders. For almost a decade, the two had kept a cordial relationship, and Marwitz even claimed in his memoirs that before his engagement to Fanny von Brühl, Marie might have harbored ambitions to marry him.[25] After serving as Hohenlohe's adjutant in 1806, Marwitz organized a volunteer corps where Marie's brother Fritz served for a brief time. In that period, Marie exchanged regular letters with him, but bitter resentments—mainly surrounding his daughter—severed the relationship. During the time of peace following the War of 1806–1807, Marwitz intended to take charge of his orphaned daughter, whom he had left in the care of Marie and Sophie von Brühl. Sophie in particular met the request with extraordinary hostility, and the family feud gradually spilled over into the already strained relationship between Baron vom Stein and

Marwitz. Listening to the complaints of his dear friend Sophie ("Countess Charles" in his correspondence), Stein lamented her son-in-law's "crudeness."[26] The little girl Fanny, who suffered the most from the family feud, grew to become, to Marie's great disappointment, a "reticent character."[27]

A staunch conservative, Marwitz rallied other Junkers around the idea that the Stein-Hardenberg reforms threatened the traditional basis of the Prussian state—the agrarian society and the nobility's dominant role. A skilled politician with an eloquent personal style, he argued that serfdom was the expression of an ancient institution bonding the peasant to the nobleman, hence dissolving it would subvert the social order. It did not matter that in reality the *Oktoberedikt* remained remarkably vague in its language and that, while the peasants became "free," little to no provisions were made about retaining the land they had cultivated for generations. Many Junkers indeed saw the loophole as quite beneficial for seizing tenured land and taking further advantage of cheap wages. Marwitz's rhetorical talent, however, won over many minds, and even Marie and Carl's close friend, Charlotte von Moltke, fell under his spell. "You cannot believe how much it saddens me to think that she is, due to her future situation, as good as lost to me," Marie commented upon hearing the announcement that Charlotte had become engaged to Marwitz.[28]

The anguish and anger about the future of the reforms came to a boiling point in the fall of 1808 with the dismissal of Baron vom Stein. In 1807 the small country of Portugal had tried to defy Napoleon's blockade of British commercial goods, the so-called Continental System, and subsequently was defeated and occupied. The emperor was not finished with the Iberian Peninsula, however. In 1808, he turned on Spain, up to this point a French ally, but also a seemingly easy victim because an incapable and corrupt government had led the country to a desolate state. What Napoleon did not expect was that ordinary Spaniards would oppose French occupation as well, and a wave of popular enthusiasm would tie up his troops in a bloody and prolonged fight. Observing the events on the Iberian Peninsula, the circle around Stein, Scharnhorst, and Gneisenau started to hope that a similar uprising could be possible in Germany too. Famously, French agents intercepted Stein's letter spelling out such an idea, and it turned Napoleon's vengeance against the powerful minister. "It seems to me impossible to love the Prussian state without holding Stein's loss as almost the biggest misfortune that could now befall it, and I thought that even [the inner opposition] should realize that only a man of such an excellent talent, of such power and incorruptibility could hold the remains of our former greatness and spread the seeds of a better future," wrote Marie to Carl, once the news became known in Berlin that Napoleon, the unquestioned overlord of Europe, had requested Stein's dismissal.

In September, the emperor had ordered Stein's family estates—now within the borders of the newly created French client state, the Kingdom of Westphalia—to be seized. In Königsberg, Friedrich Wilhelm still tried to evade the pressure, but it became obvious that the removal was only a matter of time. The news dealt Marie a double blow—not only had a close friend she admired found himself in disgrace, but her hopes for an accelerated pace of reform appeared slashed: "I would like to believe that we still have men in their qualities in no way inferior to him (although I still don't know them); but even if they existed, their merit is still unknown, their authority not justified, and precious time would be lost again with fighting thousands of intrigues and difficulties."[29]

Clausewitz, who had observed Stein in close proximity these months, had a more restrained assessment and wrote back pointing out the minister's impulsive character and political weaknesses. Despite regretting his unavoidable political demise, Carl wrote that the baron was "not like you presented him to me, firm and never changing as a diamond."[30] Taken aback by Marie's fearsome objection to these sentiments, he tried to clarify in the next letter that the criticism concerned the statesman's compliancy and indecisiveness in the first months of the reforms when he could have achieved so much more.[31] Still the countess found the criticism of Stein's character at such a pivotal moment unacceptable. The minister might have been difficult and often alienating, Marie allowed, but there were all too few great men like him in Prussia.[32] "I admit that maybe one could have behaved in these latter events also <u>completely differently</u> but then it would definitely have required a <u>completely different</u> personality."[33] For Marie, a forceful character like Stein was above and beyond normal measures, and his personal failings, which others wished away, were, in her estimation, the essential source of this forcefulness. She overlooked the apparent contradiction between his flawed character and the need to rise to the occasion, because only an extraordinary person could step out of the convention and bring change; less flawed and more ordinary people simply would not dare to challenge the rules.

Stein's uneasy character preoccupied Marie and Carl for one more personal reason. They had hoped to make him an ally in achieving Sophie von Brühl's permission for their marriage. The elder countess herself had already approached the minister with a request to find a suitor for her daughter, although she failed to disclose Marie's relationship with Carl. Despite his preoccupation with the affairs of the state, Stein managed to find the time to inquire for prospective husbands, and at that, Marie lamented, "with zeal."[34] As a countermeasure, she suggested that Carl should try to get closer to the minister since he was "probably the only one" who could convince Sophie that the young officer had a bright future in front of him.[35] Stein indeed came to know Clausewitz in these months in Königsberg and held quite a favorable view of him. As Marie's close friend, Princess Marianne, wrote back to her after discreetly probing the minister's opinion, he had agreed with Scharnhorst that Clausewitz "should be taken out of Prince August's [service] and appointed more beneficially."[36]

Yet Stein was still kept in the dark about Carl and Marie's relationship. To Carl's great dismay, now the name of Alexander zu Dohna-Schlobitten, a member of a very old and distinguished Junker family, became publicly connected with that of Marie. "The oldest Count von Dohna is highly regarded by him, and [Stein] believes that no other choice could be more appropriate," he bitterly complained.[37] Indeed just a few months later Stein suggested Dohna as his successor as minister of interior. Carl's only consolation was that he could secretly enjoy it when courtiers gossiped about what a good match Countess von Brühl would be: "Despite somewhat unpleasant occasion for me, I cannot describe how much my pride was flattered as well because of the true tenderness everyone talked about you. Krusemark spoke about the happiness that your possession would grant, and at that stared at me, so that I had difficulties not to blush and almost came to the suspicion that he knew something about our situation."[38]

How and when Marie found a way to inform Stein and his protégé that she was not interested remains unclear. Yet it must have happened in a cordial and mutually respectful way since the powerful statesman's friendship with the couple only grew with the years, and Clausewitz later cooperated with Alexander von Dohna in the creation of Prussia's local militia, the *Landwehr*. In 1831, when Marie wrote to Carl about Dohna's death, she had nothing else to add but what "an excellent man" he was.[39]

The correspondence from 1808–1809 displays one more difference in Marie and Carl's characters—and one that only deepened with the years. As he had noticed and been drawn to in the very beginning of their relationship, Marie had the quality, in her own words, "a natural gift, to ingratiate myself with people."[40] She could listen to Count von Schwerin's glorious stories about the Seven Years' War—the conflict that spelled the end of her family wealth and power in Saxony—and not only not rebuff the old Prussian soldier but even describe him as "loveable." The empathy did not make her less realistic or uncritical. In recollecting the same visit to Ueckermark, Marie emphasized the deep gap separating the reform circle from the conservative Junkers. Yet such realism did not result in a cynical or angry outlook: "Had I stayed longer, I might have felt more lively the lack of meeting points with the whole society, but a couple of days go quick, especially in a nice area."[41] Marie indeed tried to instill in her beloved this rather pragmatic approach. Especially in the case of Stein, she recommended to Carl that he try to separate the personal frustration about their fate from the political alliance.[42] Following her advice, Carl did come, over time, to value the statesman's ideas, energy, and friendship despite the initial disappointment. Yet to allow in his close circle people whose character or abilities he did not admire, was a trait increasingly hard for Clausewitz to master, and with the years even more so.

Marie put Carl's ability to "pour powerful, gratifying, and ardent words" as one of the qualities she deeply admired about him.[43] As the time passed, however, debate and the building of elaborate arguments happened for him mostly on paper. Carl remained eager to engage in disputes when the opposing view could be defended with eloquence and integrity—as his friendship and praise for the archconservative Leopold von Gerlach throughout the years revealed.[44] Unfortunately, he found such qualities exceedingly rare and had little interest in tolerating anything else. Clausewitz's spirit, as his longtime friend Carl von Gröben put it, was like a small flowering plant, the mimosa, famously closing its leaves when intrusively touched. The spirit opened up when encountered with trust and shut down when met with suspiciousness.[45] In contrast, Marie's pragmatic manner and aptness in navigating the public sphere saved her from reclusiveness, and until her death she remained an active and outspoken member of society. Among his wife's other qualities, it would be this capacity to overlook weaknesses and tolerate adversity that Clausewitz banked upon when he decided to entrust her to see *On War* published only after his death.

In the first stage of Prussia's reform period, 1807–1809, debating current affairs became an increasingly dissatisfying enterprise, and the countess turned toward history texts. Studying Herodotus and the life of Alexander the Great, she wrote to Carl, made a "somber, even sad impression" on her. Timidity, stupidity, and disunity, Marie remarked, could bring down even the greatest states. Not every hero was embraced with adoration, she lamented, quite the opposite—many had to fight their way against not only outside enemies but also the ones within.[46] In light of such reflections, the fact that Marie was so close to the reform circle, yet without any opportunity for real involvement and influence, left her feeling helpless and increasingly resentful about women's circumcised roles. Women, even if they loved "most affectionately" the Fatherland, she wrote, could not truly be deep-felt patriots because they could not actively participate in rebuilding it. They were stripped of power to take action or influence the political sphere, "the real world," in her words, and could only hope to support "the noble men in their surrounding."[47] Often the restrictions felt physically unbearable, because as a woman Marie could not even take a walk in the park in Giewitz without an escort: "This easiness to go out alone I actually do envy men as I do so envy them in other things; because after all, it's something else to be alone in nature with your thoughts, than in your room."[48]

Whereas Marie could only lament, in Königsberg her friend Princess Marianne attempted to use what power she had to influence the course of events. Marianne was married to the king's younger brother, Wilhelm, a prince also educated by Marie's father Charles. In the years after the princess's arrival in Prussia, she and Marie had grown increasingly close—they both were amateur historians, passionate art scholars, and German patriots. Marianne was actually six years her younger, but the countess boundlessly admired her personality, a perfect mix of "tender femininity and impressive dignity."[49] Soon after Carl's arrival in Königsberg, Marie shared with her royal friend the secret of their relationship and gained her support.[50]

Marianne won over the tight-knit circle of military reformers with her patronage of Scharnhorst's daughter, Julie, and then played an instrumental role in obtaining approval for her marriage with Karl Friedrich zu Dohna-Schlobitten, a young officer in Scharnhorst's service but also from an old and distinguished Junker family.[51] In the absence of her husband, who was still negotiating the terms of the peace in Paris, the princess gathered the reform circle in her salon. During these meetings, she gave Stein the impression that Prince Wilhelm was ready to lead the new war faction and embrace their plans for a popular uprising similar to the one raging against the French occupation in Spain. When, however, he finally arrived back in Königsberg at the end of October 1808, it turned out that Wilhelm was neither prepared nor willing to embrace and advocate the bold plans in front of the king.[52] "He may not have enough belief in himself to be certainly of any use," was Marie's merciless verdict. About Princess Marianne she added, "What a pity that this extraordinary woman does not hold a place, where her superb qualities could have the influence they deserve."[53]

Meanwhile the political situation around Europe had changed once again: in September and October 1808, the Congress of Erfurt officially reaffirmed the alliance between the Emperor Napoleon and Tsar Alexander I of Russia. Then in November Napoleon personally led his army in rebellious Spain and scored impressive victories. The belligerent Austria delayed its plans for war. Napoleon's growing strength increased the pressure over Friedrich Wilhelm to dismiss Stein—no friendly terms with the emperor were possible if the powerful minister continued to lead the Prussian government. In December Stein left Königsberg. While in Berlin, the news reached him that Napoleon had officially declared him an enemy of France. Afraid that his fate might be to rot in a French prison or even death, the once-powerful minister left the Prussian capital in a hurry in January 1809 and went into exile. Most likely with the assistance of Marie and Sophie von Brühl, he found a warm welcome at the residence of Marie's cousin Therese, now the married Countess von Thun, in Prague.[54]

For Marie, the disappointment over Stein's fate was lessened by the news of Carl's release, at last, from his adjutant duties. He was also promoted to a real captain. "Today, 23 February 1809, I have been appointed by His Majesty, the king, to work at the War Ministry, i.e. at disposition of General Scharnhorst," he wrote back to Berlin. However, Carl further informed Marie, as long as Prussia's payment of contributions continued, his annual income would be only 900 thaler, instead of 1,300 thaler.[55] From Berlin she answered exaltedly: "Certainly a big step toward the goal is made and one so happily at that."[56]

Carl, now Scharnhorst's closest and most devoted personal assistant, found himself elevated in the ranks of the reformers. Although Friedrich Wilhelm, holding onto his power as supreme commander, never officially appointed a war minister, as the ministry's administrative head Scharnhorst now had at his disposal the resources needed to enforce his ideas. It was a Herculean task since it demanded not only saving the Prussian army, badly shaken after the war of 1806–1807, but actually rebuilding it essentially from the ground up in a completely new spirit and operational modus. Clausewitz worked intimately with Scharnhorst, enjoying such trust that he drafted and even sent in the general's name memorandums for the development and manufacture of weapons, tactical regulations, and the introduction of conscription.[57] His promotion and position in the reformers' circle was impressive enough even for Sophie von Brühl. After Marie's close friend Luise von Voß stepped in on the lovers' behalf and talked to the elder countess, she agreed that once Carl was back from Königsberg, the two could meet in her house.[58]

Then in the spring of 1809, the balance of power shifted once again. Peace had not come to the Iberian Peninsula, despite Napoleon's victories in Spain, and the British army's failure under the command of Sir John Moore to militarily support the Spanish resistance in the winter of 1808–1809. Armed bands of fierce local fighters continued harassing the French troops, and Clausewitz felt vindicated in his earlier prediction that through hit-and-run tactics the Spaniards were actually wounding the enemy much more vehemently.[59] Austria was preparing for war again, this time in all earnestness. The vehement defeat in Austerlitz in 1805 was not forgotten in Vienna, and although very recent, the subsequent social and military reforms, similar to the ones in Prussia, promised to bring benefits on the battlefield. Emperor Francis was also afraid that he might miss a good opportunity to start a war when his budget still had the money for it and Napoleon was tied down in Spain.

Vienna was looking for allies, and Friedrich Wilhelm felt the greatest pressure to join the fight. Once more the Prussian king found himself in the place he least wished to be—between the opposing European powers and those within his state. Based on the Convention of September 1808, a supplement to the Tilsit Peace, Prussia owed Napoleon support with an auxiliary corps of 12,000 men. The war faction in Prussia, however, argued that the moment was right to join Austria in its fight. Complicating things further, in Russia Tsar Alexander remained noncommittal for a united campaign against Napoleon. With so many unknowns and risks to be taken, Friedrich Wilhelm once again decided to wait.

From Königsberg, Carl wrote back to Marie that the current events appeared to him "endlessly more interesting" than those of 1805–1806. It now seemed the moment when Napoleon, facing too many enemies on too many fronts, could be finally crushed.[60] In Berlin in the spring and summer of 1809, Marie found herself in the midst of events that profoundly shook Prussia and its monarchy. Luise von Voß had turned the informal sojourns of poets and intellectuals in Giewitz into a highly influential salon in Berlin that, based on Marie's descriptions, could hardly be called literary. In her famed biography of the most prominent Jewish intellectual of the period, Rahel Levin, the philosopher Hannah Arendt has noted how strikingly different these later social gatherings were compared to the early ones during 1790–1806. Where the first salons debated matters of mind and soul, these from 1809 were devoted to pressing issues of the day and most of all the fate of the Fatherland. Among the new generation of salonieres, the hosts and hostesses were all "persons of name and rank," and thus were able to gather members of high nobility and the officer corps. Highly exclusive, these events did not invite social outsiders like Rahel Levin or other Jewish intellectuals.[61]

In her correspondence, Marie described the evenings at Voß's residence in Berlin as less formal or organized than they appeared afterward. Luise invited "many men" and "some came also every day" around nine o'clock in the evening, while very few women—mainly Marie herself, Friederike von Moltke, and Julie von der Goltz, former lady-in-waiting of Princess Marianne and now newly wed to the officer and diplomat Count von der Goltz—were among the regulars. "My cousin [Carl von Brühl] and [Ferdinand von] Schill . . . are daily visitors; sometimes the two Arnims come, especially the poet (who in social interaction is so simple and pleasant that one could not hold him for the author of such great works), Count Arnim, the young Goltz, W[ilhelm von] Humboldt, Kettenburg, etc.," she further set the stage.[62] In other letters, Marie pointed out also Clausewitz's former instructor Johann Gottfried Kiesewetter and Prince August, now back from Königsberg, as regular guests.

The political discussions in Voß's residence did not remain without consequences. The young hussar Schill had led the light cavalry harassing the French supply lines during the legendary siege of Kolberg in 1807. Then he marched at the head of the first Prussian troops to reenter Berlin in the autumn of 1808. Schill now burned with impatience to once again raise the masses. The Voß salon welcomed this new folk hero with admiration and enthusiasm. Some of the salonieres were also associated with the *Tugendbund* or "League of Virtue," the patriotic society established in June 1808 in Königsberg and notoriously suspected by the French of preparing a rebellion. Just like many other contemporaries Clausewitz judged the *Tugendbund* to be more of a debate society that accomplished almost nothing.[63] There is no evidence that Marie ever belonged to it. Yet the French suspicion revealed the risk associated with the virulent political rhetoric and explains why the gatherings functioned more like "secret societies," in Hannah Arendt's words, than classical salons.[64]

Highly patriotic and closed to any voice of dissent, the meetings at Voß's residence reinforced an echo chamber dangerously spiraling out of control. In Berlin wherever the patriots turned, they seemed to see evidence that the masses would rise against Napoleon. In her letters to Carl, Marie revealed the lofty and fervent atmosphere among the group as she commented that the "sparkle" was still alive in the common people and "just waited the first fortunate inspiration to flare up into a bright flame."[65] The salonieres even convinced themselves that the masses had indeed chosen sides by not, in the French manner, taking down and beheading the nobility in the disastrous winter of 1806–1807.[66] The resentment and frustration in the newly created Kingdom of Westphalia, where Napoleon installed his brother Jerome on the throne, was also growing every day, and in Tyrol a peasant uprising swept the French allies. On April 10, Austria opened the so-called War of the Fifth Coalition with an assault against the French ally Bavaria. The propaganda from Vienna offered, as Marie wrote, "such beautiful" proclamations for all Germans to take arms.[67] She herself had one more reason to advocate Prussia's involvement: after Stein's interference, her brother Fritz had received a commission in the Austrian army.[68] The fact that Luise's mother, Caroline von Berg, was the queen's closest companion also gave rise to the speculations afterward that Queen Louise herself had encouraged Major von Schill to act.

Since January Schill had been receiving secret messages from the Kingdom of Westphalia's patriots, and in the spring he agreed to lead the insurrection. When at the end of April the French intercepted the proclamation for the masses to rise, aptly called "To the Germans," and threatened immediate arrest, Schill decided to act—but not before visiting the Voß salon one last time. "It deeply touched me that he remembered also about us in the last moments and at that in the hour, before he left with the regiment, came for while, probably, to take a silent good-bye," Marie wrote to Carl. "The good Schill! He surely knew what heartfelt sympathy we have toward him and with what sincere good wishes we will follow him."[69] On the next morning, April 28, without consulting his superiors, the major left Berlin with his regiment with the stated goal of launching a rebellion.

The act caused immediate uproar and heated debates across all sections of the Prussian population. With all the visitors coming to her house either to inquire about details or discuss Schill's acts and persona, Marie could barely find the time to write to Carl. The major had clearly committed insubordination and his actions threatened to destroy the authority of the king. Many, even if they hated the French, were not ready to break their oath to the Crown. As Marie wrote to Carl: "The old ladies . . . and the old staff officers make horrified faces, but the public appears in highest enthusiasm for its hero, and there must be, as sources have assured, a significant number of people following him. That those, who cannot rise above the trivial and common, find him punishable, I understand very well, and according to the law he is indeed, but in such extraordinary times, only extraordinary [actions] could help; and it's better to be saved through a daring decision than to go down with all rules." Schill's deed was so radical in Prussia's political and historic context that in the first hours after hearing about it some, like Marie, believed in the possibility of informal contact between the major and the king. "I am convinced that [Schill] would not have taken this step without important causes and without assurance that he could fulfill it with honor and for the good of his king and his Fatherland," she wrote to Carl immediately after hearing about Schill's actions.[70]

Soon enough this belief was disavowed but Marie still continued to passionately support the rebellion. Despite the implications, the radical new generation saw his act as necessary in a moment of great need. In a country where the nobility, the bureaucracy, and the officer corps strived to sway the monarch one way or another but had never openly questioned his preeminence or tried to force his hand until now, this was a striking statement. Marie was brought up at the court in a family of staunch servants of the Crown and undoubtedly realized the consequences of her words. Nevertheless, she could not help but be swept up by Schill's actions and the mood permeating the country.

The crisis in the spring and summer of 1809 raised another crucial question, one that would take decades to answer, about the clash between wider German interests and the particular ones of the Prussian state. While in their correspondence Carl and Marie often wrote of "Germany" and the "nation," these constituted idealized rather than political terms. When in the period of the Napoleonic Wars patriots and romanticists used the words, their meaning was based not upon the modern understanding of an autonomous state but rather on a cultural and political kinship and shared history. Hence Clausewitz also used the term "German peoples" (*deutsche Völker*) without seeing it as contradictory.[71] At that point neither Carl and Marie, nor their contemporaries, understood "Germany" as one nation requiring or desiring, let alone able, to undergo a process of unification to form one single mastodon state. Even the idea of a strong political integration that the patriots envisioned during 1813–1815, to say nothing of a territorial unification, went too far for great intellectual figures of the day like Goethe, as Marie discovered when meeting the poet for the first time.[72]

The question of what constituted the "German nation" only gathered poignancy with the continuation of the War of the Fifth Coalition. After the initial surprise of the Austrian attack and the subsequent French retreat, Napoleon now personally led his troops. The emperor went on the offensive in Abensberg, and now Vienna desperately appealed for allies. In Königsberg, Carl felt the burgeoning dilemma especially keenly as fellow patriotic officers started asking to be released from their service and then joined the Austrian ranks. These acts split the reformer circle, some of whom viewed them as acts of desertion that weakened Prussia. When Karl Wilhelm von Grolmann, an offspring of a great Westphalian noble family but now a leading member of Scharnhorst's team, decided to leave, for instance, Princess Marianne indignantly described him as ungrateful.

This type of reaction inflamed Carl's anger—should one demand that a man who "doesn't have some special connections to our state" let his energy and military talent rest while he could actually help "the German Fatherland"? He viewed such people, those who "bear continuously the word Prussia on their lips so the word German does not remind them of the heavy, sacred duties," with disdain.[73] Indeed, Carl wrote to Marie that he felt compelled to leave the Prussian army as well.[74] But even if the two failed to see it at that time, what benefited the Austrian interests was far from advantageous to Prussia, still rallying from the disastrous period of 1806–1807. This point was even more valid for the smaller German states. Facing extreme pressure from the two hegemonic states, Austria and Prussia, some viewed Napoleon as the lesser evil and did not rally around the pan-Germanic cause.

Despite the tensions and tumult, Friedrich Wilhelm continued to hold his neutral stance. In Berlin Marie breathlessly followed Schill's movements: "our hero," as she referred to him, was welcomed in Dassau, Röthen, and Bernburg with "pure joy," and in Dodendorf close to Magdeburg his troops swept the French garrison and "took away from them many cannons."[75] At the same time, more French victories against the Austrian army followed in Landshut and Eckmuhl. Carl viewed them as "decisive"—but the "good affair" could not yet be declared for lost, he wrote to Marie, and "now would be the right moment for an energetic and inspired conduct on the side of the Germans."[76] Napoleon continued the victorious march and ten days after his triumph in the Battle of Ebelsberg near Linz, on May 13, he occupied Vienna once more. Keeping in constant contact with her relatives in Austria, Marie informed Carl that the retreat and loss of capital had not, yet, diminished the public enthusiasm.[77] In these days of tumult, her circle's reputation for insight and fervent patriotism grew so great among the high society in Berlin that Marie, Luise von Voß, and Julie von der Goltz were invited to otherwise all-male *soupers* at Prince August's home in Belleview, "which as you might think aroused big astonishment in the elegant world." The new adjutant now serving under Prince August, obviously not knowing about Marie's relationship with his predecessor, tried even flirting with her, a comical situation that made all close friends burst into laughter afterward.[78]

Soon enough, however, the wave of public enthusiasm started to subside. Carl recognized that the reforms had not yet resulted in an overhaul of Prussian society. The majority of the people still remained passive and uninterested in the fate of Prussia, a state they did not recognize as really theirs.[79] Carl's greatest fear now became the possibility that the overhaul would be put on hold and the military reformers banned from Friedrich Wilhelm's adviser circle: "Dare [the king] on his own risk to separate from this 'good party,' because he thinks he has more reason than they; we should brazenly make an appeal to the future."[80] Carl's words sounded awfully close to insubordination and raise the question whether the radical mood in Berlin, as conveyed by Marie's letters, had started to affect his thinking. Hers might have been one of many patriotic voices Carl listened to in his surrounding; but without a doubt, it was the closest to his mind and soul. In this case, Marie's unrestrained support for Schill's rebellion clearly led Carl astray from the creed and traditional loyalty of a Prussian officer. In Carl's brazen embrace of the radical position, there might have been also a grain of intellectual competition—he had always been the more intensive and profound thinker of the two and the one who had had the chance up to that point to play an active role in political processes in the reform period. Yet now Marie was a recognized member of the militant patriots' circle, and Carl strived to belong to it too.

Meanwhile even Marie had to admit that Schill's expedition had lost its focus and appeared close to failure. The lack of any recent successes against the French could be explained by bad luck, she wrote, "but what makes me most sad for him and despairing, is his wandering back and forth without a plan. . . . How much more of ours will go down in such a way!"[81] At the time Marie wrote this letter, she did not know that Schill's fate was already decided. After taking over the city of Stralsund on the Baltic Sea, he was surrounded by French, Dutch, and Danish troops and killed on May 31. Schill's head was cut off as a trophy, and twenty-eight of his followers were executed by a firing squad. With real pain Marie wrote back to Carl on June 8 that despite her "cordial friendship" with the hussar, she, too, had to agree that "our poor friend was not up to his great enterprise."[82]

Observing how many strong and talented personalities perished in pursuit of noble goals, Clausewitz must have started questioning whether the romantic concept of *Kraftmensch*, the vexed and restless personality that populated the texts of Sturm und Drang and German Romanticism, had any basis in reality. Later on, he would devote whole passages of *On War* to reflecting on this debate about what constituted an extraordinary person, and whether a volatile spirit could fulfill an exceptional mission. In Book I, Clausewitz underscored that under the term "genius" in general one should understand it as outstanding "intellect and temperament" that revealed themselves in "exceptional achievements." He analyzed extensively the role of temperament and defined it as "an emotion which serves to balance the passionate feelings in strong characters without destroying them, and it is this balance alone that assures the dominance of the intellect." Hence Clausewitz's conclusion about what constituted an exceptional human being ran in the opposite direction of the romanticist notion of *Kraftmensch*: "Therefore we would argue that a strong character is one *that will not be unbalanced by the most powerful emotions.*"[83]

Yet in the summer of 1809 Carl still remained under the romantic spell. Encouraged by the Austrian victory in Aspern on May 21-22, which shattered the myth of Napoleon's invincibility in battle, he decided to follow fellow Prussian officers and transfer to the Austrian service. Carl started gathering the needed letters of recommendations. Because the desired position—an officer at the general staff—could be easily achieved through the help of the Austrian ambassador in Berlin, Johann Baron von Wessenberg, he tasked Marie with establishing the contact. By now Carl had gained so much trust in her abilities that he left it up to her discretion whether she would talk directly with Wessenberg on his behalf or rely on some of her friends to do so.[84] Marie, however, hesitated and delayed. She even suggested that the ambassador would not take a recommendation by an outspoken woman well, a quite improbable notion since Wessenberg enjoyed very much the company of her friend Caroline von Berg.[85] After the Schill debacle, the countess appeared more reserved and less inclined to see Carl leave his secure place in the Prussian army. Marie might have been a passionate patriot, but at heart she remained a pragmatist and a shrewd political operative, most of all interested in achieving influence and tangible results. She intuitively felt that Carl's skills were better applied in the prolonged and difficult reform process.

Next to Marie's hesitations, external events soon decided Clausewitz's fate. The Austrians did not immediately follow upon their illustrious victory in Aspern with further engagements but for the next six weeks tried instead to gather their strength for one more decisive battle. It came on July 5 and 6 near Wagram, and this time Napoleon destroyed his enemies with a vengeance. The battle went into history as the bloodiest up to that point in the Napoleonic Wars because Austria suffered almost 40,000 casualties. The Austrian commander Archduke Charles asked for an armistice, and this graceless end sent shock waves through the patriotic circles in Berlin. "I was prepared for more lost battles, for errors and missteps but not for such a pettiness, not that the noble spirit . . . would be extinct like a flash in the pan!" Marie wrote with a shaking hand to Carl.[86]

Encouraged by the long and difficult negotiations for peace, Carl himself still hoped that the fighting was not over. Everything pointed toward the unsuccessful end of the War of the Fifth Coalition, but for him to be again a mere watcher of the action was a painful déjà vu. When in August the Austrians stopped the recruitment of foreign officers, Clausewitz even contemplated going to England. On October 14, 1809, with the signing of the Peace of Schönbrunn, the Hapsburg Empire arrived at its lowest point. It lost much of its territory, including Salzburg and West Galicia. The reform circle in Vienna was dismissed and, due to the enormous war contributions, the state finances were plundered. As a guarantee for peace Emperor Francis's daughter Marie-Louise had to marry Napoleon.

In the fall of 1809, the court in Königsberg was finally preparing to come back to Berlin. Despite the long physical separation, through their epistolary debates and shared thoughts Marie and Carl had grown closer during this time, and their ideas had matured. Without grasping the consequences, both of them had moved to a more plebiscite stand—the reforms, Schill's rebellion, and the rise of German nationalism had altered the centuries-old relationship between Prussia's absolute monarch and its subjects. In startling contrast to the old regime's conventions, the young generation started to see the people as a proactive and autonomous force. If before the king's and his government's will was synonymous with that of the nation, now the people and their passions emerged as potent power demanding to be heard. Marie and Carl welcomed the enormous energy released by the public enthusiasm but also came to see its uncertain and combustible side. In 1809, Prussia's radical patriots had overestimated the people's resolve to fight against Napoleon and failed to see the logic behind Friedrich Wilhelm's firm decision to remain neutral. If anything, Schill's rebellion revealed that for success in war, next to popular enthusiasm, astute political guidance and sound military strategy were also needed.

Clausewitz would spend years analyzing the shattered illusions from 1809 and many more to come until he boiled down these observations in his famous paradoxical trinity. When it comes to war, he would argue, the people with their passions, the army and its command with their talents and chances, and the political power with its governing rationale are in a state of constant balance and interplay. And one could ignore the three elements' interdependency only at his own peril.[87]

5

Time of Love, Time of Troubles
(December 1809–March 1812)

In August 1810, Carl von Clausewitz received a long-awaited letter from Friedrich Wilhelm. Together with his promotion to the rank of major, it included the official permission a Prussian officer needed to marry. At the age of thirty, Carl finally arrived at a place of professional influence and personal happiness with Marie. Yet the world around them bore the unmistakable signs of a brief lull before the storm. The wakened forces of popular enthusiasm and their crush in 1809 rippled throughout the unstable Prussian state. Despite his glorious victories, Napoleon could not achieve a lasting peace in Europe, and the alliance between France and Russia was crumbling. A new war was just a matter of time.

In this pivotal period Marie and Carl experienced only a few very short separations. Although she mentioned receiving one letter from Clausewitz in 1811 during his stay in Potsdam, it is not preserved.[1] Their thoughts on the events of this period, therefore, can only be surmised from snippets of correspondence from different years, remaining writings of the couple, a few documents, and memoirs and writings of third persons.

When after more than three years Friedrich Wilhelm and Queen Louise finally returned to Berlin on December 28, 1809, crowds on the streets welcomed them warmly. Yet the cheers must have reminded the king all too vividly of public enthusiasm the previous spring that he had refused to harness. His return to the capital, in fact, was anything but voluntary. It had come under pressure from Napoleon, who knew that French agents could keep better tabs on the royal family and the court in Berlin than in far-east Königsberg.

As an officer of the Prussian general staff, Clausewitz also arrived in Berlin on that day in December 1809. "In the beginning he was in a very bad mood and sad," Marie recalled of their reunion at a mutual friend's home. In the company of fellow patriots, they undoubtedly discussed the political situation, and therefore Marie did not take her beloved's sad demeanor personally. Once Marie and Carl managed to be alone for a couple of minutes, she brightened his mood. Then in the beautiful starlit evening they walked together to her home.[2]

With the return of the court to Berlin, Marie became the chief lady-in-waiting (*Oberhofmeisterin*) for the king's oldest daughter, Princess Charlotte (the future Tsarina Alexandra of Russia), who was then just eleven years old. Unfortunately, no record has remained about the countess's duties. In later years Marie and the princess exchanged correspondence, and in her letter right after ascending to the Russian throne the latter ended warmly with "please remain always the old Marie for your Charlotte."[3] The new and prominent position as *Oberhofmeisterin* came to Marie not only in recognition of her education and sophistication but also due to her close connections at court as an intimate of Princess Marianne and Caroline von Berg, the queen's bosom friend. Carl, meanwhile, also enjoyed social prominence as Gerhard von Scharnhorst's closest associate at the general staff. This association conferred enough status for Carl that Sophie von Brühl could not ignore him anymore without risking disapproval of the reform circles whose opinion she valued so much.

This was one of the paradoxes of the Clausewitz couple's life: while the great political and military upheaval after 1806 troubled their minds and challenged their emotional and physical strength, it also brought them closer, forged their union, and finally allowed them to marry. The same pattern emerged over the next two decades of their lives when, despite professional disappointments, political clashes, and financial troubles, their marriage remained exceptionally strong and loving.

By June 1810 Marie and Carl's engagement must have been made public, because Princess Louise Radziwiłł and Baron vom Stein started gossiping in their correspondence about the impending marriage. The secret about the relationship had been kept so tight that for many it came as a complete surprise, including the otherwise well-informed Princess Louise. A rather agitated Stein commented that the marriage hurt "many proprieties" and recounted Sophie von Brühl's concerns about the new, unwanted son-in-law. On the contrary, Princess Louise advised the elder countess to accept Carl and recommended him as someone reliable and noble. "It is true that happiness depends on wealth and in this aspect the future is not bright for

Figures 5.1 and 5.2. *Marienkirche* in the heart of Berlin where Marie and Carl von Clausewitz married in December 1810. *Photo Vanya Eftimova Bellinger.*

Marie but to be fair to Clausewitz, he understand this problem well, while Marie doesn't see or does not want to see it. He often speaks to me with uneasiness about his personal anxieties, the sacrifices Marie would face, while she, on the contrary, regards such scruples as [signs] of weakness and affection weaker than hers," wrote Princess Louise to Stein.[4]

The wedding between Carl and Marie on December 17, 1810 at eleven o'clock in the morning at the Marienkirche in Berlin was simple but full of joy.[5] The medieval church had become fashionable among patriots because its Gothic brick building appeared so uniquely German. In the church book Carl's last name was written as "Klausewitz," and the ages of the bride and groom were also mistakenly reversed as thirty and thirty-one years old, respectively.[6] Whether this was a clerk's error or Marie and Carl felt a bit uneasy about their age difference and swapped the numbers remains unknown. The newlyweds left for their honeymoon at the quiet manor in Giewitz, generously offered by Luise von Voß. "The last day of the year 1810 we spent on our trip back from Giewitz and arrived some hours before the end of it in our affable domicile, where its beautiful furniture and some presents from our friends pleasantly surprised us. But it did not need such external appearances to make the moment, in which we entered our apartment for the first time, one of the most beautiful in our life," Marie wrote about the beginning of their life together.[7] Carl's mood was so elated that he expressed his feelings in several lyrical poems full of deep love and quiet satisfaction.[8]

Outside observers were less generous when describing the newlyweds' circumstances: "A sofa, six chairs covered in muslin, and a few other pieces made up the entire household. Marie . . . was delighted when she could entertain a few relatives or good friends with a leg of mutton," wrote Caroline von Rochow.[9] Although no record remains from this period, the couple had at least a few servants, probably a maid for Marie and a cook. Carl's rank as major brought him an annual income with additional housing allowance of 1,300 thaler, fodder for his horses, and an orderly; however he still had to purchase out-of-pocket horses and uniforms.[10] Carl also provided for his mother until her death in 1811, and then for decades he supported his sisters. Contrary to the practice in other countries or the lower classes, women of noble birth in Prussia like Marie kept full control over their dowry and were expected to use it to cover all expenses associated with their clothing, servants, and personal needs.[11] Already extremely sensitive to their unequal situation, Carl consequently refused to even debate the appropriation of

Marie's income and expenses. The Clausewitz family budget was so tight that their plans to save money and buy a small estate as an investment and retirement insurance were never carried out.

By the time of their marriage, Marie was thirty-one years old and had spent the last five of those years preparing and planning for her life with Carl. She had closely observed friends' domestic situations—how they organized their household and kept a balance between the spouses' needs.[12] Drawing upon what she had learned, Marie described her image of homely bliss as one of "true living together" where "every occurrence of daily life, every thought, every feeling" should be shared. Showing each other mutual "love and respect," the partners could remain true to their own "character, worldview, and peculiarity" and would not lose their personality.[13] Already in 1807, Marie had warned Carl that the "imperative marital obedience does not in fact belong at all to my principles, and I would resist strongly against it if it should be coerced from me with force."[14] Luckily, being a tyrant at home was the last thing on Carl's mind. After spending the last seventeen years in shabby barracks and cold bachelor quarters, he longed for comfort, love, and "woman's beneficial influence" in his life.[15]

In an era when brides were married without any knowledge about the real emotional and sexual sides of marriage, the couple was not free from unrealistic and romanticized notions. In 1809, the recently wed Julie von der Goltz tried to explain to Marie that disagreements happened in all families because "the reality could not fulfill the expectations one had build in the beautiful times of juvenile illusion." When Marie shared this story with Carl, he reacted with anger and strong disbelief as well.[16] Man and woman living in perpetual harmony, and indeed complementing each other so completely as to build one perfect human being, was the prevailing notion in the times of German Romanticism. Yet it appears that Marie and Carl managed to keep their relationship tender and loving beyond the honeymoon. The prolonged period of courtship had given them an opportunity to learn about each other, and deep mutual respect and admiration made them tolerant toward the other's weaknesses. The only truly disappointing piece of the couple's marriage became the fact that Marie could not get pregnant. Becoming a mother, Carl wrote in a poem, was "the greatest happiness on earth," and Marie impatiently waited for this to happen.[17]

In their home the couple spent most of their time together. A daily routine was set that would prevail throughout the rest of their life. In the humble living room, Marie and Carl deliberated on current events, books they read, or speeches they heard.[18] While over time "some feigned differences" occurred, they felt closer than ever.[19] The long discussions between husband and wife gave Marie assurance in her own intellectual contribution to Carl's ideas. In 1815, when she wrote about meeting Goethe and her disappointment at the poet's refusal to actively support the patriotic fervors, Marie displayed a healthy self-confidence: "I quite wished to have you there, so I could hear <u>our</u> collaborative opinion, spoken with your spirit and your eloquence because I, of course, did not have the audacity to take it upon such an opponent."[20]

Quite strikingly after 1810 in her letters, Marie never again complained about her circumcised societal role as a woman. She felt an equal partner to Carl and as such had found a place and mission in life. In the early 1800s, a noblewoman in Prussia enjoyed far greater freedom in the public sphere because she was expected to represent her family and nurture contacts beneficial for its success. Yet few husbands truly saw their wives as their equals. Remarkably, the Clausewitz couple not only realized the unusual extent of their relationship but also took great pleasure in it. "To be more than a trivial husband to you would be an extraordinary pride; every statement revealing it brings me endless pleasure," Carl wrote to Marie in an unpublished part of his letter from May 23–24, 1815.[21]

They lived, however, in an uneasy limbo between personal happiness and political fragility. Marie would later describe 1811, the first year of her marriage, as "the most beautiful in my life until now," but also as one full of anxiety and premonitions of another struggle.[22] Already in June 1810, after pressure from the French ambassador in Berlin, Scharnhorst had been forced to resign from his position at the war ministry, although he kept his role at the general staff. Then on July 19, 1810, Queen Louise died unexpectedly while visiting her father in Strelitz. The circumstances— only thirty-four years old, exhausted, and in the arms of her husband, still thinking about her children and Prussia—quickly elevated the personal into national tragedy. The untimely death became a potent symbol of all the country had to suffer under Napoleon. In 1814, at the height of the German Wars of Liberation, Caroline von Berg published the first biography of the beloved queen full of highly patriotic messages and devotion "to the Prussian nation."[23] It remains unclear whether Marie, at that time still *Oberhofmeisterin* for Princess Charlotte, escorted the latter to see her mother at her deathbed, since Marie failed to leave any account about these events. Yet the countess was surely involved in the state funeral.

Figure 5.3. Queen Louise Memorial in Berlin created by sculptor Chistian Daniel Rauch. Print circa 1900s. *Library of Congress Prints and Photographs Division, LC-DIG-ppmsca-00354, Library of Congress, Washington, DC.*

While the queen was still alive, Marie harbored rather ambiguous feelings about her. She loved Louise's vivacious character and the easiness she brought to the stiff Prussian court, and admired the dignity and courage she had shown during the horrible days of 1806. Nevertheless, in the reform years, the countess harshly judged the queen's inability or unwillingness to sway the king in the right direction. When after Stein's dismissal Carl sarcastically reported from Königsberg that "the lovable queen is more lovable than ever" and danced until 2 o'clock in the morning, Marie saw it as evidence of Louise's political immaturity and limited influence over the king. "Her situation and her surrounding should be enough for her excuse," she wrote with some understanding about the queen, who, despite the reform party's wishes, owed her loyalty first and foremost to her royal husband. Still, Marie could not shake the impression that if her friend Princess Marianne had been the queen, she would have handled the situation better and found a way to save Stein.[24]

With Louise's death, all the criticism against her was suddenly forgotten, replaced with shock and sorrow, and with every passing year tending further toward a kind of hero worship. Louise became a myth, and the cornflowers that she gathered with her children during the flight from Napoleon in 1806 were seen as a symbol of defiance and German patriotism. Just like many others Marie embraced this view of the queen, and her friend Elise von Bernstorff affably wrote in her memoirs about Madam von Clausewitz's obsessive preference for the blue flowers on her own birthday.[25]

Despite the reformers' uneasy relationship with Queen Louise, her death spelled new difficulties for them. Never an energetic character, Friedrich Wilhelm now plunged into depression and seclusion and left most of the day-to-day decisions to Hardenberg. Bearing the title "chancellor" (the first in Prussian and German history), Hardenberg gathered in his hands an unprecedented power of foreign, inner, and financial ministry. He promised to solve Prussia's troubles with a new round of fiscal and economic reforms. Expressing the state's pressing interest, the Financial Edict of October 1810 announced the end of land tax exceptions, an overhaul of the tariff and toll system, equalization of the tax burden, and increased freedom of enterprise. To smooth the opposition, the chancellor gathered in Berlin sixty representatives nominated by regional and local elites, an "Assembly of Notables," to approve and propagate the measures. This first attempt at people's representation in Prussia, however, created more problems for Hardenberg than it solved, as the assembly turned into a hotbed of antireform rhetoric. Marie's former brother-in-law Marwitz led the reactionary assault, and the assembly was quickly dissolved.

The military reformers around Scharnhorst also submitted their plans for future actions against Napoleon. They outlined preparations for insurrectionary war in the Spanish manner. While Schill's failure weighed heavily on their minds, they discussed ways to once again ignite popular enthusiasm. In reality, only a small minority of the Prussian officer corps supported unleashing the powerful forces of people's war. The idea's most fervent propagandists came from the intelligentsia. Once the hope that Austria would unite the Germans and defeat the French had died, patriots like the poet Heinrich von Kleist now turned to Prussia. Kleist arrived in Berlin in early 1810 and published *Prinz Friedrich von Homburg*, a play glorifying Prussia's historic rise and, by extension, searching to inflame nationalistic sentiment once again. Another intellectual pushing the movement was Friedrich Ludwig Jahn, who created the *Turnbewegung,* where enthusiasts gathered in a park in Berlin, addressed each other with the informal *du* to signal that they all were equal, wore loosely fitting costumes, and trained for the upcoming struggle against the French. Jahn went further than any of the military reformers, advocating not only universal service but also the idea that a national militia should be the state's main fighting force.[26] Friedrich Wilhelm observed with suspicion these developments and blatantly rejected ideas for partisan warfare. It did not help that, after Queen Louise's death, the king harbored bitterness against the war party that in the past had repeatedly made her question his character and decisions.

From a modern perspective, Friedrich Wilhelm's strategy of steering clear of yet another confrontation with Napoleon in this period might have been wise. But the policy of "wait-and-see" only increased the discontent and restlessness among the patriots. Not coincidentally in this period of heightening emotions, when Carl and Marie grew increasingly disgruntled by the Prussian government's indecisiveness, they spent much of their time among the intellectual circles in Berlin.

Marie had dreamed ever since they became a couple of seeing her husband rise to a popular and influential salonier, an idea mocked by Carl.[27] Yet during his time in Königsberg, Carl came to appreciate the sophisticated gatherings at the salons of Princess Marianne and Princess Louise Radziwiłł. As Marie wrote with some vindication, in the usual course of life, without these lively societies, he would have remained unknown and overlooked by many important personalities.[28] Despite their limited budget and humble home, Marie also entertained prominent personalities in her own small salon. Her later correspondence names some of the regular guests, all personalities that would come to play instrumental roles during the Wars of 1813–1815, especially the later commander of the legendary volunteer Lützow Corp, Ludwig Adolf Wilhelm von Lützow, and August Neidhardt von Gneisenau. The latter gained fame as the hero of the siege of Kolberg in 1807, and although Clausewitz had met him already in Königsberg, they grew closer in Berlin. Contemporaries described Gneisenau as accessible and pleasant, and although somewhat brisk and lacking in quick wit or comprehensive education, he was well read and very much interested in current politics and cultural debates.[29]

The Clausewitz couple primarily visited the salon of Luise von Voß, where Carl was introduced to Wilhelm von Humboldt and Achim von Arnim. He also grew closer to the brothers Wilhelm and Carl von Röder, the latter to become the trusted addressee of Clausewitz's *Two Letters on Strategy* from 1827. In early 1811 Arnim or some of the other patriots invited Carl to the *Deutsche Tischgesellschaft* gatherings, which met every second Tuesday for lunch in different taverns around Berlin to discuss politics and literature. Founded by Arnim and the political economist Adam Müller, the group boasted famous and influential members like the poet Clemens Brentano, the philosophers Friedrich Schleiermacher and Johann Gottlieb Fichte, the artist Karl Friedrich Schinkel, and the jurist Friedrich Carl von Savigny. The group excluded "philistines, women, and Jews," the last two restrictions as a direct challenge to the most famous literary salons in Berlin (women were not allowed in taverns in the early nineteenth century anyway). In the absence of correspondence from 1811, it would be hard to reconstruct what exactly Marie, who wanted to share everything with her husband, thought about these reactionary provisions and in general about Carl's membership in *Deutsche Tischgesellschaft*. Still, she lived in times when women often found themselves excluded and perhaps pragmatically encouraged him to use the social opportunities.

Although far from the most debated or central concern, the society's rampant antisemitism has gained notoriety in modern scholarship. It indeed appears as a sharp turn from the tolerant atmosphere of the late eighteenth and early nineteenth centuries in Berlin, when Moses Mendelssohn's towering intellectual presence and the popularity of the Jewish literary salons promised social acceptance. The prejudices never really disappeared during the Enlightenment, but it still was a striking circumstance when men from the high nobility and intelligentsia, who had been the first to visit Jewish homes, now were the first to ostracize Jews openly. Neither Carl nor Marie had ever belonged to the circles of the prominent Jewish salonieres Sarah Levy, Henriette Herz, or Rahel Levin, being one generation younger than all three. Theirs was also not the case of Brentano and Arnim, who, as the historian Norbert Miller colorfully puts it, in the evenings at salons rubbed elbows with ease who they would pathetically anathematize the next day at lunch.[30]

The trigger for this new explosion of antisemitism was Chancellor Hardenberg's energetic endeavor to finally resolve the centuries-old question about the status of Jews in Prussia. Since the first wave of reforms, the abandonment of discriminatory laws and regulations had been part of the ongoing reform debate. With the city ordinance of 1808, Jews with a protected status (i.e., those allowed to reside while paying a special levy) and property owners had been allowed to vote and be elected in town and municipal offices. With the edict of March 11, 1812, Hardenberg in one sweeping gesture granted Jews full citizenship, lifted occupational and residential restrictions, and abandoned all special taxes and levies.

The hostile and outward reactionary speeches at the *Deutsche Tischgesellschaft* confirms a pattern long observed by social scientists: the granting of political and economic rights to a minority is almost inevitably followed by hostility and even social isolation by the majority. Many members of the patriotic intelligentsia explained the recently increased intolerance as payback for the Jewish friendliness toward the French during the occupation of Berlin in 1806–1808. It did not help that the economic crisis in Prussia had forced gentry families into debt and bankruptcy, inspiring the rise once again of the hateful image of the Jewish banker, despite the fact that Jewish businesses in Prussia suffered too. Finally, the nobility's own insecurities over whether it could continue to determine the fate of the state after the disaster of 1806 fueled the backlash. From this insecurity, for instance, stemmed the curious parallel made by the *Tischgesellschaft* between "philistines" (a euphemism for the rising middle class) and Jews, both understood as soulless, without real talents and honor, and unable to develop sophisticated ideas. The granting of equal political opportunities to these two groups would presumably bring down German arts and culture, and thus they deserved to be ostracized from the intellectual elite.[31]

Not surprisingly for a couple of their background, Marie and Carl's correspondence features some virulent remarks. While it is critical not to trivialize the issue, it should also be noted that such comments are relatively few and far between compared to the tirades of their contemporaries Arnim, Müller, or Ernst Moritz Arndt. Nonetheless, they are present in the couple's writings. Traveling throughout the Russian Empire in 1812, Carl wrote with particularly strong language about Poland as a land where "dirty German Jews, swarming like vermin in the dirt and misery, are the patricians of this land."[32] Clausewitz had probably passed by a shtetl or *miasteczko* (in Polish), a settlement where over centuries Jews from Central and Western Europe had found refuge (hence the remark that they were "German" but in all likeness had spoken Yiddish—a mixture of German, Slavic, and Hebrew languages). After the Partitions of Poland, when the shtetls became also part of the more repressive Russian Empire, they were increasingly marked by poverty, discrimination, and violence. In this case

Clausewitz, otherwise so sensible to political and historic developments, failed to understand the complex causes for the Jewish misery.

Studying documents and contextual information available to him, Peter Paret summarizes Clausewitz's attitudes as positive or at least neutral toward Jews assimilated in German society and negative toward all others.[33] Some of the pronouncements may have stemmed from the influence of the poet Ernst Moritz Arndt, who, Marie's correspondence suggests, became a good acquaintance of the couple in 1812–1815. At least one of Clausewitz's virulent remarks, this from 1814 about Napoleon as "tough as a Jew, and equally shameless," bears clear marks of Arndt's thinking.[34] In his vehement hatred toward the French, Arndt famously equaled them to Jews.[35] Marie, meanwhile, as a lady from high society, had less direct contact with Jewish intellectuals and only years later mentioned interacting with them. Despite her enlightened education and outgoing personality, hers was still a world centered mostly on the royal court and its exclusive atmosphere.

The Prussian government's refusal to assume a more proactive position toward Napoleon increasingly alienated the already agitated circle of patriotic intellectuals and military reformers. Clausewitz actually assessed the role played by Chancellor Hardenberg in this period in rather positive terms, explaining that the chancellor's "personal resourcefulness, moderation, and flexibility were well suited to the task of maintaining relations with France on a bearable plane."[36] Nevertheless Hardenberg's reforms, executed in order to pay war tributes, burdened the already shrinking private finances with new taxes, forced the furlough of almost half the army, and, due to the strict following of the continental blockade for English goods, crippled the economy. And, contrary to Prussia's submissive policy, Napoleon never followed up with his part of the peace agreement and continued to occupy the fortresses Danzig, Stettin, Küstrin, and Glogau.

Throughout 1810–1811, Napoleon and Tsar Alexander's once-warm relationship gradually cooled off due to the emperor's insistence that Russian ports be closed to British merchants and goods, a move harmful for the Russian economy. The growing hostility between the two Great Powers spelled the beginning of a new war. The military reformers' circle observed the events with growing anxiety, afraid that the eventual victory of Napoleon would lead to a new redistribution of the European lands and with it the end of Prussia. Gneisenau and Clausewitz, together with Hermann von Boyen and Carl von Tiedemann (the first Scharnhorst's successor at the war ministry and the second one of his gifted students), prepared another plan that would enable Prussia to significantly contribute to the French destruction. The plan suggested that if Napoleon were to march East and thus cross Prussian territory, with partisan actions behind the enemy lines, the Prussian troops could force Napoleon to waste enormous energy and manpower to overcome the resistance. The Russian tsar would then have enough time to prepare and execute a smashing victory. If with so many sacrifices Prussia played a crucial role in the French defeat, the war party logic went, then its survival and restoration to previous glory would be secured. The irregular, bloody nature of the warfare almost certainly guaranteed that the civilian population would be involved and pay a heavy price for that. Still, the full devastation of Prussia's own territory and people was seen as acceptable by the military reformers because they believed that the country's destruction at the hands of Napoleon was unavoidable in any case.[37]

For Friedrich Wilhelm, however, the price was too high to pay and the plan was unsurprisingly rejected. The king did follow the advice of military reformers in at least one aspect and agreed upon enlargement of the Prussian army and reinforcement of key strongholds. This move elicited a swift and strong reaction from Napoleon, who threatened that if the rearmament did not stop immediately, he would withdraw his ambassador from Berlin and send instead Marshal Davout and his army. Predictably, the king complied again. It appeared that Prussia had not only failed to learn its lesson about the need for proactive policy from Jena-Auerstedt, but indeed had maneuvered itself into the worst possible position—between the fronts, without a long-term strategy, and leaving its fate in the hands of foreign powers. Once again Clausewitz observed how, without energetic and bold political leadership, even the most daring military staff was bound to fail in its plans.

In this state of heightened agitation Carl composed and partially dictated to Marie his *Drei Bekenntnisse* (Three Declarations)—a series of texts offering a comprehensive view of Prussia's current situation and possible response. The first text, written in the most exalted manner and in a form close to a poem, manifested his deep frustration with the despondence and lack of resolve displayed by Friedrich Wilhelm and the Prussian government. In the second text he explained why, in these circumstances, friendly relations with France were just an illusion and how eventually the alliance would lead to the destruction of Prussia. The third text described possible steps for national defense. The virulent and radical rhetoric made the first

Bekenntnis the most infamous one of the three, and in fact in the last days of World War II the Nazi propaganda machine would use this appeal for proactive and uncompromising policy as a call for total war. In Clausewitz's own time, the text was not published but was read in the circle of his and Marie's patriotic friends. Friedrich Wilhelm probably also saw a copy of the *Drei Bekenntnisse*, but in those restless days its tone surely would not have surprised him.[38]

Carl may have found some relief from his agitation in the face of the upcoming storm through writing his declarations, but the humiliations for Prussia only continued. On March 2, while at dinner, the king received news that French troops had already marched through Pomerania. On the same evening, just as Friedrich Wilhelm was preparing to go to bed, a courier from the Prussian ambassador in Paris, Baron von Krusemark, arrived with yet worse news. Left with the choice of whether, on their offensive eastward, the French troops would march through Prussia as an ally or as a foe, Krusemark felt obliged to sign the offered treaty for Prussia's direct involvement in Napoleon's upcoming Russian campaign. As an obvious tactic to smother any resistance, the courier was delayed, and the unhappy Friedrich Wilhelm saw no other way out than to immediately ratify the document. In doing so, the king was forced to promise to quarter and supply Napoleon's army, open all of Prussia's munitions stores and fortresses, and provide an auxiliary corps of 12,000 men. "Despair was at its height in all hearts devoted to their country. All who had declared against Napoleon were anxious, if they were not bound, to quit Berlin," Princess Louise Radziwiłł wrote in her memoirs.[39]

The fervent patriots found themselves in an especially precarious position: to stay and be forced to support Napoleon would have been against their principles, but to leave would eventually mean fighting against their own state. Princess Louise summarized the tension when she wrote that "consciences were sadly distracted between conflicting duties, and this state of uncertainty was harassing to the last degree."[40] On March 31, the day French troops entered Berlin, Clausewitz left the capital with the declared goal of transferring service and fighting for Russia. The difficult and painful decision made him literally sick and, as Carl wrote to Marie, a severe headache and a cold sweat tortured him, so he "cursed every stone over which I drove" on the road eastward.[41]

6

Exile (April 1812–March 1813)

When Carl left Berlin at the end of March 1812, he was embarking upon a very uncertain future. After almost two decades in a Prussian uniform, he was giving up a promising career path, the influence and prestige of his positions at the general staff, and the comfort of his loving home. Even in the eyes of many of his fellow reformers, the fact that the king and the country appeared poised to sink to a new and greater low than that of 1806 was not reason enough to transfer to the Russian service and eventually fight against Prussia. There were other alternatives. Carl could have instead resigned his commission and searched for a different employment; he might have stayed and waited for an opening that would allow Friedrich Wilhelm to change course and, when that happened, assumed again an active role; or he might have remained a Prussian officer, like many others, deciding that their oath to the sovereign obligated them to follow even an awful decision. Carl, however, took the most radical path. As Werner Hahlweg notes, the fact that in the Russian service Clausewitz never achieved the influence or participated in the type of action he had hoped for makes this step appear, in hindsight, especially cataclysmic.[1]

Just fifteen months after their long-awaited marriage, Marie not only did not stop Carl from leaving but in fact actively supported his decision. Peter Paret questions why Marie, otherwise such a skillful courtier, did not seek to dissuade Carl from an action that would clearly bring Friedrich Wilhelm's lasting anger upon him.[2] In his resignation letter, Clausewitz committed a faux pas that later gave the reactionary faction more ammunition against him—he failed to mention his intentions to enter the Russian service or to ask the king's permission to do so.[3] When Carl wrote his resignation letter on his way to Russia, Marie was far away and unable to advise him about the form. When it came to the content, however, one can hardly doubt that she encouraged his stand, and indeed had taken it herself. Marie had been in the epicenter of heightened emotions that produced Schill's Rebellion in 1809, had already been known to utter damning words against Friedrich Wilhelm, and saw Prussia's failure foremost in terms of weak and incompetent political leadership.

Marie's support for Carl's decision to leave and transfer to Russian service fit the pattern of her hard-nosed and unsentimental approach toward politics. For Carl to remain in Prussia and subsequently fight on Napoleon's side would have been not only morally wrong but also in vain. Even in the darkest hours of Schill's Rebellion and the Austrian defeat of 1809, Marie continued to believe that the French domination of Europe had been so flawed that it was eventually bound to fail.[4] Taking a conformist approach for the time being was not an option, because such behavior would not only prolong Napoleon's demise but also rob one of moral high ground when it came time to give the emperor a final death blow. The nature and hardship of the upcoming Russian campaign, when the possibility of death appeared very real, also made the conformist option unbearable. If Carl were to risk his life in the inhospitable East, it should certainly be on the right side of history.

In 1812, the couple profoundly believed that the only chance to help Prussia's survival required them to break away from and even fight against it. Strikingly, contrary to the shortened and edited versions of Carl's letters known until now, Marie's clearly reveal that the couple saw the transfer to Russia not as a temporary alternative to the Prussian disgrace but as a possibly permanent response. Marie and Carl actually considered leaving for Russia together and living there for an extended period of time. In the spring of 1812, Napoleon still appeared very strong, and the continuation of the Russian campaign for years was a rather plausible outcome. And in an era when life often ended abruptly, even half a decade could constitute a lifetime. Marie only regretted, bitterly, the decision not to travel right away with Carl in the spring of 1812: "Were I able to accompany you forthwith, I would have been spared at least this headache," she wrote about the lack of news. Ever the high-society lady, she also tried to establish contact with important persons, learn about prices and living circumstances, and plan their new life in St. Petersburg.[5] The finality of Marie and Carl's decision in 1812, suggested in Marie's letters, also explains why Carl committed the legal faux pas in his letter of resignation. If he envisioned a prolonged, or even complete, separation from Prussia, he could bluntly disregard the protocol.

Contrary to many other Prussian courtiers dazzled in the previous decade by Tsar Alexander's opulent visits to Europe (ironically described by Marie as their "Russian passion"), Marie bore very few illusions about the true state of Russian society and politics. Her family had traveled to and lived in St. Petersburg for extended periods of time and debated, as she shared with Carl, the ruling class's appalling abuse of its serf population and the country's riches; although, as Marie wrote, Charles von Brühl also admired Russian people's culture and spirit.[6] Marie's clear-eyed approach saved in all probability Carl from the unrealistic expectations or outright hostility and arrogance many Westerners felt toward Russian society upon arrival in the country, as no condemning statements could be found in his correspondence. Such were the momentous times of 1812 that the couple embraced the most authoritarian state in Europe in order to save Prussia from French domination.

Carl left Marie in Berlin partially because of the uncertainty of the roads eastward and the terms of his new assignment, but also due to their limited finances. He waited in Breslau for the arrival of his last annual paycheck and wrote to Marie about the nice surprise when he found that he had been paid in full, "instead of 1,300 thaler wage—1,900, so now I could be without worries." With money secured for the trip to Russia and the first months there, Carl could prepare for their life together in St. Petersburg and, he wrote to Marie, "with that indeed a great step toward our union would be made."[7]

None of Marie's letters from April 1812 have been preserved, probably lost by Carl on his way to the Russian headquarters in Vilna (today Vilnius, capital of Lithuania). She wrote almost every other day to him, and the first preserved letter from that period, dated May 12, is numbered the fifteenth. Marie had left Berlin soon after Carl for Giewitz, and stayed there until mid-July. The French once again effectively occupied the capital as, according to the terms of the signed treaty, the Prussian army had been ordered to leave and the Napoleonic troops were brought in. On May 6 the king's brother, Prince Wilhelm, and Princess Marianne were forced to give a great ball for the French Commanding General Count Nicolas Oudinot. "I had hoped I might be able to avoid the sight of the French, once more become our masters," indignantly wrote Princess Louise Radziwiłł, "but far from it, I was obliged to go into society again and attend the dinners my father gave to the French generals."[8] In June, the Russian ambassador Count Christopher von Lieven and his wife Dorothea left the country (carrying a letter from Marie to Carl with them), and none doubted the upcoming war anymore.[9]

In the formally independent Duchy of Mecklenburg-Schwerin, Marie spent her days quietly, helping the pregnant Luise von Voß care for her other children, teaching them English, reading Livy's *History of Rome*, and painting landscapes. It was at this time that, feeling nostalgic but also overwhelmed by events of the past several months, Marie began composing notes about her childhood, the early years of her relationship with Carl, and the first year of their marriage. Marie also kept in constant contact with friends and relatives and, on her husband's behalf, preemptively informed them about the letter of resignation sent to Friedrich Wilhelm.[10]

Carl was resolved to leave the Prussian service regardless of the king's response to his letter. He asked Marie, in case he had to travel without permit and thus avoid Prussian territories, to help him obtain a pass for Galicia from the Austrian Ambassador Ludwig von Bombelles.[11] In the end, Friedrich Wilhelm's cold dismissal made Clausewitz's travels easier, and although in fact the letter did not contain permission for transfer to the Russian army, Carl continued his trip without significant trouble except for arrogant behavior of the Graudenz fortress's Polish commandant.[12] Along the way, he found fellow Prussians sympathetic to his decision. One, Stein's old associate Theodor von Schön, now administering the Lithuanian region in East Prussia, even declared himself ready to serve as a courier for the couple's correspondence.[13] Carl crossed the Russian border ten days later and arrived at the tsar's headquarters in Vilna on May 20.

"I received yesterday a very friendly letter from Pr[incess] L[ouise]; she said that for a couple of days the people were preoccupied with you but then the Dresdner gathering created such a powerful diversion that none has time anymore to think of anything else," Marie reported in her letter of May 28.[14] The "Dresden gathering" she referred to, was a grandiose, thirteen-day-long celebration held in the Saxon capital by Napoleon just before the beginning of the Russian campaign, to which he summoned both Friedrich Wilhelm and Francis I of Austria. News like this strengthened Marie's belief that Carl's decision had been the right one: "Consoled a little about our separation, I always thank God that at least you were not part of these indignities."[15] On May 24, the Grande Armée, around 600,000 men strong, started its march east with Carl's two elder brothers, Friedrich Volmar and Wilhelm Benedict, among them.[16]

The beginning of the war might have distracted Friedrich Wilhelm, but troubles for the couple were far from over. Marie could not stay forever in the province—the safe delivery of Luise's baby required medical attention in the capital—and her own financial matters needed attention. Arriving back in Berlin on June 20, Marie braced herself for backlash. In the first weeks after Clausewitz's departure even her own mother, afraid of losing her widow's pension from the king, avoided discussing his resignation.[17] Others expressed oblique sympathy, while people she thought fellow patriots not only refused moral support but also behaved "in a way that sincerely enraged me."[18]

Yet once back in the capital, Marie discovered that the mood against the French had soured even more, and hers and Carl's stance was not universally condemned, as she had feared. When Napoleon's troops marched through Neumark, Pomerania, and West and East Prussia, they behaved as nothing but foes, seizing food and animals and devastating the lands. Already economically stagnant and plagued by a series of bad crops, Prussia could hardly support the march of the over half-a-million men eastward. The shortages of provisions soon weakened the French morale and led to sequestration of provisions and cruelty against the peasants. In the summer of 1812, even big landowners away from the path of the Grande Armée, like the Voßes in Mecklenburg, found themselves under enormous economic pressure and unable to cover taxes and expenses. At age thirty-two, August von Voß decided to hand the reins of Giewitz over to his wife Luise and look for a paid position in the Austrian army.[19] "You cannot believe how sad it was to see a family man leaving his own to take up such an uncertain future," Marie described the scene in Giewitz.[20] The Brühl family's estate in Pförten also suffered from bad crops and the overall stagnant European economy. While Marie received her annual interest, the money owed from previous years still could not be paid.[21]

So, contrary to expectations and with some irony, Marie reported to her husband that soon after her arrival in Berlin, she had become an object of quiet sympathy: "If anything, all our friends wish that you remember them fondly, especially Mademoiselle [von] Bischoffwerder, Julie [von der] Goltz, Luise [von Voß], aunt [Laura, the widow of uncle] Heinrich [von Brühl], and so on. Even the old [General Anton Wilhelm von L']estocq recently asked me to send greeting to you, to my great surprise."[22] Her old friend, the Swedish diplomat and poet Gustav von Brinkman, also volunteered to serve as a courier, so the exchange of letters between the couple could go on unnoticed.[23] Princess Marianne and Princess Louise never severed their friendship with Marie. As her letters suggest, Marie's influential backers at the court might have been one of the reasons why Friedrich Wilhelm held back—to punish a member of Prussia's high nobility, given the Brühl family's stature, would have been a controversial step. The king treated her less harshly than expected, Marie wrote to Carl about her stay in Berlin, he answered to her curtsy, and although he gave her a displeased expression, "that was the only evidence of wrath that I received from him."[24] Nevertheless Marie wisely prepared to depart once again from the court, this time to stay in her cousin Therese's estate close to Tetschen (now Děčín in the Czech Republic), a part of Austria's Bohemian domain.

Just when Marie thought that the storm might blow over, Julie von der Goltz, who as a wife of a high-ranking member of the Prussian government had received an inside tip, informed her about the upcoming lawsuit against the thirty-some officers who left for Russia. "Julie G. was just here to prepare me [for the fact] that you and your friends will be called in the newspapers <u>by name</u> to come back and, should you fail to appear, a formal court will be staged," Marie wrote to her husband on July 30. She emphasized the fact that the officers would be named specifically, because up to that point the reprimands had remained unspecific and inconclusive. "Earlier I was completely prepared for this but I admit . . . that I have believed that one would let the issue die down. . . . It is unpleasant for me because of the impact it would have on mama and because of all the gossip about it that will begin again," she wrote in dismay. Nevertheless, at the end of the letter Marie bravely repeated her plea for Carl not to worry about her since women had no formal political power and thus little retributions to fear: "Real ill for me could not arise from it because I cannot answer for your actions in court, so I would gladly like to defend them in front of every moral tribunal." She added that her property wouldn't be liable either (since Pförten, as an independent estate, was out of Prussia's jurisdiction), another comfort for them.[25]

The citation from Berlin's highest court was published twenty days later in the newspapers, as Julie had said. The *Kammergericht* acknowledged Clausewitz's status as an officer who had resigned his commission, but charged him with entering the Russian service without permission and demanded his immediate return and appearance before a judge. If he failed to do so or did not ask for an extension to return, the court would deprive him of all property and any inheritance he might receive in the future.[26]

Contrary to the analysis of modern scholars, Marie did not believe that Clausewitz being singled-out came directly from Friedrich Wilhelm but from the clique around him, especially since the citation appeared with some delay.[27] While acknowledging the king's personal anger, she investigated the probable instigator of the attack. Her description ("the old fool who lets hussars visit") makes it hard to pinpoint the person in question, but Marie wrote with certainty that he had submitted accusations to Friedrich Wilhelm against Carl. However, she added, the king "probably judged according to merit because <u>nothing</u> happened after this citation."[28]

Whether Marie's intelligence was correct or not, it reveals the complicated situation in the summer of 1812. Despite the old guard's fearsome reaction, his personal feelings, and the damage done to the monarchical power, Friedrich Wilhelm found himself overwhelmed by the rising forces of nationalism and in fact could do little to turn around the situation. He responded, again, in the usual hesitant manner symptomatic for his approach to political crises. Throughout his reign, Friedrich Wilhelm maintained a personal coldness against the persons who had offended him or tried to push more proactive positions; but sooner or later, under the pressure of events and personal whims, the king accepted them. Particularly Clausewitz would come to experience this pattern, even as late as 1830.

Although convinced that no real repercussions would follow the citation printed in the papers, Marie still left Berlin as soon as possible—waiting only for Luise to safely deliver her child.[29] The day after this event, she left for the Tetschen Castle in Bohemia, where she still took measures to protect her property by temporarily transferring it to her cousin, Therese's younger brother Friedrich August. The other obvious relative for the transfer—Fritz von Brühl—was at that time considering leaving the Austrian army as well and joining Carl in Russia.[30]

The sophisticated and cosmopolitan counts Thun and Hohenstein had built their home at the confluence of the rivers Elbe und Ploučnice in Bohemia. Today the castle remains the most prominent symbol of modern-day Děčín and is visited yearly by thousands of tourists. When Marie arrived, the second and last reconstruction of Tetschen Castle had been completed less than a decade previously. The residence, however, was not yet the important cultural and political center it would become when, in the second part of the nineteenth century, diplomatic congresses met within its walls and prominent figures like Fryderyk Chopin and Archduke Franz Ferdinand stayed in its rooms. For Marie, despite the comfort and the marvelous view of the Elbe, Tetschen still appeared too isolated, although she was treated with welcome kindness: "This painful, endlessly painful absence of news and the fear about the turn of the great public events set aside, I feel very well here. Genuine joy I cannot experience now anywhere, but the sincere love and heartfelt, truly touching sympathy that everybody here shows toward me, makes me feel really good, and the quiet monotonous country life in such a beautiful area allows that, at least, one loses sight of the days, without especially painful efforts."[31] To keep her body and mind occupied, Marie exercised ("I have become again a great equestrienne and also Therese has plucked up courage for it").[32] She visited Prague, Kulm, and Töplitz, and painted landscapes again. Just like she had in Giewitz with Luise, Marie helped her cousin with the children.[33] Instead of going back to their Prague residence for the winter, Therese and her husband decided to stay in Tetschen, and Marie was happy to continue her voluntary exile from the Prussian court.

In the Bohemian province, Carl's letters came with significant delay and they were few and far between. Many got lost on the long way to and from embattled Russia. The couple used several intermediaries, so the letters would not arouse suspicions coming from an enemy country, and wrote fake names and addresses on the envelopes ("Madam Fenche in Gotheberg"). They also cautiously avoided political debates that, should the letters be intercepted, might further complicate their already precarious situation. After Carl's letter written on June 20 from the headquarters in Vilna, Marie had to wait a painfully long time until September 8 when she received a letter two months old (July 18). Then on December 2 came another one written on October 27, and the next piece of news (November 10) didn't arrive until January 13, 1813. The couple repeated the most important news in letter after letter, unsure if the previous writings had been received. They sent their correspondence using alternative roads, and in all probability afterward took special care to recover the undelivered letters still in the possession of their numerous intermediaries. Due to these fortunate circumstances, the invaluable and highly personal information about Clausewitz's experience in the Campaign of 1812 has been preserved. Marie also received news about Carl through the families of the other officers in the Russian service, but generally learned the extent of events and his participation in them only partially and with significant delay.

Soon after arriving in the headquarters in Vilna, Carl realized that his situation—being a stranger in a foreign country whose language he didn't speak—made it almost impossible to navigate the hierarchy and put his mark on crucial decisions. He received a rank of lieutenant-colonel and met the emperor personally, but he quickly lost most of his illusions: "Brilliant prospects have not opened to me and I am far from enjoying the trust . . . that I had in Prussia, let alone getting the chance for it."[34] For his day-to-day accommodations in a foreign land, in all probability Carl relied on his newly hired servant, Jascha in all probability of Jewish descent. Jascha appears in Marie's correspondence only in 1813 and then in 1831, but the Slavic or Yiddish origins of the name (nickname for Jacob) would suggest that in addition to German, he spoke Russian too. Therefore, it is more likely that Clausewitz hired him going to Russia, where he did not speak the language, than coming back from it. His remarks about the shtetl in Polish Lithuania he had passed by, although virulent, suggest that the servant probably came from such. Jascha would remain with Clausewitz until the end of his life and would take care for his papers and most personal needs.[35]

Unable to stop the Grande Armée, the Russian army retreated and fell back ever deeper in the country's vast territory, burning villages and crops to deny the invader supplies and shelter. This was far from a unified or carefully prepared strategy, nor was it unilaterally supported by the Russian officer corps or nobility, and newcomers could hardly navigate the different factions. Initially Clausewitz served in the general staff as an aide to another Prussian in the service of the emperor, General Carl Ludwig von Phull, but wrote with dissatisfaction back to Marie on July 6 that he was "barely aware of the war." Carl had to admit that Princess Louise's warnings that in a foreign land he would never enjoy the same degree of influence he was used to in Prussia might hold true. He still tried to make the best of the situation: "I could barely hope to be useful here, and my whole ambition is directed singularly towards seeing the war for myself and through this, to win personally."[36]

By the time Marie read Carl's next letter, he had transferred to service in the Russian rearguard and witnessed the battles of Smolensk and Borodino, but he did not write to his wife about the horrific bloodshed. In his attempt to finally force a decisive battle upon the ever-retreating Russian army, Napoleon completely destroyed the city of Smolensk. In Borodino, the new Russian supreme commander Mikhail Kutuzov decided to make a stand, for the sake of his officers' and troops' morale, but for a terrible price—he lost one-third of his army. Yet the tsar had an enormous reserve of men to recover from the defeats, while with every passing day Napoleon was drawn deeper into inhospitable Russian territory and away from his lines of communication.

Carl slept under the open sky and suffered from the weather, dirt, lack of clean water, and hunger. He found his mood darkened by the abandoned and burned villages, and was plagued by gout and a toothache.[37] Still his conviction that Russia could not be conquered grew only stronger. Initially, as the invader, Napoleon enjoyed the advantage: he had the initiative, and led a better-trained, more organized, and modern army. But with every avoided battle and every mile deeper into the Russian territory, the French offense lost its intensity, and the balance was shifting toward the defenders. Due in large part to the scorched earth policy of the Russian army, the morale of Napoleon's troops plummeted and their fighting abilities were badly weakened. Later Clausewitz would touch upon this experience when he challenged one of the orthodox military ideas of the day—that the attacker always enjoyed all the advantages.[38] Defense, he would argue in *On War*, is after all the stronger form of warfare.

The only thing Carl feared now was that the tsar might lose his nerve and agree to "a bad peace."[39] He wrote this after Russian troops and civilians abandoned the old capital Moscow and it was almost entirely burned. After waiting for a peace offer from Tsar Alexander that never came, Napoleon now had to choose between two utterly unbearable choices. His army had to either suffer more casualties in the upcoming winter in the devastated Moscow and its surroundings or leave the city, turn around, and try to fight their way out of Russia. The emperor chose the second. On October 27, Carl wrote to Marie his optimistic prediction that "maybe action in the German Fatherland is closer than we thought."[40]

Meanwhile at Tetschen, Marie learned from her correspondents in Berlin about the death of their friend Carl von Tiedemann. Like Clausewitz a former student and close collaborator of Scharnhorst, he too had left his position in the Prussian army and transferred to Russian service. The similarities of their circumstances—Tiedemann had also left his wife (and children) back in Prussia—made Marie feel restless and the reaction of Friedrich Wilhelm's court increased her agitation. Serving as chief of staff for the Russian forces protecting Riga, Tiedemann was killed by a Prussian hussar belonging to the auxiliary corps attached to the Napoleonic army. Marie bitterly decried the ruling clique's "sordid revilement" and inability to show solemnity and grace when fellow countrymen tragically shot at one another. This strengthened her resolve to stay away from Berlin and the court.[41]

Clausewitz was supposed to take Tiedemann's job after the latter's death, but during his stop in St. Petersburg and upon meeting there other expatriates like Hermann von Boyen, Baron vom Stein, and Ernst Moritz Arndt, he changed his mind and sought assignment in the Russo-German Legion that had started to take shape. Without mastering the language, a foreign officer could only be a well-meaning adviser without real influence, and Carl's attempts to learn Russian had been unsuccessful. The opulence of St. Petersburg dazzled but also convinced him that he and Marie could not live there with their limited income.[42] Carl now longed to return to the Fatherland.

Clausewitz's change of heart in the fall of 1812, historians have pointed out, had a noticeably German overtone instead of simply Prussian patriotism. During his time in St. Petersburg he had learned about the court proceedings against him and this, together with the already deep-seated anger he held, led Carl to reject the Prussian monarchy and turn his attention instead to the glory of the German Fatherland.[43] The presence of Stein and Arndt in his close social circle only strengthened these sentiments. Arndt was the first to call for German unity, and he espoused that men owed greater loyalty to the shared Fatherland than to the princes, especially if the latter failed to fulfill their essential mission to protect the country's interests.[44]

By the time Marie received the news about Carl's new assignment, she had independently come to the conclusion that their fate was no longer interconnected with that of Prussia. This was the case not because she feared the punishment waiting for Clausewitz should he return (she didn't believe the king would ever gather enough will to fulfill it) but because the course the Prussian monarchy had taken divorced them from their loyalty. "In the extreme case we still have Austria where it is possible to live well and I have so many friends and family," she wrote in December to Carl.[45]

Clausewitz now received an offer to become part of the Russo-German Legion, a pet cause of Tsar Alexander—the unit that was supposed to incite soldiers and officers from various German territories now under Napoleon's command to defect and fight on Russia's side. While Carl waited for the legion's slow creation, he took a temporary job in Prince Wittgenstein's army, which was tasked with cutting off the French retreat north through Lithuania. The main Russian objective now was to force the Grande Armée back through the same Smolensk road it had come by, leaving them to face the already stripped-bare and utterly devastated lands during the unforgiving Russian winter. Without provisions and starving, the Napoleonic troops had to slaughter their horses, meaning the cavalry ceased to exist, and the artillery had to abandon their cannons. "Who would have thought that at the end of 1812 it would look so good as it does!" Carl wrote ecstatically to Marie on November 10. Just a few months earlier he had believed that the campaign would take years. Now, less than nine months after Carl had left Berlin, he was about to pursue Napoleon's destroyed army back to Prussia. "It could be ascribed only to human mistakes and fate if now Europe will be not be rescued. In the salvaged Europe, should we find an honorable sanctuary, so we could enjoy untroubled our quiet happiness? Our fate has never been so interconnected with the world events as in this moment," Carl captured the mood as he prepared for the final pursuit.[46]

Carl wrote again to Marie right after the last big clash at the River Berezina. There, squeezed by two Russian armies, the exhausted and starved Napoleonic troops fought their way through to cross the pontoon bridges. Carl spared writing to Marie about the most gruesome scenes but in the face of such horror, he still looked to find some comfort in sharing his experiences with her: "I am writing you between bodies and dying men under smoking debris, and thousands of ghosts like people pass by, and cry, and beg, and weep for bread in vain."[47]

On December 20, the Russian advanced units reached East Prussia and on the other side of the border met 14,000 men from the Prussian auxiliary troops led by General Ludwig Yorck von Wartenburg. An old and distinguished Junker, he had opposed the French without ever belonging to the reform party. When Friedrich Wilhelm ordered him to follow Napoleon into Russia, he dutifully followed. Yorck should have covered the Grande Armée retreat, but a meeting between him and the Russian commander General Hans Karl von Diebitsch on Christmas Day convinced him to begin negotiations. The Russian officer chosen to lay out the facts and sway the Prussian general to abandon the French was no other than Clausewitz. "I spent four days in the most horrible anxiety; we had cut off General Yorck and were ready every day to start fighting with him," wrote Carl to Marie on December 30.[48] The quick note of relief was written the day when, at the outskirts of Tauroggen (now in Lithuania), the general signed the convention that would become a critical turning point in Prussian and European history. In all probability

Clausewitz had drafted the armistice.[49] According to it, Yorck neutralized his troops for a period of two months and allowed the Russians to pass into Prussian territory.

Yorck had little doubt that his actions, committed without authority and in clear violation of the policy of the government in Berlin, were treasonous, but he still tried to defend them in a letter to Friedrich Wilhelm. The old Frederician officer argued that the situation needed to be exploited in the best possible way and, in a striking sign of the changing mood, added that the decision followed the wishes of the nation. In February, Baron vom Stein, now sent as a Russian plenipotentiary to Königsberg, convened the East Prussian Estates, thereby guaranteeing public support for the preparations for war against France. With the decision to declare all adult men regardless of their social status and religion eligible for service (except schoolteachers and clergymen) in order to create a provincial militia (*Landwehr*) of 20,000 men and a home guard (*Landsturm*), the Province of East Prussia de facto slipped from Berlin's control and began preparing for war with France.[50] Again Clausewitz assumed a crucial position by drafting a plan for the popular mobilization.

On January 21, 1813, afraid to be taken hostage by French troops in his capital, Friedrich Wilhelm left for Breslau. He called Gerhard von Scharnhorst back from retirement but, still fearful of Napoleon's vengeance, the king again hesitated for weeks to boldly and radically change course. The Russian troops pursuing the French were not as numerous as Friedrich Wilhelm was initially led to believe, and Austria, a much-needed partner for the upcoming battle, adopted for its part a wait-and-see attitude. Yet the enthusiasm among wide circles of Prussian society made the threat of an open revolt serious enough to force Friedrich Wilhelm to the crucial step. On February 27, the Treaty of Kalisz was signed, and the Prussian king and the tsar became allies.

Marie knew little about her husband's decisive role in the turn of events because none of Carl's letters after November 10 reached her. However, she followed the events closely and since the first days of January was prepared to travel to the Russian camp in East Prussia. Through her mother's letters Marie learned about Carl's appearance in Russian uniform in Yorck's headquarters, but the gossip about his high position and many medals seemed to her too good to be true.[51] Marie rushed to preempt the Wittgenstein army's march into Berlin, and while the residents of the capital teetered on whether the French garrison would fight back, she, together with her friend Caroline, recklessly ran to meet the advance guard of the Russian army. Only the insistence of the city's commandant General Ludwig von Brauchitsch that these were dangerous hours forced the women to go home and wait for the unfolding events.[52] Finally, on March 4, 1813 the French withdrew from Berlin without putting up a real fight. After a year of separation, Marie and Carl met once again a week later.

7

The Long Path to Liberation
(March 1813–August 1815)

The events of Eastern Prussia, in which Carl played an essential role, launched the period known in German history as the *Befreiungskriege* or Wars of Liberation. As the name implies, later generations saw the three-year-long destruction of Napoleon as a time full of patriotic pathos, and sacrifice, which cut across class, gender, religion, and geographical borders of various German lands and produced glorious victories. For Marie, the years 1813–1815 were indeed the most exciting, active, and eventful of her life. For the first and only time she came close to the battlefield and to Carl's experience as a soldier. Volunteering at the military hospital, Marie had the chance to leave behind her passive role as an observer and participate actively in the war efforts. Yet Carl's role in the Wars of Liberation deeply dissatisfied his ambitions and abilities and, as we shall see, created lingering bitterness. This led to Marie's first attempts to shape the narrative of his achievements.

On March 11, 1813, the day the Wittgenstein corps entered Berlin, the *Kammergericht* was preparing to issue a verdict depriving Clausewitz of all property. As Marie learned from the superbly connected Caroline von Berg, the Prussian justice minister, Friedrich Leopold von Kircheisen, personally ordered the heavy-handed move.[1] Yet Carl's precarious legal situation contrasted starkly with the enthusiastic public embrace in the first hours of his return. The recognition came even from the highest circles of Prussian society after Princess Marianne invited him to the palace and heard his take on the Russian campaign.[2] The princess had stayed in Berlin to nurse her sick toddler while the rest of the court, including her husband, fled to Breslau. These circumstances not only made her, as the most senior member of the royal family left, the nominal head of government in the capital but also won her the boundless admiration of citizens of the city. In the days following the troops' return, crowds cheered the Russian soldiers, women at the court wore orange and black cockades (the colors of the Order of Saint George, the highest Russian military decoration), and families related to Prussians in service of the tsar, like the Brühls, enjoyed particularly high recognition.[3] Berlin welcomed the arrival of the Wittgenstein corps with fireworks and, when Yorck's Prussian corps appeared two weeks later, repeated the celebration with even greater enthusiasm.[4]

On March 17, the Prussian government formally announced the break from France followed by Friedrich Wilhelm's appeal to the citizens of the country to rise against Napoleon. Despite the passionate rhetoric, the text—titled "To My People"—still carefully sought to strike a balance between Prussia's conservative faction, who wished to restore the territories the various German princes had been deprived of, and the aspirations of liberal thinkers and the middle class for more political and economic rights. These differing understandings about what should come after Napoleon's destruction underscored inner tensions and marked the Prussian approach toward war in 1813–1815.

Following the reformers' advice, Friedrich Wilhelm abandoned all exemptions for military service. Although volunteers poured into Breslau, the enthusiasm was far from shared by all people. Recruitment problems persisted, and towns where inhabitants had previously been exempt from military service protested. Taking into account the reactionary party's fears about the nobility's privileges of rank and position, the king did not call a revolutionary *levée en masse*. But by organizing its male population into a regular army, provincial militia (*Landwehr*), elite units of volunteers (*Jäger*), and local irregulars (*Landsturm*), Prussia still managed to gather an army of 130,000 troops and almost 270,000 for the fall campaign from a population of less than five million.[5]

At the end of March, Prince Peter Wittgenstein assigned the defense of Berlin to the Prussian General Friedrich Wilhelm Baron von Bülow and headed with his corps toward Saxony. Clausewitz left the capital on March 20 and made his way to the Russian headquarters in Kalisz. Marie accompanied him to Frankfurt am Oder, but despite his sincere wish to continue their trip together a little longer, she decided to turn back there. The faltering Austrian position had led her to believe that her brother Fritz might have to leave home soon and she wanted to see him one last time.[6] Carl's new Jewish companion also seems to have been a source of confusion to Marie around this time, and she tried to pry information out of Carl about his relationship with Jascha. Referring to him as *dein Israelit* (your Israeli) and *der Jude* (the Jew), Marie demanded details about his trip. For unknown reasons Jascha traveled separately to Kalisz and carried with him some of Carl's documents.[7] Maybe because Carl himself felt uneasy about their relationship, he never answered her questions. Jascha belonged to a minority that many around Europe, and especially Marie and Carl's fellow German patriots, still observed with great suspicion. Yet the attendant had suffered with Clausewitz throughout the bitter Russian campaign and now followed him into the new war.

The year of separation had weighed heavily on the couple. Before their reunion in March Marie had written to Carl about the traces that passing time left on her face and body, softening the unease with self-irony: "I am well but everyday discover more white hairs and age marks; prepare yourself to find back home an old gammer."[8] For his part, Carl had suffered badly from the harsh Russian weather and the brutal campaigning. A whole range of illnesses—gout, arthritis, toothaches, headaches—tested his will on a daily basis. Carl's hair thinned, and the extreme temperatures damaged blood vessels in his face, leaving a permanent redness that later led many to suspect him as a secret drinker.[9] To deal with the severe pains he would also start taking opium.[10]

In their early thirties, the couple still hoped for children, and their short but passionate reunion in Berlin fueled the expectations. But not long afterward Marie wrote to Carl with disappointment that "my hopes, unfortunately, went again as usual[.] I couldn't bring myself to tell you but, as disbelieving as you would be, I have to do it though, so as not to give you empty hope through my silence." She added, "One should not question God but why he denies us happiness that so many enjoy, who value it less and who . . . are also surely less worthy of it, is hard to understand. This makes me often really sad, especially the thought about the happiness that evades <u>you</u> through it[.] Would I carry this burden alone, so I would be much more peaceful about it because my heart is already replenished by you."[11] Receiving the news, Carl showed even more disappointment: "I am very sad about the emptiness of our house and I have to admit to you that I grow daily more so, but not so much because the deprivation from this happiness hurts me but because I cannot console myself that from you, from the most lovable and noble woman that have ever existed, no descendants should remain. . . . In this case heaven does not understand its own interest;

because it is completely impossible that your child, brought up by you, would not come into the world for the best of the world."[12] Two centuries later it is almost impossible to reconstruct the exact cause for the couple's infertility. However, Carl's chronic illnesses appear the most likely source of the problem.

To the personal disappointment the professional was then added. On March 19, the Prussian government had decided to end the prosecution against Carl, but the quiet move after repeated public citations left the impression that he was still in disgrace. Almost a month later, Marie, his brothers, and the couple's close friends remained unsure whether the court proceedings had really been brought to an end.[13] The celebrations Carl had experienced in Berlin in March hardly mollified the precarious state of his career. "For a year I am stalled on the same position and shift from one army to another without coming ahead," he wrote to Marie.[14] Even if Carl believed that fighting for Russia in 1812 had been the right call, as a proud Prussian officer he could not completely shake off the regrets he harbored in abandoning his own beloved country. This nagging feeling was probably exacerbated by the fact that, although he fought in some of the most iconic battles of the war, Clausewitz never enjoyed the trust and influence in Russia he had expected when leaving Berlin.

The decision of the thirty-some officers to quit Prussian service in the spring of 1812 had also created a rift within Friedrich Wilhelm's army that was slow to heal. Even if the times had changed, and history upheld their radical convictions, the returning men were not welcomed home by the majority of those who stayed and suffered under Napoleon nor, most significantly, by the king himself. If war was a completely rational and dispassionate endeavor, officers like Clausewitz, with their enormous experience throughout the difficult but staggering Russian campaign, should have been welcomed with open arms back into the Prussian army. But war remained a human activity plagued by passions, insecurities, and occasional pettiness, and never more so than in the Prussian headquarters in the spring of 1813. Some of the senior officers—by extent also members of the royal family and for the most part sheltered safely in Berlin the previous year—treated him coldly. Others, like Prince Wilhelm, were "somewhat friendly," reported Carl to Marie. It was only his former patron, Prince August, who embraced him "really warmly."[15]

Both Gerhard von Scharnhorst and August Neidhardt von Gneisenau, the latter just promoted to general, lobbied Friedrich Wilhelm to reestablish

Clausewitz back in Prussian service. Unsure exactly where Carl was at the time, Scharnhorst sent Friedrich Wilhelm's answer, together with his personal note, to Marie. Until now both documents have remained unpublished because the original was lost and the copy she made stayed in her correspondence. In his answer to Scharnhorst, Friedrich Wilhelm was harsh and unbending: "Regarding your intercession, I stopped the process against . . . Major von Clausewitz and explained to him during the notification about this decision that he could be readmitted in the service of the Fatherland only if he would acquire new right for consideration through distinction in the upcoming war." In her accompanying letter to her husband, Marie bluntly called the king's answer offensive: "It really made me indignant and I would have found it a lot less ungraceful if he were to silently ignore the offer for your services and to just give you permission to stay in Russian service." Scharnhorst, on the other hand, tried to soften the perception: "I have never misjudged your great value but I have felt it even more in these times when I have so much to do." The general added that a similar arrangement to the one in 1808, when Clausewitz remained nominally in Prince August's service but worked for Scharnhorst, could be struck again. Prince Wittgenstein was eager to please the Prussian supreme commander General Gebhard von Blücher and probably wouldn't refuse this favor to Scharnhorst, the latter's chief-of-staff.[16]

The issue might have been complicated by the question of Clausewitz's rank. In Russian service, he had been promoted from major to lieutenant-colonel. Working side-by-side with Scharnhorst and Gneisenau at the headquarters would have implied keeping the higher rank. However other officers, who had left Prussian service and fought for other countries, were forced to give up the acquired ranks when readmitted. "Grolmann, promoted here to a major seven years ago, fought two campaigns, rose to lieutenant-colonel in Spain, [and] Oppen, [going through] similar circumstances and being a colonel, have been readmitted here as majors," wrote Carl to Marie.[17] This issue was emphasized further by Friedrich Wilhelm's instance to call Clausewitz "major" in his letter to Scharnhorst. Marie's correspondence reveals that she, however, firmly opposed the idea of possible demotion. "I have to admit too that giving up a rank that might be required [for your readmission] would truly appall me, [especially] if . . . the public might see this as punishment," she wrote to Carl.[18] Marie also questioned whether Friedrich Wilhelm personally harbored any such hostility against Carl or the letter had been written by one of the king's reactionary secretaries.[19] Despite declarations that serving the Fatherland was all he wished to do, like many times before and after, Clauswitz was torn between his ambitions and the hunger to be in the middle of the action. Marie's opposition against a possible demotion dissuaded him from pressing more vigorously for his readmission back into the Prussian army. On April 22, Carl ended the discussion with the statement that he was too proud to ask Scharnhorst to lobby once more on his behalf.[20]

The old mentor kept his promise, and Clausewitz soon worked for him once again, formally as the Russian liaison officer on Blücher's staff.[21] "I have a pleasant occupation and I am needed just as a Prussian officer; I have Scharnhorst and Gneisenau's full confidence and have never had so many duties and influence when I carried the [Prussian] blue uniform as I have now," he wrote to Marie.[22] Soon after Carl could also report that even Blücher warmed up to him, especially after discovering that his subordinate had married one of the Berlin ladies greatly admired by the old general.[23] Despite the reactionary faction's continued animosity toward Clausewitz, his influence in the Prussian headquarters clearly could not be overlooked. From Berlin, Marie reported with both disgust and irony about the attempts of one of its most prominent members, Friedrich Ancillon, a Hugenot preacher and tutor of the crown prince, to get closer to her: "Ancillon spent yesterday the evening by Princess Louise and formally asked for [me and my mother] to come. . . I would love to see what a face he would put on."[24]

Despite Carl's attempts to sound positive, he rankled at the insecurity of his position, and his emotions were bound to spill over. When Marie made an inconsiderate but rather harmless joke about a medal he did not receive, Carl wrote her a messy and clamorous letter: "Through such expressions you could easily bring me to feel ashamed in front of you, a shame that would be twice as disagreeable because at the same time I would feel that there would be nothing to be ashamed of." Not surprisingly, this first part of his letter form April 22 was cut out from his published correspondence. "I will distinguish myself, this I have promised you and I will keep my word. All my dreams and thoughts [*Dichten und Denken*] aim at refuting the king and his surrounding by means of excelling." In his mind, he and Marie were one team and now her thoughtlessness made him question whether she really understood what that meant. Hence he added: "Don't be angry and forgive my lack of patience. You should be and must rise to be my protector."[25] In the next letter Carl sought to smooth the episode with a joke—he drew a medal and a general's mustache that Marie deserved for the patient way she handled his frustration.[26]

Meanwhile, Napoleon's defeat in Russia had fanned the flames of anti-French sentiments, but most of the German princes did not feel strongly enough to oppose him openly. Austria hesitated and Bavaria still could not bring itself to defect, despite the fact that fighting on the French side in the Russian campaign caused it 30,000 casualties. Saxony's Friedrich August I found himself in the worst possible position, with his country threatened to take center stage in the upcoming clash, but still hesitated to turn against Napoleon. Even in Berlin, people fretted that the French emperor might again outwit his enemies and march once more triumphantly through the Brandenburg Gate.

With the hopes for a mass uprising of all German lands put on hold, the Russo-Prussian forces marched at the end of March into Saxony, and Clausewitz wrote to his wife from Dresden. Napoleon concentrated his forces there too, but Carl attempted to calm Marie by insisting that even in a case of lost battle, all long-term advantages were on the side of the Russo-Prussian alliance. Time was now working against Napoleon as one by one the European countries overcame their fears and abandoned him. Even more significant for the Prussians, the brilliant military strategist Scharnhorst finally enjoyed recognition and influence in the joined headquarters.[27] Despite Carl's analysis, Marie wrote back to him a week later about the tangible relief in the capital when news about the first French defeats came. "[The news about General von] Dörnberg's victory in [Lüneburg] from the other day is posted on all street corners . . . and not in the dry newspaper style but in an avid, exalted one. This is indeed another time compared to when on all street corners was written: <u>Calm is the most important civic duty</u>. I quite amused myself yesterday to see on [Berlin's main boulevard] *Unter den Linden* and actually on all streets such a piece of news posted . . . and the public busy reading it zealously."[28]

On the battlefield, this first victory turned out to be short-lived as, under the threat of Marshal Davout's advancement with 11,000 men, the Allied troops had to retreat from Lüneburg on the very next day. The mood in Prussia, nevertheless, had changed, especially after the following battle confirmed the vitality of the Russo-Prussian military union. On April 5, near the town of Möckern, the forces under the command of Wittgenstein unexpectedly defeated the numerically superior French army led by Napoleon's stepson, Eugène de Beauharnais. "We celebrated the feast for the two victories in Lüneburg and Möckern . . . on Sunday with really joy-ful and <u>completely new</u> feelings," wrote Marie to Carl.[29]

Yet the allies failed to follow these advances with more aggressive strat-egy and this thawed the public enthusiasm. The Russian Commander-in-Chief Mikhail Kutuzov needed time to reorganize his army after the dreadful winter campaign, and his confidence in the Prussian army's fight-ing abilities was still insufficient. "For many days such a quietness has pre-vailed here, such a deficit of news and significant new developments that even the most decisive novelists have searched for them in vain," Marie wrote to Carl on April 18, adding that the sound of exchanged fire around Spandau, the fortress west of the capital still in the hands of French, was the only novelty she could share.[30] In his answer, Clausewitz tried to com-municate the notion of war as not just a string of battles but a complex enterprise determined by many factors. "The impatience that one has in Berlin, I can understand. . . . But I can assure that if nothing has occurred until now it is not the result of some special circumstances but caused by the nature of the things. . . . We are in fact not our own masters but are standing under Wittgenstein and then also under Kutuzov. You have very wrong impressions about the strength of our army."[31] Carl used the plural pronoun *Ihr* in the last sentence to signal that it was intended not toward Marie in particular but the public in Berlin in general. He probably believed too that his wife would share his analysis in the broader circles in which she moved.

At that time Clausewitz's second-oldest brother, Friedrich Volmar, now a major, arrived in Berlin as the new commander of the Fourth East Prussian Regiment, part of General von Thümen's corps awarded with the task of taking on the French forces in Spandau. Throughout the years Marie had occasionally met members of Carl's family, especially one of the sons of Wilhelm Benedict, who visited her often. Scattered remarks in her correspondence indicate that she had also exchanged infrequent letters with them. Now Marie finally could spend more time with her husband's family as Friedrich Volmar's wife and children joined him in his camp in Charlottenburg. Marie reported back to Carl, full of excitement, about also meeting one his sisters visiting from Burg, although she failed to state her name. To Marie's disappointment, she shared very little information about Carl's childhood. He had left so young that the sister barely knew him.[32] "You cannot believe, dear friend, what perpetual joy is for me to be among your relatives, they are so good and affectionate that only because of this, one should love them."[33]

The assault on Spandau started on April 17 with heavy bombardment, which damaged not only the citadel where a powder magazine was hit but also the surrounding civilian houses. "One part of the town went into flames...; it was a horrible view to see the whole sky lid up by blaze," wrote Marie. She visited the Prussian encampment on April 21 and in the pause between the fighting dined with Friedrich Volmar and his family: "It was a quite special, solemn, anxious feeling to know that one is so close to such scenes of horror but this tense expectancy, this lively participation was also of great interest."[34] Marie proudly reported to Carl that his brother led the successful negotiations for the French garrison's capitulation and after that escorted the surrendered troops over the Elbe.[35]

March and April 1813 were eventful months for the women in Berlin. Most men of stature had left the capital, either volunteering in the army or gathering around the king in Breslau. Marie complained to Carl that Princess Louise's salon, usually the place where important and interesting people gathered, now resembled "a real cloister."[36] Princess Marianne, who had stepped into the role of mother of the nation, initiated the "Appeal to the Women of the Prussian State," signed by eleven other female members of the royal family. Published in the newspapers and widely read, the letter announced the creation of the Women's Association for the Good of the Fatherland. It urged "wives and daughters of all ranks" to assist the war efforts by donating jewelry, money, or their time and labor. "*Frauenvereine* [women's clubs] are forming, for the purpose of providing arms for those who cannot afford to buy them, as well as such other assistance as they need," wrote Princess Louise in her diary.[37] "Those who couldn't do anything else knitted sox, stitched shirts and God-only-knows-what pieces of clothing for the soldiers. In the society one only plucked *charpie*," Caroline von Rochow wrote in her memoirs, referring to the straight threads plucked out of linen cloth and used for surgical dressing.[38]

Further involvement for women in the war effort came when a public uproar over the horrible conditions in Berlin's main hospital prompted the famous saloniere Rahel Levin to initiate the creation of another facility. Smaller but more effective, the hospital was to be led by representatives of "all classes and religions," an organization free of prejudice seeking to harness the energies and contributions of all Prussian citizens, especially the newly emancipated Jews. It was an egalitarian and inclusive approach, so liberating from stagnant gender and class norms that it sounded almost revolutionary for Prussia. When Levin sought the support of the royal princesses, however, she lost control over the hospital. The emancipating part of her idea was soon abandoned too. Feeling cheated and deeply disappointed, Levin wrote with bitterness that the new patrons "overruled everything for creating an establishment that I do not like"; but the money and the enthusiasm did not wane.[39] Particularly in modern scholarship, Princess Marianne, who came to preside over the hospital, has received harsh treatment because she circumcised the effort, putting it firmly under state control and back into the gender-acceptable and strictly hierarchical norms of the day.[40]

As Marie wrote to Carl, even in its restrained form the women's activism rubbed many contemporaries the wrong way. Still, they were not deterred. "With a fund of 10,000 thaler and many payments on a monthly basis, in only a couple of weeks a house has been completely equipped and abundantly supplied with everything needed . . . for the care of some 50 wounded. . . . Twenty ladies are at the helm and take turns with the supervision, one that cares for the domestic services lives there, everything happens without pay, all workers did their job for free . . . even all bill calculations are made by women," Marie described the hospital. "For it, the poor ladies have to suffer ridicule that some among them probably might deserve, but I find this eagerness so beautiful that I defend them with all my energy."[41]

Marie never clarified her own involvement with the hospital. But the fact that after the siege of Spandau she promptly took two critically wounded soldiers from Friedrich Volmar's regiment there indicates participation greater than that of a sympathetic bystander. Remarkably enough, just a couple of months later Marie herself visited Rahel Levin. As Rahel's description reveals, it was rather an awkward and uncomfortable meeting for both sides.[42] Still, the sheer fact that it even occurred suggests that the Jewish intellectual was onto something when she argued that the shared effort might bridge centuries-old prejudices. In later years, Marie read Rahel's *Ein Buch zum Andenken* and copied passages out of it. By then the latter, baptized and married to Karl August von Varnhagen von Else, was firmly planted within German society.[43]

Meanwhile Napoleon prepared his counteroffensive in Germany. He had managed to amass 200,000 men but, despite the impressive number, the army now consisted of new and poorly trained recruits as well as severely crippled cavalry due to the heavy losses of horses in Russia. The emperor planned to confront the Allies in a short and decisive clash before they could effectively merge forces and realign command structures, repeating his strategy from 1805 when the Battle of Austerlitz effectively won the war.

Near the end of April Napoleon led 120, 000 men toward Leipzig. Yet the inexperienced French cavalry failed in its reconnaissance mission, leaving the emperor unaware that Wittgenstein and Blücher were also on the move. Seeking to preempt Napoleon's capture of Leipzig, the Allies prepared to attack his right flank with 72,000 troops. When the Allies took on Marshal Ney's corps just outside of Lützen, they themselves did not know that the rest of the French army was still close enough to pursue and perhaps deal a crippling blow. This was a perfect example of the uncertainty and lack of clarity plaguing military operations that Clausewitz sought to explain later and is now known as "the fog of war." By the afternoon of May 2, Napoleon managed to reach the battlefield and consolidate nearly 110,000 troops. The Battle of Grossgörschen (as it is called in German after the name of the nearby village) or Lützen (as it is known in French, because that morning the emperor had toured the legendary battlefield of 1632 not far away) lasted until the darkness made it impossible for the enemies to fight. Napoleon won a clear victory, but it did not crush the Russo-Prussian coalition, as he had hoped. The Allies suffered almost 13,000 casualties, but without cavalry the French could not pursue and wipe out the remaining troops, who managed to retreat.

"I am completely fine although one small Frenchman tried to strike me with a bayonet behind the right ear. We fought furiously," wrote Carl to Marie afterward.[44] Saxony was back under Napoleon's control, and the news of the Russo-Prussian retreat further eastward from Elbe prompted the emperor to dispatch Marshal Ney and his army toward Berlin. He gambled on two possibilities—either Ney's advance would force Friedrich Wilhelm to split his forces from the Russians, march to defend his capital, and become an easy prey; or Ney's capture of Berlin would deliver such a moral blow as to put an end to the popular mobilization and break Prussia's will to fight.[45]

The news about the loss in Grossgörschen reached the capital on May 8 along with word of Ney's approaching troops.[46] Despite Scharnhorst's and the rest of the military leadership's reassurance that they had won a tactical victory, the civilian population in Berlin was terrified. Friedrich Wilhelm informed General Bülow, responsible for the city's defense, that the main body of the Prussian army would continue to fight with the Russians— meaning that Bülow could rely on only 11,500 Prussian and 3,000 Russian troops while Ney's corps numbered 84,000 men.[47] The military governor of Berlin, General de L'Estocq, received an order to pack all state archives and valuables from the palace and send them to Breslau.[48] The situation appeared hopeless, and the capture of the capital certain.

"Countess Brühl and her daughter[,] convinced that they as a mother and a wife of a Russian [lieutenant-]colonel and a known enemy of the French should be a subject of especially harsh treatment . . . made themselves hastily on the road and kindly took me with them," Caroline von Rochow recalled in her memoir. Describing the events decades later and with a changed political attitude, the reactionary party's grande dame saw the commotion in May 1813 as exaggerated and ridiculous: "In the right frame of mind one should have said that the enemy could not have interest in pursuing ordinary families, let alone individual women." Yet at the time, the reasons for the mass agitation were all too real. If, she admitted, "everyone who was somehow capable of it should grab a pick," and women passionately and effectively supported the war effort, then one should expect that "the enemy would as well attack the country in a devastating and murderous manner."[49] The self-awareness of Prussia's citizens had changed—they were no longer a passive population and could not expect to be treated as such.

In the company of her mother, Caroline, and probably their domestic servants, Marie left Berlin on May 9 heading southeast in order to avoid the approaching French columns from the southwest. The presumed destination was again the residence of Therese von Thun in Tetschen. The women found the roads full with other refugees, the postal stations out of fresh horses, and the inns, where they had to wait for hours or sleep through the night, terribly uncomfortable. From other Berliners, among them the Hugenot preacher Ancillon, the ladies learned the uncertain piece of news that the capital might be saved.[50] On May 18, Bülow read with disbelief the reports that Ney had turned his whole army around. Indeed, it was a case of misunderstanding that became a strategic blunder—Napoleon needed a part of the army as support for his operations. But the language of the recall order was unclear, and Ney marched back with all of his troops.[51]

Despite hearing that the capital had averted capture, the women still decided that it was too dangerous to reside in such an obvious target of Napoleon's revenge as Berlin. They continued their trip through Silesia and stopped in Hirschberg (now Jelenia Góra, Poland) only to discover that the war theater had moved very close to them. Bautzen, where Napoleon's

115,000 troops clashed with the Allies' 100,000 troops on May 20–21, was just seventy-five miles away. When they heard the echo of fired volleys, Marie and Caroline climbed the tower of the local church but could not see anything. The military hospital in Hirschberg took some of the wounded, and on the next day the women went to the funeral of the first soldier who died there.[52] Napoleon won the battle at Bautzen, but the Allies managed once again to escape full destruction. The Russo-Prussian persistence constantly frustrated and blunted the French assault strategy.

Marie, Sophie, and Caroline moved further southeast to Landeshut (spelled in the correspondence as "Landshut," now Kamienna Góra in Poland), a small town closer to the Austrian border. "We have been reassured that the mountains surrounding us here and the close proximity to the border will make Landshut a reliable shelter for at least some time ... Madam von Gneisenau who lives only few steps away relayed the comfort that I will receive news about you," Marie wrote to Carl on May 26.[53] He was only twenty miles away in Schweidnitz (Swidnica) and answered hastily on May 31, advising his wife to leave the area because another battle or troop movements might occur in the vicinity. Even so, Carl urged the women to remain calm because the enemy was badly weakened and incapable of dangerous moves: "If one could remove oneself in moments like this from the army, I would come personally to Landshut to calm you down."[54]

The condition of Sophie von Brühl, who full of anxiety had fallen sick, made a prompt departure impossible, however. For the moment, the women also had nowhere to go: "Therese cannot take us in. We received yesterday her answer, all her friends of Dresden have taken refuge by her and she has more than thirty people in the house," Marie informed Carl.[55] Because Marie and Sophie had hurriedly left Berlin before receiving the annual income from Pförten, their shrinking finances now made a stay in a bigger, safer city on their own impossible. Hearing from his wife Caroline about their difficulties, Gneisenau arranged for Clausewitz to be released from Blücher's staff and see Marie for a night.[56]

Once Sophie felt better, the women moved to Liebau (Lubawka) where Madam von Gneisenau, following her husband's advice, resided. Brought up in a simple and deeply religious Silesian gentry family, Caroline Neidhardt von Gneisenau, born von Kottwitz, was a woman who devoted her time and interest mostly to her family and the church. She had been engaged to another officer who was killed in a duel. When Gneisenau went to inform her of the man's death, he himself fell in love with the unhappy fiancée.[57]

Under normal circumstances, Caroline von Gneisenau was exactly the type of woman Marie would have subjected to harsh criticism for her lack of involvement and interest in the pressing political issues of the day. But the tumultuous months had taught Madam von Clausewitz the value of having "a reasonable affectionate person" around in times of need.[58] In Liebau, the women also received kind invitations from both Madam von Stein and Countess von Westphalen zu Fürstenberg, Therese's sister-in-law, to stay in their homes in Prague (they chose the latter's spacious home).[59]

On April 8, a courier woke up Caroline von Gneisenau in the middle of the night with the news that a temporary armistice had been signed. She immediately rushed to inform Marie.[60] Despite his victories, Napoleon agreed to the truce negotiated by the still-neutral Austria in order to regroup his badly weakened army. Clausewitz believed that his defeat was immediate and criticized the Allies' decision to take a break from the fighting: "The enemy is losing on a daily basis hundreds as prisoners and deserters. . . . If we are afraid now of Napoleon, we deserve to be whipped."[61] However, the armistice also gave Prussia an opportunity to consolidate and reorganize its own forces.

Marie and Carl anticipated this process with uneasiness, uncertain what it would mean for them. At Blücher's headquarters Gneisenau and Clausewitz had worked together so well that the general asked the king once again to have Carl transferred under him.[62] The request was denied. At that point, the Russo-German Legion had finally taken shape with Clausewitz as its chief-of-staff. One comfort Marie and Carl could find in this situation was his new salary—Great Britain financed the enterprise and thus the officers enjoyed a higher annual income, 2,500 thaler in Clausewitz's case. The news prompted Marie to comment sarcastically that they could finally make the down payment for their dreamed-of small manor.[63]

At the end of June, Marie arrived together with her mother and Caroline in Prague, only to encounter a sad procession at the gates and learn from the mourners the devastating news that Scharnhorst had died. "I haven't felt this way since the death of my father, it seems to me as if I have lost him once again, and as if all our hopes, all that is dear and sacred to us, have been buried with him," Marie wrote full of sorrow to Carl. Scharnhorst had received a wound in the foot in Grossgörschen, not serious enough to stop him from traveling on a diplomatic mission. However, an infection had subsequently developed, and on June 28 in Prague he succumbed. Marie had heard about his critical state while still on the road but believed he would recover, and even fantasized caring for him. In Prague Scharnhorst's adjutant Wilhelm von Röder, with whom Marie had been a friend since 1808, showed her the room where the general died. Marie asked to see Scharnhorst's body but the casket was already sealed. As a sign of their close relationship, she visited his crypt.[64] Before the funeral, Röder had arranged for a death mask to be made, which he gave to Marie for safekeeping. After the war the sculptor Christian Daniel Rauch would use it for his famous statue of Scharnhorst.[65]

In the summer of 1813 Prague had become the place to be for German patriots. Under the terms of the armistice French, Russian, and Prussian representatives gathered there to discuss peace with the still-neutral Austria as intermediary. Many of the prominent German intellectuals found themselves in Prague because they either sought to escape the troubles of war or wanted to be closer to the events—the publicist Friedrich Gentz, the diplomat Wilhelm von Humboldt and his wife Caroline, the poets Clemens Brentano and Ludwig Tieck, the composer Carl Maria von Weber, Rahel Levin and her brother Ludwig Robert, among many others.[66] Marie and Sophie visited Madam vom Stein's salon almost every night to learn the events of the day and discuss them with other prominent members of the society.

The congress not only unhappily coincided with Scharnhorst's death, but the presumed perseverance of Napoleon's power over Europe appeared as a terrible betrayal of the general's legacy. For Marie, the events also increased the frustration she felt about Carl's career: "I am afraid that even the readmission in Prussian service now will be less desirable for you[.] [What does it hold] for you other than the sad sight of seeing your friend's lifework again destroyed[?]" These unfavorable circumstances, Marie feared, made Carl's prospects to be reestablished back in Prussian service also appear bleak.[67]

Despite the patriots' fears, none of the parties in Prague was really ready for peace. The negotiated end of the armistice on August 10 came without the diplomats coming to terms. Marie had already left the city by the end of July to reunite with Carl, and together they traveled to Giewitz. In this brief period of calm Clausewitz wrote his account of the spring campaign, *Der Feldzug vom 1813 bis zum Waffenstillstand*. Giewitz not only provided the couple with much-needed quiet time but was also fairly close to Carl's new assignment in Grabow.

The Allies used the two-month-long armistice to swell their numbers and better train and equip the new recruits. The Russo-German Legion now became a part of the Army of the North led by the Swedish Crown Prince Carl John, the former French General Jean Baptist Bernadotte. Faced with an extinguishing royal bloodline, in 1810 the Swedish Diet elected the celebrated officer, who was already disillusioned with Napoleon. The newly minted crown prince aimed at securing his own position, and he knew that the easiest way was by gaining Norway, by that time in possession of France's ally Denmark. Hence, he allied with the anti-Napoleonic forces. After the end of the truce Austria also officially entered the anti-Napoleonic coalition, and with a total of 480,000 men against Napoleon's 450,000 the balance of power now clearly tipped toward the Allies.

On August 9, Carl left for the Russo-German Legion's headquarters in Grabow, seventy miles west of Giewitz. He reported back to Marie that after meeting his new commanding general, Ludwig von Wallmoden-Gimborn, he had been appointed chief-of-staff not only for the legion but also for the whole corps led by Wallmoden, some 22,600 men. "Since then I am buried in paperwork because now I am missing almost all of my staff and generally the whole structure of the army is still very new."[68]

The so-called Trachenberg Plan (named after the Silesian palace where it was conceived) for the fall campaign divided the Allied forces into three armies (Main Army, Army of the North, Army of Silesia). The strategy took into account Napoleon's still-considerable prowess and thus envisioned gradually weakening the emperor by defeating his generals. None of the three allied armies was supposed to meet the French alone but, when encountering the enemy, would retreat back quick and deep, letting the other two encircle and defeat it with overwhelming power. According to the plan, the Army of the North's mission was to engage the French forces in the north, protect Berlin, and pressure Napoleon's main army in the south. Meanwhile in Saxony, when given an opportunity, the Allies would encircle the emperor with superior numbers and force a decisive battle upon him.

Relatively close to the northern theater of operation, Marie, in the company of Luise von Voß and her mother Caroline von Berg, expected the beginning of the fall campaign with uneasiness. The ladies did not even try to hide their nervousness: "Luise asks that in case a sudden departure becomes necessary you send us a fast courier through Wahren," Marie informed her husband.[69] Carl also sent almost half of his first paycheck back to his wife so that she would not suffer the same financial distress if she had to flee from the French again.[70] Luise, in her role as the family estate proprietor while her husband was in the army, had little choice but to stay in Giewitz until the very last moment. In Marie's case, she deliberately chose to be closer to Carl and the war theater. The separations and torturous stretches without news during the Russian campaign and the spring of 1813 had led her to forsake the comfort of the peaceful hinterland. Marie had also observed how Friedrich Volmar's wife Christiane Friederike stayed closer to the frontline and provided him with care and comfort. Marie was now convinced that she, the high society lady, should follow the widespread practice among many common soldiers' spouses: "During the stay of your sister-in-law in Charl[ottenburg] I said to myself often how much happier it would make me too to be close to you during the war. In such proximity, the sole moments of fear are probably horrible but also how many beautiful ones one enjoys . . . every return is a jubilation, every hour lived together a bliss."[71] To Marie's delight, Carl not only agreed but found solace in having her in the vicinity. His wife's stay in Giewitz was indeed his idea.[72]

The Allies' strategy brought initial successes at Grossbeeren and Bad Hegelberg, but in Dresden on August 26–27 Napoleon surprised his enemy and gained an impressive victory over a force almost double his own. The French general Dominique Vandamme caught up with the retreating army near the town of Kulm on August 29–30. Despite the fierce assault the Russian commander Count Ostermann-Tolstoy managed, at a critical moment, to rally his men and hold the position until the nightfall. The fighting continued on the next day, but this time Russian, Prussian, and Austrian troops had a clear advantage. During the French retreat even Vandamme fell into the hands of the allies and became a prisoner of war.

Marie, who knew the area since her childhood and had just spent time in Kulm the previous year during her voluntary exile, was in shock over the victory's heavy price. The Allies lost almost twice as many wounded and dead as the enemy, among them her old friend Wilhelm von Röder, with whom she had mourned Scharnhorst some weeks previously. "The human capabilities are not enough to bear all the feelings of joy, admiration, fear, and woefulness that . . . almost always simultaneously arise, and I feel quite sick and exhausted by it. . . . My heart is torn when I think about the poor unhappy [Madam von] Röder," she wrote to Carl.[73]

With the intensified campaign, it became apparent that Clausewitz served in the least-significant theater of operations. "Until now we haven't had one real battle and we have avoided them on purpose because we already found a way to keep the enemy at bay or at least to disrupt its plans," he wrote to Marie on September 1. Carl emphasized the importance of this strategy of restraint: "The balance of power and other circumstances make such an approach essential, and if anyone were to call us idle and indecisive and believe the reason for it to be found in the character of Count Wallmoden, you should brazenly think him an incompetent judge."[74] Carl's careful explanation and assumption of external criticism suggest that he might have expected her to disseminate information about the real conditions under which the Army of the North operated. By that point, Marie supported an impressive net of correspondents—beside the prominent friendships with Princess Marianne, Princess Louise, and Gneisenau, she regularly wrote to her relatives and the Stein family as well as countless other spouses of officers searching for news about their loved ones.

For an officer as ambitious to show his strategic competence and valor on the battlefield as Clausewitz was, the lack of real action became a source of endless frustration and desperation. Among ceaseless maneuvers and boring marches west, the only time the legion clashed seriously with the enemy was the Battle of Göhrde on September 16, when with 12,000 men they surprised only 3,000 French. For his participation in it Carl finally received the rank of a full colonel.

Severe gout attacks also led to long sleepless nights and darkened his mood, already low because of the lack of action. Carl's "greater irritability" even let Marie question, if she wished to avoid openly fighting with him, whether she should really undertake a visit to Grabow she had been planning for some time.[75] Yet she knew he depended on her warmth and lasting optimism more than ever. Once Marie arrived, Carl could finally find some peace: "How delighted I was when I noticed that after we had just gone to bed and I was still talking to you, you had fallen asleep in my arms and dreamed so sweet. Your head rested on my shoulder and I felt so happy under the pleasant burden."[76] As so many times before, the hardships only strengthened their marriage. "I've never loved you more," Carl would write to Marie on another occasion, "than in [the moments of] greatest happiness and deepest misery."[77]

In October, Napoleon started to concentrate his troops around Leipzig, Saxony's commercial and industrial center. In Paris the public opinion had begun to turn against the prolonged and bloody campaign. Napoleon knew that French supplies were running low and that the Allies' strengthened armies threatened to make a retreat west impossible. A decisive battle and eventually victory, the emperor believed, would slash his enemies' morale and, even if the outcome did not end the war, would open a safer path back to France. Thus, on October 16 at Leipzig with an army of around 190,000 men he took on the Allies, numbering 200,000 at the beginning of the battle but, thanks to the constant flow of reserves, more than 300,000 by its end. "The Battle of the Nations," as the clash of October 16–19 came to be known, was the single largest military engagement in Europe up to that point. On the first day, Napoleon almost snatched a victory only to be driven back on October 18 into Leipzig's suburbs by a fierce assault. Early on the next morning he ordered a retreat, which later in the day tragically came to a halt when a corporal mistakenly blew up the Elster Bridge before all French troops had left. Some of the trapped men drowned, others were cornered and killed, and many became prisoners of war. Napoleon lost over 70,000 men: 34,000 dead or wounded, 30,000 captured, and some 5,000 deserted. The Allies also paid a high price for their decisive victory: 54,000 troops dead, wounded, or missing, and many of them—17,000 men—Prussians.

Gneisenau, who had become chief-of-staff for Blücher after Scharnhost's death, sent a short note to Marie after the clashes on the northern front on October 16 (the so-called Battle of Möckern), informing her that it had ended "in a draw."[78] The general's next letter on October 24 brought even more gruesome details, but also contained language of Prussian military reemergence and national revival: "You know the beautiful trails around Leipzig. They were the battlefields on October 19. There everything was covered with dead, maimed, wreckage, cannons, ammunition cards, and arms. The earth was soaked with blood. The most amazing thing was that the triumphant soldier stayed in the columns he was ordered and no looting occurred. . . . How happy I am, you can understand. There is no more blissful feeling than the fulfillment of national revenge. We march irresistibly now towards the Rhine to free this river of the Fatherland from its chains."[79]

Marie received these letters while shuttling back and forth between Carl's location and the estate of her old friend and former Mecklenburg envoy in Berlin, August von Lützow, in Ludwigslust, some twenty miles from the Russo-German Legion position. Unfortunately the diary she kept for the fall of 1813 (now preserved at the University and State Library in Münster) did not contain many details about what she observed and did in the legion's headquarters. "On the afternoon of [October] 27, I became acquainted with Mister von Stülpnagel and then Gen. Wallmoden and Gen. Dörnberg visited me. We were by Madam von Alvensleben," she wrote, her last sentence indicating that she was not the only officer's wife in the military camp. Her other entries were similarly short and devoid of detail: "Friday, the 29 was the review of the infantry." "Tuesday, November 2, I went for a walk with C. on the banks of Elbe, it was a nice evening, the view of the herds coming back made us dream about the province and the pleasure of genial quietness. Count Dohna and Gen. Dörnberg spent the evening with us." On the morning of November 13, she recorded, "we went together for a walk and made all kinds of plans for the future." That same afternoon, news came that the French troops, led by Davout, had left Stecknitz, "and unfortunately soon after [the rumors] were confirmed."[80] With the French army on the march, Marie had to leave the camp.

Her diary from 1813 ended soon after, but until the spring of 1814, Marie continued to follow her husband. We have no information on where exactly Marie stayed or what she did since from October 21, 1813 until March 4, 1814 she did not write any letters to Carl. They simply saw each other often enough for him to send a courier with news (i.e., the six known Clausewitz letters from the period) but not to expect any long letters back. In later correspondence Marie mentioned staying in the regimental head-quarters in Winsen, the small town just outside of the French-controlled Hamburg that the legion attacked early in 1814.[81] From Carl's letters one could infer that often they sought for her places to stay outside of the military camp since the conditions of the temporary quarters of an army on the march simply did not allow female presence ("I stay with six officers in one room," he reported on November 16).[82] Nor would it be hard to guess from Clausewitz's state of mind that he also preferred to visit his wife somewhere in peace and comfort. In these days Marie often painted the surrounding landscapes, and Carl calmed his nerves by observing her.[83] In all likelihood, she would have continued following the legion, now with marching orders for Flanders, if Sophie von Brühl's weak health had not prompted her to return to Berlin in March 1814.[84]

The certainty of Allied victory and the desire for more aggressive moves than Marie had witnesses on the field clashed right away with the fears and pessimism in Berlin. The victory in Leipzig had not brought Napoleon's defeat, causing instead the Allies to continue with a bloody and pro-longed offensive in France. Many people pushed for a peace agreement as quickly as possible. Austria's concerns about potential Russian domination over Europe flared up again, and Prussia's Friedrich Wilhelm once more took a cautious position by declaring himself less interested in toppling Napoleon than in preserving his men's lives. The patriotic circles, as Marie reported back to Carl, contemplated with anxiety and anger the news from Chatillon, where French and Allied delegations debated peace. "I have taken solace in the hope that the small advantage that [Napoleon] had, has woken up all his arrogance, and that in the end this would lead him to his destruction. . . . It seems now that my anticipation has not deceived me."[85] In the first half of March, when Marie wrote this letter to Carl, the French delegation had already rejected the peace talks.

With the end of the war in clear sight, the couple also started to look for a more secure position for Clausewitz than the legion, a unit outside the reg-ular structure of both Russian and Prussian armies. The two possibilities at that point appeared to be the Netherlands and the Electorate of Hanover. In Berlin Marie took upon herself the task to learn from friends and acquain-tances about the conditions in both countries. She wrote letters, arranged to be introduced to Dutch ladies, and visited the house of General von Phull, at that point the adviser for the crown prince of the Netherlands. None encouraged the idea of Dutch service because of the Prince of Orange's empty pockets and preference for French officers; Hanover had even less budget to hire foreigners.[86] For the most part, Marie suggested patience: "It would be, I believe, something different if you were to go together with the Legion and under certain preconditions"—meaning Carl retaining his position as the legion's chief-of-staff or even assuming full command.[87]

Marie did not leave it all to fate, however, but continued to inform friends and family about her husband's achievements and ideas. She gently wrote to Carl that "the ones who [knew him] intimately" recognized his enormous contributions in the struggle against Napoleon. In reality, Marie herself could not accept his lack of public recognition. To Gneisenau, she bitterly complained that Clausewitz "during this glorious period remained sadly deprived of joy."[88] When a newspaper published unfavorable news about the legion, Marie acted swiftly and got in touch with the publisher. The recanted article on the next day was her small triumph: "You'll find it childish . . . but at least it should show you how happy I am to be useful in some way for you and your friends."[89]

In the capital Marie went to the opera, enjoyed fashionable salons, and even visited the Saxon royal family. Once Napoleon was defeated and pushed out of Saxony, Friedrich August and Queen Amalie, staunch French allies since the defeat in Jena-Auerstedt in 1806, had been taken to Prussia. Although the luxurious surroundings of the Hohenzollern palace could hardly be called a prison, they trembled with fears about the future of their dynasty and tried to gather information and gain any allies available. In this context, Queen Amalie's eagerness to meet Marie, curiously mentioned in the latter's correspondence, could be also read as an acknowledgment of Marie's access to military and political developments.[90]

In the first months of 1814 Napoleon was retreating back to France and the Allies relentlessly followed him. Then, in the second half of March, they intercepted the emperor's letter informing his wife Marie Louise about his intention to draw the Allied armies away from Paris and fight them near Marne in the northeast. While sending the cavalry to deceive Napoleon into thinking that his plan worked, Tsar Alexander and the Austrian commander Karl Philip Prince of Schwarzenberg led the majority of the coalition troops toward the French capital. The battle for Paris started on March 30 but by the next day, convinced by the generous terms offered by the tsar, the city surrendered. Napoleon, who had already realized the deceit and hurried to save his capital, was in Fontainebleau, some thirty miles away, when he heard the news. On April 4, facing the inevitable, the French emperor abdicated. The Allies also rejected the demand that his infant son should keep the crown. When the news about Paris's surrender and the end of the war arrived in Berlin a week later, Princess Marianne invited Marie for the official lunch at the palace. However, the celebration that afterward the guests watched from the palace windows turned out to be rather unorganized and disappointing.[91]

Meanwhile on April 11, 1814, the Prussian ministry of war issued an order readmitting Clausewitz back to the Prussian service with a rank of colonel.[92] It had taken a little over a year, but he kept his rank (contrary to his own expectations and others' experiences).[93] Carl could boast a significant role in the inception of the Convention of Tauroggen and in the Prussian headquarters in the spring and summer of 1813, as well as fighting bravely in Grossgörschen. But Clausewitz's absence from the great battles in the fall of 1813 and spring of 1814 would forever darken his perception and that of later biographers of these momentous days.

With the end of the hostilities Carl asked Marie to leave Berlin, travel west, and spend the upcoming months once again with him in the military camp while the peace in Europe was negotiated. Despite his earlier predictions that Napoleon would be defeated by the summer, she had planned a longer stay in the capital and had even rented an apartment there. Hence Marie now found it difficult to leave in the beginning of May. She also intended to visit her old friend Charlotte, now a stepmother of her beloved niece, to rekindle their relationship in the name of little Fanny.[94] It was not until the end of May that Marie left for Carl's new camp at the Rhine. Once again lack of correspondence between them from the period makes it almost impossible to reconstruct the couple's life. The few clues from other sources suggest that Carl and Marie spent most of the summer of 1814 in Aachen, the legion's temporary headquarters, where Carl also visited the spa for his seriously weakened health.[95] According to Carl's letter from April 19, they planned to live quietly in the residence of their old friend Johann August Sack, now the head of the provisional government of North Rhine.[96]

In June, the legion was finally put under Prussian command, but almost two-thirds of its cadre was either discharged or left on its own. Clausewitz became a commander of one of the two remaining brigades and, later on, provisional commander of the whole corps. In August, the legion was sent to Hesse to maintain public order, but whether Marie went with them or stayed behind remains unknown. Her worries about Carl's future, shared with friends in Berlin, reached Gneisenau and prompted him to write to Carl. The war minister Boyen, Gneisenau informed his friend, had plans for Clausewitz but he would have to be patient because the whole Prussian army was in a state of overhaul.[97] Marie's later correspondence suggests that in this period Carl also started working on *Portrait of Scharnhorst,* later published as the second part of *On the Life and Character of Scharnhorst.*[98] Then, in the middle of the couple's vacation in 1815, again in Aachen, came the news about Napoleon's return from the island of Elba.[99]

The events were far from unexpected. Already the previous year Carl had judged the terms of the emperor's abdication too generous. The enormous pension of two million francs per year (Clausewitz mistakenly thought it to be six) that Napoleon received allowed him to support a political faction back in Paris. This, together with the emperor's popularity among the French officers, Carl lamented, would make it impossible for the new king to take over the military. "What is more natural than for the party of the dissatisfied to turn their eyes toward him? How easy it will be under such circumstances, in case of division, for [Napoleon] to step up at the head of a powerful party!" Carl angrily wrote to Marie.[100] The Congress in Vienna, which in September 1814 started the negotiations for peace and the new European security design, had turned into a dysfunctional gathering. The contradictions among the uneasy anti-Napoleonic coalition came to the forefront, and the compromise for the future political structure of the continent stalled. Using the distraction, less than a year after his abdication Napoleon landed at Golfe-Juan on March 1, 1815. The emperor swayed the armies sent to intercept him and promised the masses a constitutional reform and direct elections for an assembly. Napoleon triumphantly marched in Paris on March 19.

In preparation for a new campaign, Clausewitz was transferred to the general staff and shortly after became chief-of-staff of one of the four corps that now comprised the Prussian army under Blücher. The III Corps received as a commander Johann Adolph von Thielmann, a gregarious Saxon in the Prussian service, with whom Carl built a close and pleasant partnership. In April, Marie accompanied her husband to Blücher's headquarters in Liege, Belgium and they stayed there until the beginning of May. Then the couple traveled further south to Diekirch in Luxembourg where the III Corps had its headquarters.[101] Since the preparation for the new campaign was in its final stages, Marie left around May 10.

Initially she planned to travel to Kassel to the residence of Wilhelmina Caroline, the electress of Hesse-Kassel that Marie, in all likelihood, had met and became close to in Prague in 1813. On the road, Marie learned that the man hired to accompany her had deserted the *Landwehr* ("such a good patriot," she commented sarcastically to Carl) and this made the company undesirable. With the roads unsafe for a lady, she was forced to stay longer in Cologne until a new escort was found.[102] By this point in her life, Marie had become so accustomed to finding her way in an unfamiliar environment that the trouble turned into a pleasant sojourn. In Cologne, which had just been seized as a part of the Rhineland by Prussia, she quickly built a relationship with the commandant, Baron von Ende, and received news from him about the troop movements. Marie also spent time visiting the houses of prominent Rhineland families. After taking part in the official ceremony where the city paid obeisance to the Prussian king, she climbed to the still-unfinished top of the Cologne Cathedral. Marie wrote to Carl about the mood in the formerly free city where people by that point wished themselves "content with any lord, even the King of Prussia, only not Napoleon."[103] The poet Ernst Moritz Arndt, publishing at that time the magazine *Der Wächter* in Cologne and hoping for appointment at the future Prussian university in Rhineland, dined with her as well.[104]

Eventually Marie abandoned her plans to go to Kassel, but instead received an invitation to spend some time in Düsseldorf with Scharnhorst's daughter, Julie von Dohna. Julie's husband, Karl Friedrich, served with Clausewitz, which meant that trips to and from the camp and the flow of information would be easier, in addition to the fact that the women had a close personal friendship. Meanwhile the III Corps marched into Belgium to join the rest of the Prussian army still waiting for an Allied plan of operation. The war had yet to begin and Marie, together with other officers' spouses also staying in Düsseldorf, visited the corps' temporary headquarters in Ciney in the first days of June. Her letters give very few details about their stay, except that the women had to leave just a couple of days later—an order that came from none other than Clausewitz, the corps' chief-of-staff. Two days after their arrival back from Ciney, Marie wrote to him: "Everyday officers . . . travel from here to the army and it makes my companions sigh . . . I wish to sigh too, as you can well imagine, but I can also see that you were right to send us back [from the headquarters] and that a longer stay of women with the army would be inappropriate now."[105] Even if he had been the one to order the women to leave, Carl still deeply regretted Marie's absence: "As I went back to my room, I felt so sad to see it without you; now that you have lived in it. I miss you twice more because everything reminds me of you."[106]

Clausewitz's decision to send the women back turned out to be the correct one. Napoleon was already on the move with an aggressive offense into Belgium aimed at attacking Blücher's troops and Wellington's Anglo-Dutch army separately before they could unite and overwhelm him. The first clash came on June 15 in Charleroi just seventy miles west of III Corps' headquarters in Ciney, followed by the double victories of Napoleon in Ligny against Blücher and then Marshal Ney against Wellington near Quatre Bras. The emperor, with the bulk of the French army, now pursued the Anglo-allied army toward Brussels, while Marshal Grouchy with the right flank came after the Prussians. The ensuing battles on June 18 by the villages Waterloo and Wavre were simultaneously fought. At Wavre, despite a ferocious and ultimately successful French attack, the III Corps

Figure 7.1. A newly found drawing of Carl von Clausewitz. For over a century and a half it had been in the possession of descendants of Carl's siblings. *Artist unknown. Private Collection Bernd Domsgen/Olaf Thiel.*

held long enough to enable Blücher to both gradually transfer 50,000 troops to support Wellington and prevent Grouchy from helping Napoleon.

Waterloo, of course, was the critical battle. Later Clausewitz wrote an exhausting analysis highlighting the crucial role the Prussian army had played at Waterloo. Wellington, commander of the Anglo-allied army, perceiving the text as an attack on his own glorious legacy, felt compelled to answer with an account as well.[107] On June 18, by waiting to attack until midday Napoleon made an unforgivable mistake. Despite the repeated and ferocious French assaults, the Allied center held strong and broke only around six o'clock in the evening. By that time, the Prussian troops had already arrived on the battlefield and changed the balance. Wellington now could rally his men, repulse the French, and force them into a full-blown retreat. The Allies chased Napoleon and his troops mercilessly once more toward Paris.

"That the III Corps also played a prominent role by this unbelievably glorious clash, makes us very happy," Marie wrote back to Carl after learning about the decisive victory of June 18, adding, "My head hurts from too much joy."[108] Bursting with pride about the performance of the Prussians in Waterloo and the III Corps' desperate but crucial defense at Wavre, Gneisenau wrote letters describing the events in detail. One of them went to Marie with an explicit request to make it known to prominent people and the public. "I have read and reread aloud your letter so often that I know it almost by heart.... Despite this, [it] (of course with the required exceptions and how you asked, anonymously) will be published tomorrow in the local newspaper," Marie reported back to Gneisenau.[109]

Completing his defeat and embarrassment, Napoleon also lost his carriage and luggage on the battlefield. The trophies, captured by the Prussian Major von Keller, arrived in Düsseldorf as a present for his wife, and Marie and Julie von Dohna rushed together with a huge crowd to see them. "It was highly curious and entertaining to see all these things being unpacked, whereof many still carried clues of recent use." These included Napoleon's toothbrush colored by red tooth powder, his golden shaving and hygiene kit, night lamp, and a set of six golden cups. Writing with her usual irony, Marie added that all the guests gathered at Madam von Keller's home were eager to drink from the cups, "but of course not for [Napoleon's] health but for his end." She received as a souvenir some of the incense in the emperor's night lamp, and Julie was given a table napkin.[110]

Soon enough, however, the women were confronted with the bloody aftermath of the Allied victories. The small and tight-knit group of army spouses staying in Düsseldorf started to receive shattering news about loved ones who had perished in the battles. The women had to hide the news about the death of an officer in Waterloo from his pregnant wife, fearing for her health; the husband of Marie's friend Sophie von Schwerin was also dead; and even Napoleon's captured carriage was used to bury men dying in the military hospital.[111] Confronted by so much death, Marie's letters to Carl now assumed a darker tone: "I had to do so much these days that I did not know where my mind was[.] I cared for the sick, comforted the unhappy, visited the wounded and even if I could not yet contribute a lot, at least I have devoted my whole time to these tasks. [Madam] von Stülpnagel was so shaken through <u>three</u> death cases in her family which she learned at once and [for which she was] fully unprepared that we were afraid she would get really seriously ill."[112]

Napoleon's aggressive assault in Belgium had surprised not only the Allies but also their whole rear-support system; now the heavy losses—over 24,000 Allied casualties from Waterloo alone and another 2,500 in Wavre—overwhelmed the military hospitals in Belgium and Rhineland. The German writer Helmina von Chezy, traveling in the summer of 1815 to gather and distribute donations to hospitals, wrote about shortages of bandages and especially *charpie* for surgical procedures. In her account she also mentioned meeting Marie and Julie in Düsseldorf, "both passionate benefactresses of the wounded and the sick."[113]

The women were overwhelmed in caring for the soldiers. As Marie wrote to Carl, "I was today, yesterday and the day before very busy in the military hospital so that I am quite tired from it and actually have more desire to sleep than to write." She noted that they were becoming more helpful in their service, so perhaps the doctors would not look at them "so suspiciously like in the first days when they seemed to think of our visits as nothing more than an insulting distrust against them." The women had arranged a system whereby the doctors would provide "their own lists of the badly wounded and determine which particular refreshments should be given to them, and we have taken over this distribution in order to make certain that it happens on time and diligently."[114]

Marie admitted that some of what she witnessed was hard to bear, but added that it was "also a great joy to provide at least some help and even through some friendly, affectionate words also to do good to the poor people." She also bemoaned the numbers of wounded they were faced with, and the fact that some had to travel so far before receiving any treatment. "It seems really irresponsible that so badly wounded, like there are now and then, have been carted so far away, and that now, when the armies are ceaselessly going forward, it still continues. Yesterday again three hundred arrived, among them many were badly wounded. . . . What an atrocity! It is outrageous that these matters are not better provided for."[115]

On the march to Paris, Carl wrote to Marie letters with exhausting length, some of them even seven to eight pages long. He often tried to cope with the darker feelings troubling his soul by describing the destruction and suffering he encountered in the French countryside, now fought over and trampled by foreign armies for a second time. Yet like many other Prussian soldiers Carl still found the time to tour the Compiègne Palace, some fifty miles outside of Paris, extensively renovated in 1810 for the official arrival in France of Napoleon's second wife, Empress Marie Louise.

Marie Louise's quarters truly shocked Carl—the walls of the bedrooms and bathrooms covered with enormous mirrors, he wrote to Marie, "breathe sensuality and female lavishness."[116] Despite enjoying a marriage that many outsiders in his time would classify as extraordinary and unconventional, when it came to the sensual and sexual side of it, Carl remained a shy man.

Napoleon abdicated his throne for the second time on June 22, but the provisional government in Paris was not ready to give in. As Clausewitz would conclude later, the center of gravity—the source of strength and the most important component to attack—was not the emperor but the French army and the capital.[117] Finally, the Prussian victory at Issy against Marshal Davout, the last engagement during the Campaign of 1815, opened the road to the French capital. On July 7, the Prussian troops marched once again into Paris. Clausewitz arrived there two days later but wrote to Marie that he was so busy that he did not have time even to go out and buy her a beautiful shawl.[118] Soon after he left for the city of Le Mans in the northwest.

In these early weeks of occupation, the fear of popular insurrection was still high and Marie had to wait before traveling to France. "I barely know how I will endure the next suspense-filled months when the peace will be negotiated. With you it would be easier for me," confided Carl.[119] Marie lost patience and, forsaking all propriety, wrote openly: "Make so that we sleep soon in one bed, you surely need it badly."[120] To help the time pass by quicker, she decided to visit Baron von Stein and his family at his residence in Nassau. To her surprise, she also found Goethe there, the poet she had adored since her youth. Here excitement soon turned into disappointment, however, because he refused to support the patriotic aspirations for the German states' greater political integration.[121]

At last, in mid-August, Marie received her travel passes and was reunited with Carl once more.

8

"The Happiest Time
of Our Lives"
(August 1815–December 1818)

The two decades of war that devastated the continent and irrevocably shifted the geopolitical structure of Europe came to a formal end in Paris on November 20, 1815, when the new French government signed peace treaties with the four major powers in the anti-Napoleonic coalition, Russia, Prussia, Austria, and Great Britain. In very personal terms, for Marie and Carl this put an end to the long and frequent separations full of uncertainties and terrible fears. The peace now promised them opportunities for social and professional rise. Yet even before the Treaty of Paris was signed, it became clear that the hopes for more political and economic rights across Europe would not be fulfilled, despite the fact that precisely these hopes energized the common people to fight against Napoleon. Neither Marie nor Carl were completely surprised by the events, but the enormous social and cultural rearrangement taking place in the first years after final victory still challenged their intellectual and moral powers.

In the summer of 1815 France was an occupied country, and once more the question of how to pacify it absorbed the Allied forces' attention. Soon enough bad precedents were set that raised questions about whether the coalition was up to the task of setting Europe on a more sustainable path. As a part of the III Corps, Carl was directly involved in implementing the various policies, while Marie, who came to be with him in his operational area in Le Mans in the north, assumed the role of companion. Throughout the 1815 Campaign, Marie had written that after all the humiliation and hardship Prussia and she herself had suffered, the French deserved little sympathy. Marie openly wished for Napoleon's death and the complete annihilation of his army as the only guarantee for peace (although she admitted that both desires were rather unrealistic) and argued that steep reparations would be the least punishment the civilian population deserved.[1] Her opinion was far from unusual, as the subsequent actions of the occupational forces displayed.

Confronted with the realities on the ground, however, Carl sharply divorced himself from this view and came to believe that the policy of revenge, especially that characterizing the Prussian approach in the coalition, was both unsustainable and dangerous. In a letter to Gneisenau, he wrote that initially his troops had been welcomed in Le Mans "with open arms" but requisitions, confiscations, and humiliations, "unknown in these lands since the Hundred Years' War," had alienated the civilian population and brought it close to insurrection.[2] Carl's anger, as so often, was directed toward the Prussian government and its inability, once again, to capably manage the task at hand. Where the British came as "a punishing master, proud, cold, and completely pure," the Prussians acted "with a passion for revenge and retaliation" and thus sowed the seeds of resentments and future clashes in Europe.[3]

No record remains to indicate whether the time in Le Mans softened Marie's position toward the French. But she, like Carl, was happy to leave the occupied country behind and to assume their new assignment in Coblenz. In the fall of 1815, the couple arrived in the headquarters of the General Command of Rhine (later called the VIII Prussian Corps) led by August Neidhardt von Gneisenau. In his privileged position as a celebrated war hero, Gneisenau now enjoyed the freedom of selecting his immediate team and unsurprisingly picked Clausewitz as his chief-of-staff. It was a pleasant assignment for Carl, now thirty-five and a colonel. He not only served under a close and valued friend but was also able to settle down with Marie in a beautiful surrounding near people whose company they sought and enjoyed. When looking back to the time in Coblenz, Marie often described it as one of the happiest in their lives. It was also during this period that Carl started formulating his idea to write a comprehensive war theory.

Situated where the Moselle River picturesquely confluences with the Rhine, in 1815 the city became the seat of government for the newly acquired Province of Grand Duchy of the Lower Rhine. During the Congress of Vienna's long negotiations in the winter of 1814 through the summer of 1815, Prussia had relinquished much of its former Polish territories to Russia and had been compensated with lands in the west (Rhineland and Westphalia) and parts of Saxony (Torgau and Wittenberg). Although German-speaking, the Rhineland in the southwest differed greatly from the other Hohenzollern domains—it was predominantly Catholic and its free cities were used to enjoying greater autonomy and self-government. Moreover, for the last thirteen years under French rule, the citizens had come into contact with a much more liberal and progressive regime. In the first part of the nineteenth century, the Rhineland was a predominantly agricultural region, yet to become the industrial powerhouse that it remains today.

For the newcomers, Coblenz's natural beauty, gregarious characters, and seemingly endless vineyards in the surrounding area nurtured an atmosphere of personal optimism, intellectual ease, and poetic endeavors. Marie and Carl received a comfortable apartment at the Von-der-Leyenschen Hof, picked to serve as the command's headquarters and just minutes away from where the Moselle merged into the Rhine. Archbishop Johann von der Leyen built the residence in the sixteenth century (thus the name), and later inhabitants repeatedly modified and expanded it. Four large wings connected through a large atrium, although today only the southern one is still standing due to heavy bombardment during World War II. The living quarters at the massive residence should have been reserved only for Gneisenau, but since he stayed in Coblenz for the most part without his family, the general generously offered the rooms to his senior officers.[4]

For Marie, this was her first experience living outside of the court and in a military garrison for a prolonged period. In the beginning of their relationship, Carl had wondered if she, with her society background, could ever live far away from the busy capital and in the secluded atmosphere of a provincial town where he might be sent to serve. When on his way to France in the winter of 1807, passing by unremarkable and dull places, he wrote that his chest tightened at the thought of offering her a similar existence: "Would Marie be able to take upon her to follow you to such a town, in the case that fate tosses you there for few or more days of your life? . . . I was too fearful to answer straight [this question] by myself, yes, I am even more fearful to seek an answer from you," he wrote at the time.[5] Marie's answer probably caused him greater uneasiness, indicating that she had neither thought about the possibility of leaving Berlin nor had a realistic idea about life in a garrison town.[6] Indeed when later passing by one of these towns in Mecklenburg, she romanticized living there with Carl. The

Figure 8.1. The only remaining southern wing of the Von-der-Leyenschen Hof in Coblenz. *Photo Vanya Eftimova Bellinger.*

"parochial surrounding" and the "remoteness," Marie wrote, would bring them even closer together and grant them "the happiness to be all for one another."[7] Carl, who remembered his life in the Neuruppin garrison only with bitterness, must have shuddered reading this.

With the Prussian state's consolidation and rise in political prominence throughout the seventeenth and eighteenth centuries—processes intimately connected with the strengthening and professionalization of its army—a unique and distinct garrison society had come to life as well. The system of a standing army required soldiers to move and live permanently in fortresses and regional detachments. In different periods the apparent contradictions between military service and domesticity forced harsh regulations regarding soldiers' right to marry. Being at full disposal at the sovereign's will, the long separations, and restrictions in freedom of movement required permanent living quarters, better pay, and support for families when the husbands were gone, all issues that the administration struggled with. Nevertheless the realization that a married soldier was a more disciplined and reliable one compelled the state to provide military families with a limited number of benefits and even offer support for wives and children in need, measures that later became the basis for wider welfare programs.[8] Yet economic hardships, diminished quality of life, isolation, and boredom remained a constant feature of garrison life. In varying degrees these problems continue to afflict even modern standing armies, despite social progress and economic improvements.

When Marie followed Carl during the Napoleonic Wars, he barely could hide his surprise about how easily she embraced life in a military camp. "Here in Aalst I cannot really promise you a lot of amusement; because the place is small and quiet," he wrote to her from the Russo-German Legion headquarters in Belgium after the end of the hostilities in 1814, "however I am already accustomed [to the fact] that you gladly share the loneliness with me."[9] Soldiers' wives following their husbands on campaigns was nothing unusual in the early modern times, and many of them assumed important roles as laundresses, sutlers, or nurses for wounded or sick troops. Ladies from the high nobility, however, were much more limited. They could, at most, visit the army only when it settled down in the breaks between the fighting seasons before attracting criticism. "All officers' wives go to their men in the winter quarters. I am convinced that they all will come back pregnant and then will scream and want to arouse public pity," Count von Lehndorf, chamberlain at the Prussian court, snarled in his diary in 1756.[10] Yet the revolution in warfare since 1792 also changed the equation for women. The Napoleonic armies' practices of requisitioning supplies rendered the role of sutler irrelevant. Yet the shared patriotic fervor made it acceptable for other women to play a more visible role at the rear. The society as a whole still saw women's increased participation as unique and restricted to the unusual time in war, as the historian Karen Hagemann convincingly argues.[11] Still, as Clausewitz's own experience revealed, many military men welcomed and came to depend on women's involvement.

After 1815, Marie became even more integrated in Carl's work and career as a senior officer. Although not nearly as fast-paced as Berlin, Coblenz was a far cry from the isolated and desolate garrison towns that Carl once feared. Marie not only lived in the immediate vicinity of his office at the Rhine Command but also had an opportunity to participate in spirited debates about the future of the Prussian state and the affairs of the new province at hand. In the afternoons the officers and their wives strolled around Coblenz, and when Gneisenau and his staff traveled around the province, they often took the women with them. Almost every evening the military men, Prussian officials, and local intellectuals gathered together, and since the general's wife preferred to stay in Silesia, Marie frequently played the hostess. She usually welcomed the society for a more informal encounter around her tea table.[12]

Being geographically separated from the main body of the Prussian lands, the Lower Rhine required especially able officials to govern and, at least in the beginning, this included many fascinating and prominent personalities. In Berlin, the direction of the state became a cause for rising political polarization but in Coblenz, bound by the close personal encounters and the need to work in concord, the different factions found ways to curb their dissent. Some of the men in Coblenz represented the "old Prussia," like the sixty-three-year-old Governor Karl Heinrich Ludwig Baron von Ingersleben, a pedantic carrier bureaucrat. Others were gregarious and cosmopolitan characters like the president of the appellate court, Karl von Meusebach, in his free time an influential literary scholar. After Meusebach's death, the Prussian government spent the exorbitant amount of almost 15,000 thaler to buy his precious private collection of books and manuscripts for the Royal Library (now the State Library in Berlin). The poet Max von Schenkendorf, whose patriotic songs made him famous during the Napoleonic Wars, served in the civil administration in the Lower Rhine as well. As it happened, just ten miles way from Coblenz, the retired Stein lived in his family estate, and the Clausewitz couple visited him often.

Gneisenau's staff, Marie wrote, was a "small but so tightly bound circle."[13] Wilhelm von Scharnhorst, the oldest son of Clausewitz's former mentor, had fought against Napoleon in Portugal and Spain. He would later marry Gneisenau's daughter Agnes. Another decorated soldier was lieutenant colonel Carl von der Gröben, as it happened a former student of Clausewitz's, with the battles of Leipzig, Ligny, and Waterloo under his belt. Franz August O'Etzel was just a major, but in his life before the army he studied chemistry in Paris, became acquainted with the French scientific elite, and observed the eruption of Mount Vesuvius with Alexander von Humboldt. Back in Berlin, he associated with Romantic writers like Chamisso, E. T. A. Hoffmann, Brentano, and Arnim and in 1808 founded a fencing and swimming school to prepare young men to fight against Napoleon. In the 1830s O'Etzel would play an instrumental role in setting telegraph lines in Prussia and would become its first telegraph director. The friendship between Gröben, O'Etzel, and Marie and Carl von Clausewitz persevered throughout the years, and these two men would be the ones to help her in publishing his works posthumously.

Among the wives, Marie was by far the most prominent member of the Coblenz society. Henriette von Schenkendorf, the poet's wife, was a quiet but beloved person.[14] Intelligent and well-connected, Ernestine von Meusebach also became a friend of Marie's for life, and later in Berlin in the 1830s Marie would be the only one outside the family with whom Ernestine would confide about her husband's psychological breakdown.[15] Selda von der Gröben was the daughter of the famous general Wilhelm von Dörnberg and a great beauty. Both Marie and Carl grew closer to the spirited Emma von Jasmund, a professor's daughter from Göttingen and a friend of poet Arnim before she married Carl Wilhelm Friedrich Theodor Gustav von Jasmund, the officer who acted as Clausewitz's adjutant.[16] In such company, Marie was obviously an exception—unburdened by child-rearing, with extensive experience living close to the center of power, and an outspoken interest in politics.

Gneisenau understood his position in Coblenz as one having rather political functions. Being the head of the military force in a province geographically, religiously, and historically distant from Prussia was an uneasy task, but born in Saxony, Gneisenau himself was an outsider among the Prussian elite. He opened Von-der-Leyenschen Hof and made it the meeting point for Rhine society, foreign dignitaries traveling from and to France, and members of the Prussian administration. The most prominent and controversial of these guests was the fiery publisher of *Rheinischen Merkur*, Joseph Görres, who famously advocated for democracy and unity of Germany. Gneisenau even tried to help Görres when the latter received a ban on publishing in January 1816. "All the parties ate daily at the general's table that was often expanded by many more invited guests," the staff officer Ferdinand von Stosch remembered with nostalgia.[17] Yet the approach had, quite literally, a steep price because Gneisenau's allowance as a commanding general was far too insufficient to cover the sizable lunches and dinner parties. He paid out of pocket many of the expenses and complained later that if he had stayed a little longer, the "command in Rhine would have almost led me . . . to bankruptcy."[18]

The Clausewitz couple found comfort and pleasure in the spirited atmosphere and leap of intellectual and political optimism. It should not come as a surprise that this genial surrounding also nurtured Carl's idea to start work on a book studying changes in the nature of warfare and capturing his own experience in the Napoleonic Wars. In an official letter from August 16, 1816, Gneisenau wrote to War Minister Hermann von Boyen about an idea for his chief-of-staff to compose a field manual for officer corps with chapters on battles, attacks, sieges, and the like. The general asked that in order to work on it, Colonel von Clausewitz be allowed to maintain his position at the Rhine Command but be freed from some of the most tedious bureaucratic tasks.[19] Whether this rather limited and practical concept was the beginning of *On War*, one can only speculate. With the departure of Gneisenau from Coblenz, the idea for the manual seems to have died. Instead Carl started to work in his free time on a much more complex book.

Despite the prevailing mood in Coblenz, the years 1815–1816 saw far from seamless progress and tranquil intellectual meditations. Instead of ushering Europe into a new "era of justice," as Princess Louise surmised the hopes of her contemporaries, the Congress of Vienna shattered the radical ideas for greater liberalization in various countries.[20] Modern scholars like Henry Kissinger have come to see its legacy in a more positive light because the balance of power it created between the major European players kept the continent from being engulfed by another great war for almost a hundred years.[21] Yet for contemporary German patriots, the Vienna Congress under the Austrian foreign minister, Prince von Metternich, squashed the dreams for political unity. Metternich saw the enthusiasm of the masses and growing German nationalism as the gravest threat to the future of the multilingual and multiethnic Austrian Empire. His solution was to combine over three hundred small German principalities and territories into thirty-nine larger states, and then organize them into a German Confederation dominated by Austria and Prussia (in this development the Brühl family estate Pförten also lost its independent status and became part of Prussia). The confederation was a loose and weak union with almost no institutions (only the Federal Diet in Frankfurt am Main) and hardly the strong political body, proactive and able to pursue reform policies, of which the patriots had dreamed. Even if the influential hereditary dynasties came out of the Vienna Congress strengthened, the new European design and Prussia's gain of considerable territories still presented enormous challenges. The infighting between the reformist and reactionary factions, barely muffled during the war period, now broke out again and increasingly polarized the public.

The changing political climate in Berlin echoed all the way to Coblenz and caused worries and setbacks. In events that shook up the provincial administration in the summer of 1816, Marie happened to play an active although not crucial role. When taking the Rhine Command, Gneisenau made it clear that he did not plan to stay for too long. Plagued by gout and physical exhaustion, he couldn't ride his horse anymore and missed his wife

Figure 8.2. Portrait of General Gneisenau by Marie von Clausewitz. ©*Deutsches Historisches Museum, Berlin.*

and adolescent daughters. Gneisenau's portrait of 1816, painted by Marie herself (her only remaining work of art and now part of the permanent exhibition of the German Historical Museum in Berlin), shows a man with a weary expression and meditative, sad eyes. Despite the medals and the general's uniform, it is an image far different from his better-known vivacious and resolute demeanor. Longing for a peaceful life in the Silesian province, in the spring of 1816 Gneisenau wrote "an unfortunate letter," in Marie's words, asking for relief. Insisting on keeping him in the government, Friedrich Wilhelm offered a temporary leave from command until the general recovered his health. The reactionary party, however, used the opening and convinced the king to replace him permanently with General Albrecht Georg von Hake.[22]

When Gneisenau left Coblenz in mid-July 1816, Marie accompanied him until Frankfurt am Main where they said a final goodbye and separated. The general continued to Carlsbad where he hoped to cure his gout, and Marie to Berlin to see her mother and brother, but also with the secret agenda to gather intelligence and support for Gneisenau's return to Coblenz. Marie's six letters from her stay in the capital in July and August are the only remaining correspondence between her and Carl from the period. Apart from them, the intensive letter exchange with Gneisenau is the most significant source of information about the couple's life in 1816–1818. The spouses often wrote separate letters to Gneisenau, and he also kept distinctly different approaches in his responses to them. Sometimes Gneisenau debated the same subject with both Carl and Marie, but mostly he remained collegial and matter-of-fact with his protégé—hence their numerous lengthy and informative letters—and confidential and warm to his wife. Nonetheless, the general did treat his relationship with Marie as special. While he kept a regular correspondence with several other prominent ladies (Princess Louise, the poetess Amalie von Helvig, and the socially conscious Countess Friederike von Reden), his writings to Marie outweighed them in volume and content. While Carl, despite his closeness to Gneisenau, wrote in a very courtly manner, always addressing his former superior with "Your Excellence," Marie often substituted "Your Excellence" with "dear friend"—although she was still more restrained in expressing thoughts and feelings with him than in her letters to Carl. Marie carefully kept the gender boundaries and often cared to apologize about the "audaciousness to say my opinion about things that are so above my horizon."[23]

The circumstances of Gneisenau's permanent replacement came as the result of the growing reactionary atmosphere at the court. The hawkish faction not only opposed reforms in Prussia but also used the ideological polarization and rumors of secret Jacobins as an instrument to neutralize other possible contestants for influence over Friedrich Wilhelm. The term "Jacobisn" derived from the name of the most radical political faction during the French Revolution, but in its widespread use in the first half of the nineteenth century in various German states it came to describe everyone supporting a progressive or liberal agenda. The latter, the reactionary faction claimed, would bring the same chaos and violence from which the Reign of Terror and Napoleon had emerged. Afraid for their privileges and way of life, and deeply shaken after the social and political overhaul during 1806–1811, the reactionaries mercilessly and forcefully attacked even the slightest sign of progressive support. Gneisenau was one among several well-known political figures and proponents of moderate reforms slammed by nasty campaigns and who, as a result, had their public stature greatly diminished.[24]

When Marie arrived in Berlin, she had to walk a very thin line to prevent her inquiries from making her and her husband the next target (Carl indeed was already a subject of suspicion).[25] Marie wrote to Gneisenau on July 23 that she had kept "quiet" while the king and his courtiers were still in Berlin (it was the end of the social season) but nevertheless found a way to confer with other prominent reformers and attempted to get closer to the wife of the war minister, Antoinette Amalie von Boyen.[26] At that point, Marie reported to Carl, many of their friends remained convinced that Gneisenau's relief of command was just a misunderstanding or would be overturned once his health improved. Hence her hope that if the general found a way to talk directly with the king, all would be resolved.[27]

By the end of August, Marie sounded more disillusioned and advised Gneisenau not to take another position without a promise of real power. Friedrich Wilhelm had offered him a seat at the Staatsrat, the council that only sent recommendations and reports to the king and the cabinet. "To be sure you would create some good things and prevent some bad, however, not enough so that this sacrifice would be worth it. Unfortunately, you had sufficient evidence about how imperfectly your advice is followed, and this would be even more the case when you give it to them without being authorized by an official function," Marie wrote.[28] One can only speculate whether her opinion played a role in Gneisenau's initial decision to decline the seat in the Staatsrat (he also wrote to Carl asking for his opinion and suggesting there might be a position for the protégé there).[29] Marie's assessment turned out to be correct. The general, after much convincing by Chancellor Hardenberg, finally agreed to oversee foreign and military policy at the council. However, Gneisenau lacked real power to implement his ideas or to halt policies with which he did not agree, just as Marie had warned. In 1819, the *Landwehr* lost its separate status within the Prussian army, but no one even bothered to consult Gneisenau about it.

Back in Coblenz, Carl found himself increasingly at odds with his new commanding officer. Opportunistic and uninterested in military reforms, Hake had been deeply disliked by Scharnhorst. To the staff in Coblenz, his appointment as Gneisenau's successor appeared to be a clear break with the current direction. "My worldviews are so different than those of General Hake, hence it will be impossible for him to give me his full trust," Carl concluded. Then he added even more unpleasant details about the commander, who expected of his chief-of-staff "a trained poodle to watch every move of his mind."[30] Soon after arriving Hake lost too some of the goodwill of the Lower Rhine's citizens when he converted a building promised to become a secondary school into military barracks.[31] Marie described her opinion especially colorfully by writing to Gneisenau that with Hake's appointment, in Coblenz "a dry pedant is placed next to an imbecile writing machine," the latter description probably referring to Governor Ingersleben.[32] The ultimate sign that the times had changed was Hake's order that the door to the garden of Von-der-Leyenschen Hof be nailed. Through this door staff and friends had wandered freely into Gneisenau's personal quarters, and with a few swift hammer strokes the new commander put an end to the residence's open policy. Seeing this as a barely disguised personal insult, Carl moved out.[33]

When Marie came back to Coblenz in the fall of 1816, she was aware that Gneisenau would not be coming back. With his absence the pleasant life at the Rhine had lost much of its magic but still remained rather spirited compared to dull Berlin. Prussia's celebrated victory over Napoleon had come with a heavy price tag—not only in lives but also in economic wealth. When Louisa Catherine Adams stopped in Berlin in 1815 on her way from St. Petersburg to meet John Quincy Adams in Paris (he had just negotiated the peace between the United States and Great Britain in Ghent), Princess Louise informed her that no new fashionable dress or expensive jewels were needed for the high-society gatherings there. "That the great people of Berlin had suffered so much from the War, that there was no pretention [sic] of style among them," remembered Madam Adams.[34] Caroline von Rochow clarified that the "rather meager and dry" social life in the capital was not only due to the nobility's impoverished state but also because many talented men had taken assignments in the new provinces.[35] Feeling bored and weakened in health, Caroline followed her friend Marie to the Rhine and spent some time with the Clausewitz couple.[36]

Despite being a courtier to her core, Marie had also discovered the everyday liberties of provincial life. When she appeared in Berlin, Sophie von Brühl was shocked by her daughter's unladylike appearance. She was "fatter, burned by the sun, and with more wrinkles in the face." Only the fashionable white dress Carl had bought her in Paris saved her from further criticism.[37] Back in Coblenz and now without her role as the formal hostess at Von-der-Leyenschen Hof, Marie could enjoy her domestic bliss even more. For the first few months after moving out of the residence the couple had to live temporarily in the house of a friend, "*en bivouac*" in Carl's words, since their new home—Governor Ingersleben's old house—was still inhabited by the governor's family.[38] The couple kept their spirits high with frequent visits to the home of Baron vom Stein and his wife. In the fall, the Jasmund family headed for Berlin and, as Carl wrote, Emma von Jasmund's departure left "a big vacuum."[39] After Gneisenau's removal, Carl often debated books with Meusebach and they ventured to the Rhineland with their families.[40]

In December 1816, the mood in the Clausewitz household finally brightened when they moved into their new home, "simply" decorated but with a "quiet allure" that seemed to fit their life. Marie loved to paint Rhine landscapes, while Carl spent less time on official business and more, as he confided to Gneisenau, on his own ideas.[41] "In Coblenz, where he had many duties, he could devote only a few hours now and then to his private studies," remembered Marie in the preface of On War.[42] Freed from the pressure of time and the need to write a practical manual, Carl could concentrate on the content rather than the form. In the "Note from 1818," later published in the prelude to On War, he described his early manuscript as not following "any preliminary plan" except for his intention of writing "short, precise, compact statements, without concern for system or formal connection."[43]

Around the couple the world was far from tranquil. The year 1816 went down in history as "the year without a summer" when the eruption of

Mount Tambora in Indonesia led to crop failures, hunger, and epidemic diseases on an unprecedented global scale. Carl traveled repeatedly throughout the province and recorded heart-breaking accounts of misery and suffering due to the hunger he encountered.[44] But in personal terms, the peaceful and intellectually active time in Coblenz made Marie particularly happy and content. It was apparent to those around her as well, and in a poem composed that Christmas Meusebach described her as an "elevated, beautiful lady."[45]

Yet both Carl and Marie must have recognized that their time in Coblenz could only be of a temporary character, and they never lost interest in acquiring a new position closer to the center of power. Almost immediately after assuming a public position again, Gneisenau also attempted to arrange a post in Berlin for his protégé. In September 1817, he first suggested that Clausewitz should apply for the newly opened post as director of the War College in Berlin. The job carried mostly administrative tasks with little influence over the curriculum, and while Clausewitz would be promoted to major general, it did not offer bonus pay beyond that for the rank. In addition to desiring to have Carl and Marie closer, Gneisenau admitted that he might need his former chief-of-staff's military expertise when it came to swaying the politics in Berlin.[46] Although initially Carl seemed excited about the position, the hurdles cooled his enthusiasm soon enough.

In the increasingly hawkish atmosphere in Berlin, moderate reformers found that not only were their ideas opposed but also their personalities were a subject of relentless hostility. Clausewitz, too, was subjected to an extensive scrutiny when he applied for the War College position, initiated by those who were unsure whether one "could entrust [him with] the youth."[47] The humiliating inquiry took almost five months and at one point, both Marie and Carl let their frustration become known—much to Gneisenau's disappointment. On December 23, 1817, instead of sending Christmas wishes, Gneisenau wrote an emotional letter, barely hiding his disappointment in the frivolous behavior of "you two partners." Irritated by the inquiry, Carl had written to War Minister Boyen that he would prefer to stay in the Rhineland. To make things worse, Marie, rather testily, informed her friends at the court that they would rather not go to Berlin. In such behavior, Gneisenau saw not only a danger for his own plans but also a potentially damaging turn for Clausewitz's career: inconsistency would make him even more untrustworthy in the king's eyes.[48]

In the end, General von Hake's positive report and Gneisenau's intensive lobbying convinced Friedrich Wilhelm, and in May 1818, he finally signed the order for Clausewitz's appointment.[49] In the fall of that year, the couple packed their belongings, said goodbye to their friends, and embarked on a new life back in Berlin.

9

A Decade in Berlin (1819–1829)

When Marie and Carl arrived in Berlin, the country was poised to take a sharp reactionary turn. In the years since his death, the Restoration period has always shaped the perception of Clausewitz's last decade—the standard narrative puts him as a genius who saw his career aspirations diminished and, finding himself on the opposite side of the prevailing political mood, struggled against this marginalization. From the point of view of later commentators, these unfavorable circumstances actually allowed him to concentrate on writing his theory of war. Yet when compared to the sources rich in details about the couple's spirited social life, this notion appears, if not completely incorrect, then significantly distorted. As Marie's letters clearly indicate, she and Carl never really retreated from the public sphere, and writing *On War* was not a substitute for his stalled career but a parallel intellectual endeavor. It was also one they undertook together, and although Marie clearly was the junior member helping with research and copywriting, she nevertheless remained an integral part.

Before assuming his position at the War College, in the autumn of 1818 Clausewitz received an assignment as commandant of the Aachen Congress. The first of four international gatherings modifying the European balance of powers after the Napoleonic era, the main objective at Aachen was the end of the occupation of France. In the three years after Waterloo, the new French King Louis XVIII had managed to consolidate his grip over the once-tumultuous country. The diplomats thus managed to quickly agree on the end of the Allied occupation, but the debates concerning all other unsolved questions or directly related to the results of the Vienna Congress came to a less successful end. Clausewitz's post at the conference required him to attend to the order and security of the city, but he wrote to Gneisenau that these turned out to be fairly manageable tasks. His hopes therefore were to gain recognition from the attending heads of state and diplomats and, together with his wife, to find "several friends and acquaintances from the second tier." While his promotion to major general pleased him, Carl remained reserved in his expectations ("at least I don't have to overcome a silent spite anymore").[1]

The most important acquaintance Carl and Marie managed to make was that of Christian Günther Count von Bernstorff, the new foreign minister of Prussia. Carl described him as "noble, pure, and good but also dull and tired."[2] The distinguished Danish diplomat Bernstorff owed the offer to transfer to Prussia to the polarized climate and infighting between the hostile factions in Berlin. Chancellor Hardenberg picked the bright but restrained outsider in 1818 as a way to avoid another political confrontation with the different factions in Prussia while having an experienced administrator occupying the position. The acquaintanceship with Bernstorff that began at Aachen was renewed once again in Berlin, mostly thanks to the count's wife Elise, who took the initiative and invited the Clausewitz couple to her home.[3] In the absence of a significant letter exchange between Marie and Carl, Elise's extensive memoirs, together with the correspondence with Gneisenau, remain the primary sources of information about their lives in the period 1819–1830.

Bernstorff's wife Elise was actually his two-decades-younger niece, not an unusual arrangement in the early nineteenth century, and her mother Countess von Dernath lived in Berlin as well. In age and temperament Elise was closer to Marie and Carl than to her overworked elder husband. Modern historians often find Elise's extensive accounts of lunches and decorations, conventional portraits of contemporaries, sentimental tone, and overly excited descriptions of social life in Berlin tedious reading and thus have mostly overlooked them.[4] Yet Marie, just like the energetic Bettina von Arnim, valued the countess highly, and even men of Clausewitz and Gneisenau's caliber wrote her warm letters, suggesting that, while more traditional in her views, in person she was a pleasant and interesting woman.

Even before meeting them, Elise was indirectly connected with the Clausewitz couple since one of Carl's uncles had emigrated to Denmark and, after his death, her parents adopted his children Gottlob and Charlotte (Charlotte, however, died in 1816).[5] The countess met Carl and Marie in January 1819 and wrote down as first impressions "her sweet-natured individuality" and "his melancholic, even stiff earnestness." Soon enough, a friendly relationship developed between Elise and the couple and, as she wrote, "even my husband participated quite genially."[6] The happy and

Figure 9.1. *Elise von Bernstorff, geborene Gräfin von Dernath,* Ein Bild aus der Zeit 1789 bis 1835. Aus Ihren Aufzeichnungen (*Berlin: Ernst Siegfried Mittler und Sohn Verlag, 1899*).

ever-expanding Bernstorff family became a substitute for the children Carl and Marie could not have. Later in life Marie supported and was very close to the now grown-up and married girls. Carl was particularly fond of the beautiful and intelligent Thora. In the summer of 1830, when the already married Thora visited her family in Berlin, he wrote touching lines: "That I will see Thora one more time makes me very happy and I ask you to explicitly let her know; who knows if I'll see her again in my lifetime. Even if we have not nurtured and brought up this smart person, we have always watched her growing up with pleasure."[7]

Following the conference, Marie and Carl arrived in Berlin a few days before Christmas 1818. They moved into the director's quarters in the War College's building at the heart of the capital. At that time, the school stood on the opposite side of Spree River from the Berlin Dom and within walking distance of the palace (that building was destroyed during World War

Figure 9.2. Christian von Bernstorff. *Elise von Bernstorff, geborene Gräfin von Dernath, Ein Bild aus der Zeit 1789 bis 1835.* Aus Ihren Aufzeichnungen (*Berlin: Ernst Siegfried Mittler und Sohn Verlag, 1899*).

II and today the site is occupied by a modern office building and hip cafes). The director's quarters and office were situated in the short subdivision at Burgstrasse 19, with a lovely view of Berlin's many famous landmarks. Elise von Bernstorff wrote in her memoirs that from Marie's windows one could gaze right into the oldest wing of the palace.[8]

Before the couple's arrival, Gneisenau repeatedly offered to furnish the flat, but Carl declined and admitted being excited to personally decorate their new home.[9] The comfortable major general's income of 3,000 thaler plus allowances and no rent to pay surely allowed the small and childless family some luxury. Their invested interest in domestic comfort was also a sign of the so-called Biedermeier period that had just begun. The soaring pace of industrialization brought with it growing urbanization and a rising middle class that slowly but surely started to dictate tastes. At the same time the cultural exhaustion from the Napoleonic Wars and the Restoration's increasingly hawkish political climate turned people toward safe domestic spaces.

Figure 9.3. Modern-day Burgstrasse 19 in Berlin where the War College and the director's quarters used to stand. *Photo Vanya Eftimova Bellinger.*

While their life was comfortable, Carl's work was less than fulfilling. Trivial and few, his duties as the administrative head of the War College obviously did not match his drive. He was responsible for the school budget and payroll and maintaining discipline, and it would be fairly safe to assume that at age thirty-nine, neither Carl nor Marie saw the position as the final quiet harbor of his career. In 1819, after just a few months at the college, Clausewitz began to consider pursuing the typical second-career path for senior officers—diplomatic service. Yet it was the worst possible time for a moderate reformer in Prussia to seek a new governmental appointment. On March 23 of that year in Mannheim, the radical student Karl Sand stabbed to death a diplomat, August von Kotzebue, and this sensational political murder ushered in a sharp conservative turn in the German Confederation. The older diplomat and popular playwright had become a hated figure among the militant nationalists, both because of his fashionable melodramas, which they saw as corrupting the true German spirit, and his ridicule of their craze for and idealization of the Middle Ages. In the protagonists of this tragedy, two political philosophies also clashed—Sand represented romantic patriotism taken to its extreme, while Kotzebue was an agent of the old conservative but also more cosmopolitan worldview.[10]

Having fought for their country's liberation and believing that this gave them the right to determine its future, the German youth—like Sand—found the European balance of power after the Vienna Congress deeply disappointing, and with the following years even more so. The despair led to an increasingly radical and uncompromising tone against every dissent. The glorification of the Middle Ages, fallaciously perceived as the most pure Germanic times, also woke up barely forgotten prejudices. Especially members of the patriotic student fraternities, the so-called *Burschenschaften*, embraced a very narrow definition of patriotism, passionately willing to separate their idealized state from everything cosmopolitan, un-Christian, and un-German, and thus grew increasingly antisemitic and militant.

The sharp and unfortunate turn was not lost on fellow patriots of the older generation. In the fall of 1818, Carl denounced the militant tone and even suggested to Gneisenau that the government should get involved and curb it.[11] Later, Clausewitz vividly wrote in his essay "Umtriebe" (Agitation) about the "passionate hatred against those who thought differently" and the haste and immaturity of the German youth.[12] At the heart of the ideological clash, as the historian Matthew Levinger observes, was the fact that, just like the reactionaries, the militant patriots envisioned a state where the power was "ideally unanimous," rather than shared among competing groups of society.[13]

The murder in Mannheim quickly became the subject of a heated political debate about the character of the patriotic movement and the limits of violence. Intellectuals sympathetic to the idea of German unity saw Sand's crime as a radical act but were still ready to justify it in the name of the noble cause. The murder was, as the famous letter of University of Berlin professor Wilhelm de Wette stated, motivated by the purest inspiration.[14] Following Kotzebue's assassination, Sand unsuccessfully attempted to kill himself, and after taking him into custody, the authorities carefully nurtured him back to health, prepared a trial, and then publicly executed him. This chain of events made Sand a martyr in the eyes of the radical German patriots. Among aristocrats and conservatives, the political murder and the sympathetic reactions triggered shock waves and created a state of paranoia. Elise von Bernstorff, the wife of the foreign minister, wrote in her memoirs that a poor student she employed as a secretary gave her "a panic attack" when he walked into her husband's room, dressed in a coat resembling the "Old German costume" that Sand was painted wearing.[15]

In what became known as the "persecution of the demagogues" or *Demagogenverfolgung,* the government responded to the murder and the subsequent radical reactions with unprecedented measures. University professors were arrested and dismissed, Ernst Moritz Arndt was banned from holding his lectures in Bonn, and Friedrich Ludwig Jahn's gymnastic societies were closed. The German Confederation might have been loosely designed but its chief architect, the Austrian foreign minister Metternich, knew how to use the inner mechanisms to maintain control. With the support of Prussia, he created the so-called Carlsbad Decrees for the entire confederation, by which such reactionary measures as tougher censorship and surveillance became the norms of the day.

During the crisis many moderate reformers called for a more nuanced approach, but their voices remained unheard. Suggesting in a letter to Princess Louise that Clausewitz shared his opinion as well, Gneisenau took a position in the middle. On one hand, he argued that the radicals should be "chastised" but the witch-hunt stopped. While on the other, Gneisenau dismissed fears about the Carlsbad Decrees strengthening the influence of reactionary Austria in the Confederation as "exaggerated."[16] This indirect defense of tougher censorship and surveillance measures was related to the moderates' horror over the violence that the popular enthusiasm had produced. In the polarized atmosphere of 1819, however, the principle of "you're either with us or against us" became the rule of the day. Carl complained to Gneisenau that he increasingly avoided debating these issues: "It is not a question of being pelted by accusations, against which one might defend oneself, but simply of being pelted, which at a minimum leaves stains."[17] Despite Gneisenau's support for the decrees, the police searched his correspondence for involvement with the radical patriots, and their associate from Coblenz Gröben was interrogated.[18]

The lack of correspondence between Marie and Carl in this period makes it almost impossible to reconstruct Marie's thoughts and actions in these turbulent times. In the emotionally heightened period of the anti-Napoleonic resistance, she too had glorified the Middle Ages ("pious, heartfelt, naïve times").[19] Marie had argued, extensively and eloquently, that waking up and unleashing patriotic enthusiasm was the crucial element in the fight against Napoleon ("Let this beautiful zeal finally ignite us too! Or more accurately, let the one already existing be used at last and skillfully directed!!").[20] But she had also seen German nationalism as fairly different from the French revolutionary fervor (not only "strong and arrogant" but mostly "frivolous").[21] Whether it was a shock for Marie to see the people's passions take an ugly militant turn, not unlike the way the Reign of Terror and French expansionism outgrew the Revolution, one can only speculate.

Despite the rude awakening, other accounts suggest that Marie never turned into a cynic or allowed her worldview to sway into the expected reactionary turn. "My dear Marie passionately desired from my husband and from us that we should be happy along with her that the world is making progress and is becoming smarter and better," Elise von Bernstorff wrote in her memoir about Marie in 1824. The countess added that her friend had brought this "enthusiastic hope" from the last century when "this sentiment was common."[22] As these descriptions reveal, Marie had remained faithful to the ideas and hopes of her youth. Despite the Reign of Terror, the Napoleonic Wars, and the *Burschenschaften*, she continued to be a passionate apologist for human freedom and progress. However, this put Marie at odds with most of Berlin high society, which was growing so reactionary and conformist that even an intelligent and cosmopolitan person like Countess von Bernstorff found Marie's strong progressive views an annoying personality feature.

The issue at the core of these disagreements was far more complex than simple disapproval of Marie's vocal opinions. The real point of contention was the same question that divided German society as a whole in the decades after 1818. The Reform era, at its core, followed the enlightened principle of human perfectibility—people could be guided through education and better laws to become responsible citizens of the state. When in January 1821, the conservative statesman Otto von Voß–Buch declared that "people will never attain maturity," this signaled a clear break not only with the reform movement but also with Enlightenment's leading premise. The broad population, so Voß and the reactionary party's argument went, would always remain unable to become equal and mature citizens, and therefore the state should be organized on a strict authoritarian and hierarchical principle.

In this polarized atmosphere Carl's bid for a diplomatic career was bound to fail. He wished to become an ambassador to London, the country that, with its constitution and parliament, was now seen among the moderate reformers as the example Prussia should follow. In his essay "On the

Political Advantages and Disadvantages of the Prussian *Landwehr*" from 1819, Clausewitz passionately pleaded that after the people had fought for their state, they now also deserved their representative body, the parliament. Just like the king of England could rely on and gather strength from the parliament, he argued further, so Prussia should harness the energy and passions of its citizens. This was especially true because, as a middle-sized power at the heart of Europe and surrounded by dangerous enemies, Prussia could not really afford to disarm its militia, the *Landwehr*. Even if, as some reactionaries suggested, the militia might become the fertile ground for popular discontent and even a revolution, the solution could hardly be to deactivate it. "Honest and intelligent treatment—this alone can maintain and strengthen loyalty and devotion in the army, the *Landwehr,* and the people," Clausewitz reiterated, revealing the reason behind his desire to closely study democratic institutions, as an appointment in London would allow.[23]

When Carl's wish to become an ambassador became known, he found himself the subject of vicious attack. In the beginning, it seemed probable that Clausewitz would receive the position—he had the strong support of Bernstorff, Gneisenau, Wilhelm von Humboldt (by then minister of civil affairs), and Chancellor Hardenberg. Gneisenau even wrote to Gröben in November 1819 that his protégé had been appointed ambassador: "[Clausewitz] is very pleased about it; Madam von Clausewitz less so."[24] In mid-December, however, under the pressure of the courtier faction led by the Hugenot preacher Ancillon, now personal adviser to the king, and opposition from the British ambassador Sir George Henry Rose and the ultraconservative Duke of Cumberland, Friedrich Wilhelm withdrew the appointment.[25]

The fifth son of George III, the Duke of Cumberland, who later would become the king of Hanover under the name Ernest August I, was married to the widowed sister of the late Queen Louise, Friederike of Mecklenburg-Strelitz. Cumberland resided in Berlin because he had plunged into debt in Great Britain and was also deeply disliked in London, where his marriage had been opposed by Queen Charlotte. In the Prussian capital, Cumberland's home was one of the centers of political and cultural life. He was well informed but, according to Caroline von Rochow, "mainly [a] feared" man.[26] The Brühls' long-lasting affiliation with the court of St. James—Marie's aunt was once a governess of the duke's sisters, and Sophie remained a prominent member of the British expatriates circle in Berlin——could not smooth the opposition from Rose and Cumberland. This fact also hinted that the campaign went well beyond personal dislike but was part of a greater political scheme. Even Marwitz, Marie's former brother-in-law and a vocal reactionary leader with neofeudal and antilib- eral views, thought the attack on Clausewitz misplaced and based on oppo- sition for opposition's sake.[27]

With only her rather guarded letters to Gneisenau preserved, it is again hard to reconstruct Marie's true reactions. She had to interact with the reactionary faction on a daily basis in Berlin's ensnarled high society, some- times even more so than her husband. Caroline, Marie's old friend and frequent companion during 1813–1816, was now married to another con- servative leader, Gustav von Rochow, and according to her memoirs was intimately involved in the faction's discussions and plans.[28] Caroline von Berg served as the chief lady-in-waiting for the Duchess of Cumberland.[29] The duke and Clausewitz also must have known each other fairly well since Marie's diary from the fall of 1813 captured several lunches and talks between them.[30] These personal relations and everyday interactions with political opponents surely made the treatment her husband received sting even more. Right after losing the appointment, Carl wrote bitterly to Gneisenau that "every day I progressively realize, or actually every day I feel that I have, except Your Excellence, no real friend and none to lean on among the prominent people in the state and the army."[31]

As ambitious and outspoken as Marie was, it could not have been easy on her to see Carl publicly attacked and humiliated. Yet surprisingly, Marie's discontent remained unrecorded in the accounts of the time. Despite Gneisenau's remark about her uneasiness concerning the appointment in London, in all likelihood she truly wanted her husband to receive it. Her qualms could be easily explained by the inevitable separation from her aging mother and friends in Berlin.[32] In later years, Marie expressed regrets about Carl's missed career opportunity suggesting that, despite her per- sonal anxieties, she had supported it.[33] Remarkably, contemporaries' mem- oirs failed to capture livid reactions on Marie's part in 1819–1820 against her husband's detractors. This might have been, however, a deliberate show of restraint from her side.

The foreign minister Bernstorff nominally kept Clausewitz's name in the pool of possible candidates for diplomatic service, and the hope that the hostility would blow over and Carl might be appointed subsequently to the embassies in Munich or Copenhagen continued to linger. In 1823 when the king once again rejected his candidacy, Carl gave up his dream of diplomatic service altogether.[34] Clausewitz's humiliation was by far not unique—some of the reform circle's most emblematic figures, like Humboldt, Hermann von Boyen, and the Minister of Justice Friedrich von Beyme, were denied positions, forced out of power or resigned in frustration.

Friedrich Wilhelm had promised to consider the possibility of creating a constitution, and in 1819 Hardenberg presented the king with his ideas. The proponents, in the majority, saw the constitution less as an agent for bold social reforms than as an instrument to clarify the relations in the state. Hardenberg argued that the creation of a national representation would actually solidify the monarchical authority as the overarching power in Prussia. Gneisenau backed up the idea, adding that the various provinces could be held together only through a "constitutional ribbon."[35] While still supportive, the militant outburst in 1819 was laying heavy on Clausewitz's mind. In his typical dialectic style he pointed out that a constitution would not strengthen the state per se and, although democratic institutions usually harnessed people's passions, political processes would never be completely free of irrational forces and emotions that could temporarily block or slow the government's ability to act decisively.[36] It should also be added that despite their liberal attitudes, the reformers remained weary of granting too many popular rights because of doubts that broad parts of the people were mature enough to exercise them.[37] In December 1820, the king established a committee to resolve the constitutional question but, still fearing a revolution and increasingly relying on his hawkish courtiers, he appointed mostly conservatives to it.

In the end, Friedrich Wilhelm rebuffed the nobility's insistence on full reinstatement of their privileges and turning the clock back to the pre-1806 state of economy and politics. But he also decided, in 1823, against adopting a constitution. Thus historians like Levinger argue that the terms "Restoration" and "Reaction" are rather inaccurate for the period since crucial reforms from the Napoleonic era were not completely repealed; but the king, haunted by fear and insecurities, tried to consolidate his authority.[38] To some degree Clausewitz might have agreed with this argument—he wrote to Gneisenau in January 1820 that "our horizon is coming more and more to eclipse—not exactly through thundery clouds but thick, dull, damp sky."[39] Then in October of that same year he reasoned that despite even the most retrograde rhetoric, only a true political genius, one that did not live in Prussia in the 1820s, would be able "to throw the things back to the old conditions."[40] Still, the public discourse had taken an increasingly distorted and even grotesque turn—Clausewitz wrote in disbelief to Gneisenau about a debate he had with a young noble still arguing that serfdom was the nobility's political right ("positive law") and that it carried a certain "sanctity."[41] It was exactly this dullness and the lack of progress, when just a few years ago the victory over Napoleon promised so much, that led to the overly pessimistic tone of Clausewitz's writings of the period. The news of Napoleon Bonaparte's death on Saint Helena in May 1821 even filled him with a sense of nostalgia.[42]

Bad news seemed to pile up in the first few years of the 1820s. Due to the growing budget crisis in Prussia, Gneisenau dutifully offered the elimination of his post as governor of Berlin, which the king accepted, although he insisted that Gneisenau should keep the title and the official residence. Since the old general now had to pay for his stays in Berlin out of his own pocket, for Marie and Carl this meant longer separations from their dearest friend. Then in 1822, Gneisenau's daughter Agnes died giving birth to her second child.[43] The Clausewitz couple traveled to Gneisenau's home in Silesia to stay with the grieving parents. Marie became the godmother of the little girl and throughout the years, as her letters bear witness, spent a lot of time with Agnes's orphaned children. Then, in the fall of 1822, the disheartened Chancellor Hardenberg died too.

Despite the gloom that appears to hang over these years, Carl and especially Marie kept busy social schedules. Contemporary accounts repeatedly mentioned *die Generalin* (or madam general), as Marie became known, participating in various events often accompanied by her husband but also alone. Marie was even teased by friends as "the female Natzmer," after the royal favorite of that time.[44] Accounts and letters suggest that the Clausewitz couple spent their time with the poet Achim von Arnim and his vivid wife Bettina, Prince Antoni and Louise von Radziwiłł, Princess Marianne. They visited the homes of the legal scholar Friedrich von Savigny and the poetess and saloniere Sophie von Schwerin.[45] Marie and Bettina von Arnim already knew each other from their charitable work during the Wars of Liberation—and Bettina had heard the former praising her in front of mutual friends.[46] Described as a woman of "radiant cheerfulness and wittiest esprit," Bettina lived with her seven children in Berlin while Achim spent most of his time writing and taking care of the estate in Wiepersdorf, fifty miles south from the capital.[47] The relationship between Bettina and the Clausewitz couple was rekindled in the 1820s thanks to their warm recommendation by Carl's old friend from Coblenz, Meusebach. Like many others before, he advised Bettina to look beyond Clausewitz's public image as "a cold, sarcastic hero" since he possessed, in reality, an "affectionate, dear, and deep nature."[48] When she wanted to encourage her husband Achim, Bettina quoted Marie's admiring discussion of his work.[49]

Marie and Carl also spent a lot of time at Gneisenau's manor in Erdmannsdorf in Silesia (today the village, now called Mysłakowice, is part of Poland). The old war hero had enlarged and modernized the château in a beautiful classical style and liked to invite many of his friends for long summer vacations and gregarious parties. Princess Elisa von Radziwiłł wrote in a letter about "a long (not to say boring) soiree at Gneisenau's, where the half world is invited." Understandably, the twenty-two-year-old daughter of Antoni and Louise Radziwiłł found the guests in Erdmannsdorf, many of them twice or three times her age, not quite exciting. Yet she added that "the Clausewitzes will be my comfort," singling them out as the most interesting visitors.[50] In 1828, the relationship between Gneisenau and the couple became even closer when Marie's brother Friedrich fell in love and married the general's daughter Hedwig.

But the public space in which Carl and Marie spent most of their time in that decade was Elise von Bernstorff's salon. To change the public perception of them as recent transplants in the Prussian state, the countess took it upon herself to welcome and gather in her home influential and interesting guests. Elise's preoccupation with social decorum, often irritating for modern readers, was therefore part of a sleek and highly successful strategy. Indeed, soon after foreign minister Bernstorff's arrival in Berlin, the family and his wife's salon had firmly established themselves among the capital's political and cultural elite.[51] Elise welcomed predominantly diplomats, bureaucrats, and politicians, and in her correspondence with Carl from 1830–1831, Marie described the dinners and conversations at the house as her most significant source of information about current affairs. The Bernstorff salon was also perceived as elitist, and the countess herself was not free of hauteur.[52] These circumstances would explain why Carl was reluctant, for instance, to introduce his brothers, less skilled in courtly manners, at the exclusive gatherings.[53]

In this circle, Marie's passionate political advocacy became more visible. In her correspondence with Carl from 1830–1831, she emphasized the caution with which she approached the foreign minister and his prominent guests[54]—but this does not seem to be how her behavior was usually perceived by others. There are no indications that Marie herself saw her political interests as increased or unusual. What was shifting, rather, was the world around her. Elise von Bernstorff in particular captured over and over again in her memoirs the unease Marie seemed to create. In 1824, Marie debated the Greek Revolution with foreign minister Bernstorff so fervently that Elise admitted becoming "almost worried."[55] Bernstorff did not support the creation of a Greek state independent from the Ottoman Empire, despite his pity for the fate of the rebelling people. Marie's political activity was, then, far from harmless or irrelevant, as she was trying to convince the very man responsible for Prussia's foreign policy of the rebellion's virtue and positive impact on the world. At that, during the uprising's most crucial stage when it badly needed international support.

Marie's involvement with the plea of the Russian reformer Nikolay Turgenev was perceived in a more positive light. Turgenev was a suspected member of the reform circle that produced the Decembrist Uprising in 1825, when, instead of the more liberal Grand Duke Constantine, his younger brother Nikolai assumed the throne (Constantine had actually voluntarily refused the crown). After 3,000 rebelling officers and troops refused to swear allegiance to the new Tsar Nikolai I and their attempt to reignite a mass uprising turned out to be unsuccessful, Turgenev had managed to escape abroad. He was sentenced in absentia to a lifelong stay at Katorga, the penal labor camps in Siberia. Tsar Nikolai showed no mercy to the men who opposed his reign, but Marie still tried to ask for leniency for Turgenev through her friendship with the Hohenzollern dynasty. The Russian reformer had served once under Stein, and his brother, the historian Alexander Turgenev, enjoyed close relations with many European intellectuals (the famous novelist Ivan Turgenev was his relative as well). Thus a number of other Prussian reformers like Stein and Gneisenau became involved in his case but to no avail until Tsar Nikolai's death.[56]

Especially in the second part of the 1820s Marie also eyed another possibility for political influence for her and Carl. Just like in every other hereditary monarchy ruled by an aging sovereign, in Prussia courtiers with aspirations and ideas had started to gather around the person next in line for the throne—in this case Crown Prince Friedrich Wilhelm. Marie and Carl harbored few illusions about how indecisive and averse to social and political reforms the future Friedrich Wilhelm IV was. In 1810–1812 Carl had lectured the royal offspring in the matters of war and military affairs and even summarized his most important lessons in writing right before he left for Russia. But after Clausewitz's return from the Russian campaign, the seventeen-year-old prince did not welcome back his tutor with love and trust. Marie commented on the future king's behavior in those days with barely hidden bitterness and anger: "It is not simply apathy or indignation that I felt but also true pain to see the crown prince so crude, so dry, so unable of great noble consideration.... If he follows the footsteps of his father, and he already has made such progress in his anxiousness [Geisterscheu], his dryness, his love for mediocrity, he could become even worse."[57] Yet in 1816 Clausewitz accompanied the crown prince during his tour throughout the Rhineland province and the relationship was rekindled. In the 1820s the military theorist occasionally lectured again to his former student. Marie's correspondence from the early 1830s suggests that she and her mother also often enjoyed the company of Friedrich Wilhelm's wife Elizabeth Ludovika. Intelligent and interested in the arts, the young princess must have grown particularly fond of Sophie von Brühl because she visited the seventy-year-old courtier at her home.

Some of Carl and Marie's best friends also comprised the future Friedrich Wilhelm IV's intimate circle. The archconservative Leopold von Gerlach, with whom Carl served and held long and vivid debates in 1813–1815, was now the prince's trusted adviser. Carl von Gröben, the officer the Clausewitz couple had come to love and treasure in Coblenz, became Friedrich Wilhelm's adjutant in 1829. Since Queen Louise's death in 1810, Marie's old friend and once fellow lady-in-waiting, Caroline "Mademoiselle" von Bischoffswerder, had assumed the role of substitute mother for the crown prince. Throughout his life he visited her room, poured out all his personal and political troubles, and searched for advice.[58] It would be safe to say that Marie, always so sensible in the matters of court and influence, was the one actively searching to deepen hers and Carl's relationship with the future ruler and his consort.

Yet even women from the younger generation found Marie's outspokenness and political activism rather bothersome and openly expressed their suspicion against her.[59] Probably the most unsympathetic description of Madam von Clausewitz's political activities came from a French agent visiting Berlin. In 1826, he wrote a report on the Prussian army for the French ministry. The report pointed out Clausewitz's qualities as a staff officer, his friendship with Gneisenau, and especially his negative attitude against France. In this regard, Marie's views seemed significant enough to be mentioned as well: "His wife, whose opinions were even more extreme than his, encouraged him for a long time in this attitude."[60]

After the proactive role women had played in Napoleon's defeat, in the Restoration era the society expected them to slip quickly back into their traditional duties. From nearly 600 female organizations in various German states (at least 414 of them in Prussia) at the height of the fighting, only one in ten continued afterward.[61] Even the patriotic ladies granted the *Luisenorden* or Order of Louise, the award initiated in 1814 by Friedrich Wilhelm in memory of the beloved queen, were now not beyond reproach. "I cannot hold my anger how people sometimes badmouth *Luisenorden*, to be sure because of jealousy, but it still hurts," the lady-in-waiting Albertine von Boguslawska wrote in 1826 to her mother Wilhelmine, one of the first awarded for her charitable work during the Wars of Liberation. After witnessing the hostility and mockery accompanying the ceremony that year, Albertine was happy that her mother had not attended and bitterly added that such distinctions "were not created for our society."[62]

Remarkably, the person that was closest to and probably most affected by Marie's outspokenness and activism, Carl, did not appear concerned or bothered by it. There is no evidence in their later correspondence or in Bernstorff's memoir that he ever tried to rein in or discourage his wife. Carl's embrace of Marie's political acuteness also had significant consequences for the continuing relevance of *On War*. As gender historians have noted in recent years, the military treatise was written in a realist philosophical language without the heroic pathos or empathic talk of manly honor that may be off-putting to modern readers. Yet compared to the decade in which it was created—when universal conscription led to the strong correlation between service in uniform and the right to citizenship, and entwined ideas of masculinity, politics, state, and nation—this is a rather paradoxical situation. Stefan Dudink and Karen Hagemann argue that by the time Clausewitz wrote his seminal work, ideas of masculinity had shaped the discourse of politics and war so firmly that he did not even need to evoke it explicitly.[63]

However, read in the context of Marie's unabashed political activism, another explanation becomes obvious. Clausewitz, without a doubt, saw military and civil service as masculine activities. After all, he had argued, just as Dudink and Hagemann point out, that the *Landwehr*, the militia harnessing the will of the male population to defend the country, should become the base for institutions of popular democracy. But it would be rather difficult to assume that Clausewitz held the same opinion for the realm of politics. When it came to their most broad definition of debate, building grassroots movements, or influence peddling, Marie's passionate involvement would have made it simply impossible for her husband to view politics as a sphere reserved for men.

Furthermore, throughout his correspondence and writings Clausewitz left enough evidence that he took women's roles in political and public spheres seriously. He recommended Madame de Staël's books to Marie, and his wife remained a lifelong admirer of the French intellectual.[64] After 1826, Clausewitz wrote a commentary on the published correspondence of Madame de Maintenon to the Princess des Ursins arguing that one should not dismiss the book simply because these were "the words of a woman." Quite the opposite, he stated; even if Madame de Maintenon in particular had "no talent whatever for matters of state and for war," she was so close to Louis XIV and the French court that her letters bore invaluable information about the War of the Spanish Succession.[65] To understand the royalist attempts at counterrevolution in France, the so-called War in the Vendée, he studied the memoirs of Victoire de Donnissan de La Rochejaquelein, the widow of one of its leaders, and found them "fairly interesting."[66] Carl even read the memoirs of Madame du Barry, Louis XV's legendary and influential but otherwise far from intellectual mistress.[67]

This complex understanding of politics put Clausewitz at odds with his contemporaries' increasingly exclusive views, which were patently colored by exaggerated masculinity. It also led him to write *On War* in an objective tone free of moral judgment, and to deliberately avoid the language of male heroism, bravado, and sacrifice—undoubtedly a circumstance that makes the treatise sound so modern and pragmatic in our time. Clausewitz's claim that "war is no pastime; it is no mere joy in daring and winning, no place for irresponsible enthusiasts," is clearly a direct criticism of foolish and dangerous glorification.[68] But it is also a visible attack on the romanticized, masculine notion of combat. In this appeal to understand war in all of its violence, danger, and destruction, Clausewitz also encompassed a call to grasp the complex realities of society and politics.

During the decade they spent in Berlin, the Clausewitz couple devoted many hours to their interest in the visual arts. It remains unclear whether Marie continued to paint but she regularly went to the annual Great Art Exhibition in Berlin.[69] In the summer of 1821, she and Carl made a trip to Dresden, and he finally had the time to admire the magnificent art collection that Heinrich von Brühl had once helped gather. When a committee was created to raise money for the creation of a monument for Scharnhorst, Carl became an active member. He closely cooperated with Prussia's most famous artists like the architect Schinkel and sculptors Christian Daniel Rauch and Christian Friedrich Tieck.[70] Carl even drafted the initial design for the tomb of Gneisenau's deceased daughter Agnes and let Schinkel perfect it.[71] In all probability in this period Clausewitz also wrote essays on the subject of appreciation of fine arts, architecture, and interior design.[72] His interests in aesthetics and the psychological mechanisms of creation and perception must have been well known among close friends, because Elise von Bernstorff counted on his opinion when it came to her house décor.[73]

What Marie had started with her tedious aesthetic lectures two decades ago had come to bear unexpected fruits. Remarkably often Clausewitz used art metaphors in *On War* to explain war's complex nature in simpler and visually more compelling terms. "Architects and painters know

Figure 9.4. Gerhard von Scharnhorst's grave in the military cemetery in Berlin. *Photo Vanya Eftimova Bellinger.*

precisely what they are about as long as they deal with material phenomena. Mechanical and optical structures are not subject to dispute. But when they come to the aesthetics of their work, when they aim at a particular effect on the mind or on the senses, the rules dissolve into nothing but a vague idea," he wrote in Book II. The same way, Clausewitz suggested, moral factors in war were difficult to pinpoint but any military action should take them into account and aim at them as well.[74] Similarly, he relied on an art metaphor to explain the difference between his famous concepts of absolute and real war and the need to understand the theory about the former in order to be able to wage the latter. "Just as the tone a painter gives to his canvas is determined by the color of the underpinning," so knowledge about the possibility of pure violence, unrestrained by resources and political considerations, should underpin the understanding of the real war.[75]

Carl devoted most of his energy and time on his treatise to the discussion of the transformation of the nature of warfare. According to the account of his adjutant Steinmann von Friederici, Clausewitz kept a strict daily routine. Every morning, he labored in Marie's company at her drawing room until 9 a.m. when the doorman, a one-armed veteran, announced the arrival of the adjutant with the daily paperwork to be signed. After this short interruption, Carl continued his work until lunch, with the exception of the days when he occasionally lectured his former student, the crown prince. "From twelve o'clock on, visits were received and returned. Field Marshal Gneisenau usually arrived several times each week, and would stay until 2:00 in the afternoon. Lunch was served around that time. Frequently [Clausewitz] had guests, but never more than six or eight persons. These were mostly men of great intellectual distinction. Here the general's mind, his wit, his slashing sarcasm blazed in bright flames. . . . The afternoons were devoted again to writing, the evenings, with rare exceptions, were spent at the home of Count Gneisenau or Count Bernstorff, unless there was an invitation to court or to a larger dinner. The general and his wife would almost always return by eleven o'clock."[76]

This rigorous writing routine was interrupted by Clausewitz's participation in army maneuvers, and occasionally by various sicknesses continuing to plague his poor health.[77] In June 1822, Elise von Bernstorff noted that Carl suffered a "stroke-like accident" that temporarily paralyzed his right hand. The countess added that Marie still came to a party that Elise had organized for Marie's birthday, although on her own.[78] In 1827, Elise wrote that Carl was sick "for a long time," seemingly with a more serious illness as Marie could not participate in social events.[79]

Unfortunately, the lack of sizable correspondence between the couple in that period makes it almost impossible to reconstruct the circumstances leading to Clausewitz's groundbreaking discovery of two types of war, limited and unlimited, around 1827. Even more regrettable for modern scholars is the fact that Marie did not leave any record about Carl's attempts to overhaul the already written parts of *On War* in the light of this development.

In addition to working on *On War*, Clausewitz also wrote essays about current issues although most of these texts remained unpublished until his death. In the polarized political climate, he probably worried, not without reason, that his ideas might be distorted and he was reluctant to engage in senseless debates. In all probability, Carl circulated them among friends, which would explain the overly cautious tone of some of these essays.

When it came to *On War*, however, it seemed that Clausewitz decided deliberately to work on the manuscript without time constraints or the pressure of public opinion. In the preface, Marie wrote that she had tried to persuade him to publish the manuscript in a timely manner: "To complete his work was his dearest wish, but it was not his intention to communicate it to the world during his lifetime. When I would try to dissuade him from this decision, he often responded, half jokingly, but perhaps also with a presentiment of his early death: You shall publish it."[80] Carl knew that in the worst-case scenario his wife would see his work to a successful end and thus he could allow himself the comfort of writing without externally imposed pressure. In hindsight, considering *On War*'s ambition to describe the phenomenon in its totality, this was a decision of enormous consequences.

Clausewitz was a disciplined writer, but far from spontaneous or quick to capture his ideas on paper. He took time to think through and perfect his texts, edited and reedited them, kept notes and repeatedly came back to them, and in some cases overhauled content completely. Werner Hahlweg suitably calls this process "composition in many stages."[81] When Clausewitz had to work under the pressure of a deadline or immediate necessity, his writings, although still eloquent in building an argument—like the essay *Der Feldzug von 1813 bis zum Waffenstillstand* ("The Campaign of 1813 until the Armistice")—lacked the sophistication and complex worldview that mark his revered texts.

Bearing in mind her husband's messy writing routine, Marie strived to preserve all of his manuscripts. Throughout their correspondence, she insisted, sometimes obsessively, that Carl sent her his drafts and all other writings for safekeeping.[82] Not without a reason, because, as Marie's letters in particular reveal, papers were often lost or misplaced, and debated ideas left unwritten.

The most insightful remark about his routine comes from an earlier period and concerns *On the Life and Character of Scharnhorst*. Scholars have usually reviewed this text as a way to understand where Clausewitz's ideas found their roots, especially since the essay was finished during his time in Coblenz when the military theorist also started working on *On War*. In her letter of May 16, 1815, Marie discussed an early version of the essay left with her for safekeeping: "I dared to look in your papers for the unfinished essay about Scharnhorst, partly to read it thoroughly once again, partly, as you allowed me, to share it with [Julie von] Dohna; but I didn't find any decent beginning to it and must almost fear that one sheet of paper is missing." She described sifting through all of his papers for the lost page, "to no avail." It is clear that Marie understood the value of this essay, and her concern over potentially lost material is striking. "In case this essay already has another beginning other than the quite piecemeal one, which on the page simply reads <u>Intellect</u> without referral to S.'s name on it, then something must be missing[.] And I ask you, very much so, to look if that sheet did not go by chance in your briefcase and to send it to me, it would be a pity if something of it would go lost[.] But it seems also possible to me that you haven't written yet an actual beginning but only sketched your thoughts as they emerged."[83]

The story about the Scharnhorst manuscript reveals that Marie knew, or believed she knew, its content well ("to read it thoroughly once again"), but was not involved in the actual writing, the de facto process of putting these ideas on paper—hence her wondering about the missing beginning or whether the pages in her possession were only sketches of thoughts. Together with Marie and Carl's declared love for lengthy deliberations, this would suggest that the military theorist usually put his ideas on paper after presenting, debating, and synthesizing them in the presence of his wife. By listening to or vigorously debating with her husband, she knew his ideas well, although often without actually, physically seeing what was written in his manuscripts. In 1831, Marie made a similar statement noting that she had recognized Carl's thesis and writing style in an anonymous newspaper article, but could not be sure since she had not witnessed the text's composing. Hence, Marie asked her husband whether her guess was correct.[84]

These clues about Clausewitz's writing routine would also explain the circumstances surrounding the creation of *On War*. In her "Preface," Marie wrote that "we shared everything," so "a task of this kind could not occupy my beloved husband without at the same time becoming thoroughly familiar to me." Indeed, some of the pages of *On War*'s manuscript, together with notes and references, bear Marie's handwriting.[85] Despite her involvement, she still described the discovery of the final revisions as a tedious process that also required the help of her brother Fritz. If Marie were so involved in Clausewitz's work, logically it would be expected that she would have known where to find the corrections right away. This apparent contradiction can be solved only if one assumes that Marie participated in the deliberations, research, and process of writing but often without closely following what her husband put on paper as the final version. Later on, it would be exactly these circumstances that gave her the authority to authenticate the revisions buried among other papers as indeed the last ones Clausewitz had envisioned.

Especially interesting, in this regard, is the newly found draft of Chapter One, Book I at the military history museum in Coblenz (*Wehrtechnische Studiensammlung*).[86] The text is, as the two scholars studying it, Paul Donker and Andreas Herberg-Rothe, point out, nearly identical to the published version of *On War*.[87] This fact makes the manuscript a strong candidate for the revised version of Chapter One, Book I that Marie mentioned in her "Preface." Among the surprises, the draft divulges, are the section headings of Chapter One written on the left side of the pages, for the most part in Marie's clear handwriting with some additional corrections done by Carl. Generally the sectional headings contain wording found in *On War*'s main text. Yet the most famous of them, Nr.24 proclaiming "War is merely the continuation of politics with other means," is an exception. Clausewitz's chief premise of war's political character is extensively examined throughout his treatise but never so clearly stated as in this sectional heading. Written solely in Marie's handwriting, Nr.24 is, of course, a revised version of his pronouncement in the Note of 10 July 1827 that "war is nothing but the continuation of policy with other means."[88] Still, it is the laconic sentence in Chapter One that most readers of the treatise remember. Its careful wording in Marie's handwriting not only reveals Carl's constant drive to revise and polish his texts while searching for the clearest and most economical form. It also raises the possibility that Marie actively participated in the process of crafting Clausewitz's famous sentence in the form we know it today.

By the end of the decade in Berlin, both Carl and Marie still believed there would be enough time for him to finish his groundbreaking theory. They had survived the Napoleonic Wars and had lived long enough for Carl to distill on paper the most important lessons from them. Although plagued by different illnesses, he had managed to recover every time. The couple had weathered the decade of reactionary turning but still expected to play an active role in Prussian politics.

10

The Last Years Together
(December 1829–November 1831)

In the winter of 1829, Carl von Clausewitz officially asked Friedrich Wilhelm to be relieved from his administrative duties at the War College and return to service in the regular army. The ensuing period in the couple's life was marked not only by professional challenges and separation but also by political tumult that led them to believe in the possibility of another major European war. Surprisingly, Marie and Carl found themselves defending positions at odds with many of their progressive contemporaries. These attitudes continue to perplex readers to this day. Carl's surprising death makes his last two years appear particularly tragic in hindsight, as he set aside his work *On War,* believing that it was his duty to help put out the flames of another European clash. The July Revolution, however, created shock waves without seriously damaging the balance of power. Yet the military theorist ran out of time to finish his lifework.

The immediate reason for Carl's departure from his position at the War College remains unclear. Paret suggests that his tenure had been viewed as unsuccessful, and as a field-grade officer he longed to go back to service with the troops.[1] Rudolf von Caemmerer describes the administrative duty as "not serving [Clausewitz] well" and intimates that it continued longer than it should have.[2] Even if Carl had done nothing wrong at the War College, a decade at the same post and rank, and at that away from line duty, would be damaging for any officer's career. This, of course, raises the question of why he stayed for so long and what role his ambitious wife played in this decision.

The traditional explanation, usually given in light of Carl's failed ambitions for a diplomatic career in the first half of the 1820s, is that the polarized political atmosphere hampered his career rise. Yet even if the decade had started with personal assaults and crushed dreams, Marie and Carl's busy social calendar clearly disavows the prevailing perception that they were publicly marginalized or politically inactive. One possible answer as to why Carl remained at the War College for so long is, of course, that after two decades of war and subsequent political tumult, the couple had finally become conformists and cherished their pleasant personal life and the free time for him to write. Indeed, in this period Clausewitz produced a staggering amount of texts—next to the exhausting and colossal work of *On War*, he also composed numerous essays ranging from historical events to current political developments, studies of military campaigns, and even art theory.

Another little-known account written by Paul Erman, professor at the War College, reveals that even if the director had little influence over the teaching process, he was still very much interested in it and regularly visited the lectures.[3] Recently discovered letters that Carl wrote to his nephew Carl Leopold likewise do not show him to be extremely unhappy or insecure about his situation in the late 1820s. In March 1827 Carl applied for the king's confirmation of his family's nobility status, a move that on the surface could be read as evidence of fear of more reactionary attacks and the need to preempt them. Carl's lengthy explanation to Carl Leopold as to why he felt compelled to search for clarification in this contentious family matter tells a different story. Carl, as he wrote to his nephew, did not worry for his own position as he was now "too high in rank" to become the subject of attacks and rumors about lack of noble birth. But he wanted to secure the privileged ranking in writing for his nephews.[4] Friedrich Wilhelm indeed confirmed Carl's belief that he had achieved certain eminence in Prussia—the king avoided a lengthy investigation into the matter and simply sent a cabinet order stating the family's noble status. If the decade had started with bitter personal disappointment, by its end Carl appeared more at ease with his place in the wider world.

Objective reasons might have contributed to the couple's peaceful existence in Berlin too. After the bitter polarization and personal assaults among Prussia's warring factions, in second part of the 1820s the cabinet and the courtiers also turned their attention toward rebuilding the state. In order to revive the economy, the government in Berlin continued the policy of deregulation. Following the establishment of a homogeneous customs regime for all its territories in 1818–1821,

Prussia's politicians and diplomats tirelessly worked for the creation of a Germany-wide customs union. Finally becoming a reality in 1834, this customs union would serve as the economic blueprint for the unification of Germany almost four decades later. In this atmosphere and without any immediate threat looming over Prussia, the military was hardly a priority. Carl, with his great interest in political and state matters, might very well have preferred administrative duty in the capital to service in a faraway garrison. Certainly Marie enjoyed her busy social schedule at the heart of Berlin's high society, and greatly preferred having her husband in the capital with her as a change from their many and difficult separations.

Finally, however, after ten years Carl obviously felt the need for a career change and requested a return to active service. The king granted his request. The only appointment offered, as the head (inspector) of one of the three subdivisions of the Prussian artillery—called "inspections"—was a disappointment. Carl had hoped to command an infantry division, but even so, being back among the troops revived his spirits. Before taking over the II Artillery Inspection, which had its headquarters in Breslau, the capital of the province of Silesia (modern-day Wrocław in Poland), he went on a working trip with the head of I Inspection to familiarize himself with the new duties. In this new period of their life, with Marie remaining in Berlin, the couple resumed their correspondence, although Carl's letters from 1830 have remained unpublished too.

Marie, as engaged in Berlin's social life as ever, kept him informed about the rising commotions in Europe. Although liberal and nationalistic forces had repeatedly shaken the reactionary design of the Vienna Congress, they did not put a real strain on it for over a decade. The first serious danger came in July 1830 when, after a prolonged conflict with the Chamber of Deputies, the unpopular King Charles X of France dissolved the body and suspended the country's freedom of the press. The uprising in Paris that followed went into history under the name "Three Glorious Days."

After Napoleon's abdication and the subsequent restoration of the Bourbon monarchy under Louis XVIII, Louis' younger brother Charles X assumed the throne in 1824. Since taking power the seventy-one-year-old king had managed to attract much criticism on the European stage. When the uprisings and political crisis in Paris led to his abdication, many saw his deposition as well deserved—but also feared what would fill the vacuum.

"Your wife, to whom I have sometimes tried to excuse Charles X, has defeated me; she had judged the character of this king better," Gneisenau wrote to Carl on August 18. Charles X had gained many critics with his reactionary law against blasphemy and provisions for indemnities for confiscated properties during the French Revolution. "Once he even answered, when confronted with the dangerous prospects of his measures, 'I prefer to mount the horse than to ascend the scaffold.' But [the king] did not keep his word and mounted his horse only after his cause was lost in Paris, and at that to escape," Gneisenau commented further with bitter irony. In the wake of these events the situation appeared so complex that, as he added, no one had a clear vision for the future, and the diplomats could just as well "decide by drawing a blind lot."[5]

In August 1830, the more liberal King Louis-Philippe I of the House of Orleans was sworn in as the new ruler of France and the constitutional monarchy. But the revolutionary spark in Paris threatened to turn into a wildfire when other dissatisfied peoples around Europe began to view the current political crisis as an opportunity to change their own situation. The political class in Berlin was particularly worried about the independence aspirations of the United Netherlands' southern provinces, which were predominantly French-speaking and Catholic (modern-day Belgium). Berlin saw the Dutch kingdom as the keystone of their defense against a possible assault—it was a staunch ally that the French had to cross before attacking German territories. Support in Brussels for offering the crown to another prince of the House of Orleans only strengthened fears about the balance of powers tipping strongly in Paris's favor. Hotheads in Berlin now openly urged a preemptive strike in Belgium, a suggestion that made the danger of French intervention and, with it, another European war even more feasible. In the fall of 1830, the Prussian government appeared to face an unbearably complex challenge: they would be damned if they did interfere in the Belgium affair, and doomed if they didn't.

Marie and Carl's last summer together in Berlin suffered under growing worries about political tumult. "The revolts in Brussels and Leuven as well as the news about riots in Aachen filled all minds with new worries in the beginning of September, and during the fall maneuvers by Potsdam the tension was so great that one expected a declaration of war any moment," Carl wrote in his diary.[6] Sometime before his departure to Breslau, he went once again over the draft of *On War*, and then left it in Marie's care.[7] In their last days together in Berlin, Elise von Bernstorff organized a goodbye party in her garden. When a flock of white pigeons flew over their heads, she wrote, everyone felt as though it had "carried away on its wings a long and beautiful past enriched by the most intimate friendship."[8]

Carl left for Breslau on September 7. For almost a month he had to travel, meet officers and troops personally, and inspect garrisons and weaponry. Hence Carl preferred that Marie stay in Berlin for the time being. His new position came with a family perk, since Marie's brother and his wife, Fritz and Hedwig von Brühl, already lived in Breslau (Fritz had transferred to the Prussian service in 1828 and now as a major held the command of a hussar regiment). Carl moved into a temporary apartment in a building housing the families of other military and government officials. Despite its massive structure, the house's small court forced guests to disembark from their carts on the muddy street. The Clausewitz couple's quarters on the second floor were also insufficient for their needs, and the orderly's tiny bedroom had to serve as the dayroom for the other servants. Despite Marie's protests, Carl unpacked and set up the furniture without her, but as compensation offered his wife the most beautiful space, the only one with a terrace, as her drawing room. He also designated the spacious and light-filled corner room as the salon where the couple could receive and entertain guests, part of the social functions that his new position as artillery inspector required. Carl suggested to Marie that the next spring they could move to another apartment, closer to downtown and more adequate for their status.[9]

Days after his departure, Marie wrote from Berlin with troublesome news.[10] Like Aachen, where on August 30 textile workers had taken their discontent over wages and working conditions to the streets, the Prussian capital was now swept by riots too. In contrast to events in the western provinces, the so-called *Schneiderrevolution*, or "tailor revolution," also had political demands in addition to the social. In its response to heated political rhetoric among tailor apprentices, the Berlin police overreacted, and the arrests brought thousands of other disgruntled young workers out to a protest in front of the palace. The situation escalated on September 17, when the army was hastily called, and then turned into riots. The next morning, Berlin's high society expressed shock and disbelief upon hearing what had happened—angry mob and street fights were something new for the strict and hierarchical Prussian state. On her way home after a party at the Bernstorffs' house on September 18, Marie saw blood on the streets and on buildings close to the palace, spilled on the second night of unrest.[11] Finally on September 20 the authorities managed to restore order in Berlin.

The protesters of the *Schneiderrevolution* had directed their anger mostly against the reactionary clique strangling the state and blocking the prospect of greater political representation through a constitution. In any other situation, Marie and Carl probably would have shown some understanding for the voices of dissent. After all in the early 1820s, Carl had advocated the creation of institutions of popular democracy in Prussia. In stark contrast to the prevailing attitudes among the aristocracy from previous times, the couple had also started to mention the names of their servants and wrote with understanding and sympathy about their struggles. When the lower classes took their discontent to the street, however, Marie and Carl had only scorn for them. "I find this curiosity even in the best of times beyond comprehension because first, it has at its core disregard of the law, and second a kind of pleasure in posing for which every decent person should have only abhorrence," Carl wrote to his wife. Still, with outright schadenfreude he also took a shot at the Prussian government, which had just revealed its utter incompetence to put down the riots: "It seems to me . . . that the Berlin authorities have made themselves completely laughable with their all too big institutions and all too little impact."[12]

Days later Carl himself participated in the containment of unrest that erupted in Breslau on September 27 and took on an antisemitic character. Although he briefly noted the pogrom-like riots in published excerpts from his diary, the fact that his correspondence with Marie from 1830 remained unpublished has led historians to overlook these events in his life. In the known excerpts Carl briefly wrote that he closely observed the "mob rows" and was able to "draw some basic principles about procedure in such occurrences."[13] Despite its shortness, the quote suggests that the events left him with lasting impressions. The more comprehensive analysis of his correspondence with Marie extends our understanding of these impressions, hinting toward the broadening of Clausewitz's ideas about the application of military force against civilians—ideas that only lack of time and his early death prevented him from exploring. In *On War*, the military theorist rather briefly—and from a modern point of view, many would say insufficiently—discussed the way troops could suppress unrest among civilian populations and restore peace and order.

The two unpublished letters from September 27 and 28, 1830, reveal Carl's experience in greater detail and also illuminate his thoughts about the application of military force in the sensitive matters of riot and crowd control. Probably to calm Marie, he wrote in the first passage that when it had come time for Breslau to have its own version of one of "these infamous citizen fights [*jenen berühmten Bürgerschlachten*]," it turned out to be "very boring." Nonetheless the time when Carl composed the first letter, noted at its upper corner as "twelve o'clock at night"—right after the events—suggests that they had shaken him profoundly.

Breslau, a long-standing center of textile production, experienced the effects of intensifying industrialization after the end of the Napoleonic Wars. The peasantry, still suffering from the effects of the unfulfilled Stein-Hardenberg reforms, became cheap labor for the new factories in the cities. At that time no one thought seriously about workers' rights or living conditions, or how industrialization would change the society. In 1830, when the plebs' dissatisfaction with encroaching capitalism mixed with age-old prejudices, they held the big Jewish merchandising companies, like the ones in Breslau, culpable for the workers' misery.

"It has been rumored for a while, as I've already written to you, about a campaign [*Feldzug*] of the tailor apprentices against the Jews," Carl explained to Marie in his first letter of September 27–28.[14] He doesn't appear to have spent time thinking about the roots of the problem, but neither was there a hint of hostile or virulent comments about the Jewish population deserving its fate. The description of the events reveals Carl's opinion about the riots as a socially evil and unwanted act. It also suggests that by that time he saw the minority as a part of the German state and thus deserving of protection from the mob. The wide participation of Jewish volunteers in the Wars of Liberation had made it hard for moderate reformers to cling to centuries-old prejudices. Enterprising Jews had also entered Berlin's high society and, thanks to their commercial success, now even married the daughters of old but impoverished noble houses. Marie wrote to Carl about participating in one such engagement of a friendly family (Knuth), where the happy groom, a baptized Jew, owned a cotton factory and a beautiful house. Mister Goldschmid, she described, "is clever and looks pretty pleasant, but quite Jewish." Then Marie concluded that aside from his origins, he appeared an excellent choice for marriage.[15] As the story revealed, prejudice certainly had not disappeared even in Prussia's progressive circles, but the acceptance of Jews had also become possible.

In Breslau on September 27, as Carl wrote to Marie, he was spending the evening with Fritz and Hedwig von Brühl when at about eight o'clock the news about "300 to 400 people . . . marching through the streets and smashing left and right the windows of the Jews" came. Instigated by public gatherings throughout the day, the young tailor apprentices targeted predominantly Jewish neighborhoods and also stormed a Jewish-owned warehouse. The city government called upon the local garrison, where Marie's brother served, to control the crowds. "Since I was right there by Fritz, I borrowed a horse and a rapier from him and moved into the city with his regiment," Carl described. One part of the corps guarded the armory, military commissary, and the prison, while the other moved through the streets and, despite some sporadic resistance and hand-to-hand fighting, reestablished order by eleven o'clock.[16]

Expecting another night of rioting into the next day, Carl wrote to Marie that he did not support the idea that it should "be nipped in the bud by the early intervention of cavalry." He clarified, however, that the reason he resisted the use of cavalry was not because he thought it ineffective. Quite the opposite, Carl felt that "enough cases reveal that the earliest is always the best, namely the mildest." He elaborated further that "just yesterday we saw that the simple display [of military power] quieted the storm." As in his general theory on war, Carl advocated a proactive approach with the maximum force available—the sheer display of heavy horses, flashy uniforms, and blazing weapons would psychologically overwhelm and dissuade the rioters from further actions. Hence it would turn out to be the mildest measure because it would save more bloodshed and destruction. Despite his convictions, Carl objected to using cavalry to scare the crowd in Breslau "because the authorities are not united in their opinion."[17] During the debates about how to proceed, the Silesian provincial president had argued that the military could provoke a greater backlash and thus make the situation worse. This lack of unified political support for stronger military actions became, for Clausewitz, a reality he could not overlook. In this uprising as in war, policy remained the overarching force, and the military had to take its lead from such policy, even if the soldiers did not agree with the politicians' reasoning.

On the next evening, September 28, Carl wrote to Marie that the riots in Breslau were effectively over. During the day, the tailor apprentices had boycotted work but the arrests of the leaders, to Carl's surprise, put an end to the riots.[18] The heavy-handed approach with greater military presence and cavalry assault turned out to be unnecessary.

The possibility that the wave of popular uprisings would incite another European war grew with every passing week. In the fall of 1830, the distraught Marie and Carl also openly opposed the secession of the

Netherlands' southern provinces, now known as the Belgium Revolution. He used particularly strong language to express his objection to the revolutionaries' violent means to achieve independence: "Who wants to live in a land where the law has to watch when a biased passion is put above it?" He did not have, Carl declared, "even one compassionate drop of blood in my veins for those Belgians."[19]

It was, however, the couple's blatant opposition to the Polish aspirations for independence that truly surprised many in their moderate circle. Especially in the case of Marie, even her closest friend Elise von Bernstorff had a hard time understanding it. As Elise recalled, "[Marie] would have sympathy for every other peoples that would rise, indeed she would urge participation in other rebellions, only not for the Poles."[20] On November 27, the so-called November Uprising broke out when a group of cadets from Poland's military academy revolted against Russian rule. Although the uprising occurred in the part of partitioned Poland dominated by Russia, formally known as the Kingdom of Poland, soon after it excited popular enthusiasm and support in the Prussian-controlled Grand Duchy of Posen. For Marie and Carl, just reunited in their new home in Breslau, this turbulence brought another separation when it forced Carl to leave in haste for Berlin.[21] Surprised by the attack of angry cadets, the Grand Duke Constantine, the Russian emperor's brother and viceroy in the Kingdom of Poland, had barely escaped capture. Friedrich Wilhelm scrambled to find an answer to the growing violence east of his borders, and appointed Gneisenau, promoted to field marshal in 1825, as commander of the army about to be mobilized. As he had before, Gneisenau asked Clausewitz to serve as his chief-of-staff.

Believing the troops would be on the move soon, Carl left Marie in Breslau while he headed to Berlin. Once there, he discovered that the political debates and the military preparations would take longer than anticipated. Carl sent for Marie. On her way back to the capital, Marie carried in her luggage the sealed manuscript of *On War*, deeming it too valuable to be left unattended in Breslau.[22] By Christmas 1830, the couple was reunited back in Berlin and celebrated just like many years before with the Bernstorff family.[23]

The "sad time," according to Elise von Bernstorff, transformed the mood among moderate reformers. Polarized opinions separated old friends, and "repeated disgruntlement" became the prevailing tone.[24] The arena for the growing embitterment was the Polish-German house of Prince Radziwiłł, a man who represents perhaps more than any other the history and dilemmas of the Polish question. A Polish patriot, Antoni Radziwiłł had always harbored hopes for the restoration of his partitioned homeland. He also remained a realist, however, and before 1815 advocated that Poland, if it could not be independent, should exist in personal union with Prussia governed by a viceroy. During the Vienna Congress Radziwiłł put all his time, skills, and energy into convincing Alexander I of Russia and Friedrich Wilhelm to unite most of the Polish territories and grant them an independent government, albeit within the borders of Prussia. Instead, Friedrich Wilhelm gave up most of his lands in the East and made the prince governor of the remaining Grand Duchy of Posen. While the Prussian rule was rather light-handed, in the Russian-dominated Kingdom of Poland Grand Duke Constantine trampled the rights guaranteed by the Polish Constitution.

The uprising therefore was met with mixed feelings among the liberal parts of German society. Progressive newspapers eagerly embraced the Polish cause against the mighty and retrograde Russian Empire, reporting not only in detail about the events but also, as in an article in *Karlsruher Zeitung,* declaring that the Germans should show "how high they admire patriotism, love for freedom, and valor."[25] Marie's old friend Countess Pauline von Neale wholeheartedly advocated for the Polish aspirations and gathered other Poland sympathizers and Polish émigrés in Berlin.[26] Even Elise von Bernstorff, who otherwise had stopped believing in human perfectibility, now felt pity and understanding for the cause. For other parts of society the November Uprising presented a true realpolitik dilemma because Poland was France's natural ally. Eventual liberation of the Russian-dominated Kingdom of Poland would spark aspirations for national unity, and Prussia would find itself not only losing parts vital for its economy and security but also, in the case of a future European war, forced to fight on two fronts. Carl developed this argument in his essay "The Condition of Europe since the Polish Partitions," most likely written while he was still in Berlin in early 1831 and circulated among friends. As Peter Paret and Daniel Moran point out, despite his fears Clausewitz did not advocate for Prussian intervention against the Polish rebels, and even less so for one against France. Rather, he openly and comprehensively articulated the opposition to deciding "for" or "against" public support for the Polish cause solely based on "moral grounds." In these tumultuous times, he advocated foremost for a prudent foreign policy based on Prussia's national interests.[27]

While Carl preferred to express his opinions on paper, Marie passionately debated them at Princess Louise's salon. Elise von Bernstorff held Marie solely responsible for "the discord that soon crept into the Radziwiłł's palace."[28] The remark was obviously an exaggeration because even without Marie's outspoken opposition, the Radziwiłł family found itself in an unbearable situation testing its loyalties and nerves. Their hearts, naturally, had sympathy for the Polish cause but in their dual existence as members of the Prussian royal family, related also to the Russian Tsar Nikolai by his marriage with Tsarina Alexandra (former Princess Charlotte), they had to avoid impressions of open support. Then, in early 1831 Prince Antoni's oldest son Wilhelm declared himself a Prussian patriot and as an army officer went to support the Prussian rule over the Duchy of Posen. The situation grew even more nerve-wracking when one of the leaders of the uprising, Prince Adam Czartorysky, asked for the hand of Radziwiłł's daughter Wanda. Princess Louise fell physically sick because, as Elise reported, "Father and daughter want, and the mother fears this party."[29]

Without the context of Marie's letters, scholars have struggled to understand Clausewitz's position on the Polish question and some have even described it as evidence of boundless hatred for the Poles.[30] To be sure, the couple used disparaging words about the country and its people, but their correspondence also shows a strain of sympathy. Marie, whose family once was proud to be part of the Polish *szlachta*, did use the term "the worst-off village in Lower Lusatia," that is, the region between Prussia, Saxony, and Poland populated by Slavic people, as a euphemism of dysfunctionality and misery.[31] Similarly distasteful, when confronted with the poverty in northeastern Poland during his travel to Russia in 1812, Carl used some of the strongest language found in his papers: "The whole existence of the Poles is as though bound and held together by torn ropes and rugs." The shocking conditions led him, in a truly patronizing manner, to conclude that "the partitioning of Poland was an act of benefaction," which might actually "deliver this nation since hundreds of years persisting in such a state." Carl also added damning words about the Polish nobility: they were "vain egoists" fighting for independence so "this existence that the Poles had until now might remain permanent."[32] The negative view, while harsh, was not completely baseless. The missteps of the *szlachta*, its unprecedented privileges stifling the development of the cities and the middle class, and notorious abuse of the peasants were all widely criticized in the enlight-ened Europe. What Carl failed to understand were the Polish resentments against being used as pawns in the hands of mighty, and far from altruistic, neighbors.

It should come as no surprise that when the already-established negative views about the *szlachta* and its inability to master political leadership inter-twined with fears about a wider European crisis, Marie and Carl could hardly spare empathy for the Polish aspirations for independence. Especially Marie described the rebellion against the vast Russian Empire as not only senseless but also potentially dangerous if Paris were to get actively involved: "I cannot suppress the fear that the French could also undertake some type of diversion to the benefit of [the Poles] that in fact would not help them much but could be very harmful for us."[33] Believing that their circle did not fully grasp how dangerous the situation was, Marie pushed for publication of Carl's second written article on the subject, "Reduction of the Many Political Questions Occupying Germany to the Basic Question of Our Existence."[34] Carl had offered the manuscript to the German press, but once he had to leave Berlin, he entrusted his friend and Prussian Privy Counsel Friedrich Eichhorn with finding an outlet. Marie now wondered why Eichhorn had failed to con-vince influential newspapers to make it public. The text's arguments for hard-knock politics probably alienated liberal editors, and despite Marie's efforts to involve even the Russian ambassador, it was never published.[35]

While the intellectuals and courtiers still debated about the differ-ent facets of "the Polish question," in Berlin the government's prepara-tions for answering the challenges in the West and in the East were moving painstakingly slow. In February the Russian army, under the command of General Diebitsch, marched toward Warsaw but could not crush the rebels. Finally in March the Prussian troops under the command of Gneisenau, officially named the "Observation army," moved into the Duchy of Posen. The army's tasks were to hold off a possible crossing and resup-ply of Polish troops in the duchy. Gneisenau settled down in Posen in the company of Clausewitz, his son August, his old comrade from the Coblenz days, O'Etzel, and Marie's young cousin Wilhelm von Brühl as adjutant. Gneisenau also called his son-in-law Fritz von Brühl, but the latter was seriously ill.[36] Marie wished to join them too, yet this time Carl firmly refused. Despite Gneisenau's eagerness to again assume military command, Carl dreaded his old friend's failing health and wanted to devote his time exclusively to the latter's needs.[37] The Prussian officers had decided to stay away from the local salons swirling with political intrigues, Carl explained, but if a society lady of Madam von Clausewitz's caliber were in Posen, this self-imposed isolation would have been impossible—a point that even she had to reluctantly concede.[38]

Marie's absence pained Carl but her lengthy letters about daily life in Berlin, news about political developments, and outright gossips served as his most important source of entertainment. Otherwise, Carl wrote, he led a "monotonous life" and the war theater was mostly a "bottomless source of irritation."[39] In Berlin, Marie visited the atelier of Christian Daniel Rauch, who had just finished his proposal for a monument of Frederick the Great. Unsure of receiving a positive reaction from the king, the artist reached out for the support of Berlin's high-society ladies.[40] Today the "Alter Fritz" is one of the most famous landmarks of the German capital, although the design is slightly different than the one Marie saw.

On her own, Marie also looked around for a new position for Carl. The European political crisis spelled the need for reshuffling ideas and people and thus created new opportunities. The personnel changes at the foreign ministry gave Marie especially great hope and she started circulating Clausewitz's name—only to be shut down by her own husband.[41] At that point Carl still believed there would be a war with France, and declared that he did not wish "to end up as the only military man in the salons and hold lectures for the ladies about possible operations."[42] The episode suggests that Marie was less content with her husband's plans to end his career in line duty but hoped instead to see him in high politics.

In the spring of 1831, the unease about the events in the East was already spreading among Berlin's high society. Elise von Bernstorff, who traveled to the Rhineland closer to the French border, asked Carl for a warning if an all-out war was about to start.[43] Marie developed a contingency plan in case she and her mother were forced to face again hardship and uncertainty. For some time she even considered letting her well-paid maid Albertine go but then decided against it. In times of war the sharp-tongued servant would hardly find another job.[44]

Some, like the poet and saloniere Sophie von Schwerin, believed that a second prolonged eruption of all-out violence was upon Europe, and viewed it as "a great cataclysm of the civilized world." Marie sent a copy of the letter containing Schwerin's statement to Carl. He strongly disagreed. His response is intriguing, as it illuminates Marie's involvement in the writing of On War and Carl's application of his already-developed idea of two types of war (limited and unlimited) to the current crisis. Schwerin might have described world affairs in general in a way "really very beautiful," Carl wrote in his letter, but he did not believe that the time they were living in constituted an altogether "new era" because such an era had already begun with the French Revolution. He reminded Marie that he had debated the issue with her before: "There would surely be enough disarray and crisis, and you know that I am convinced that I would not live to see the end of it." In other words, a new era of unlimited warfare had started after the French Revolution, but even in this era not every clash unleashed all-out violence; some conflicts would remain limited. Europe was far from a stable and peaceful continent, and it would go through multiple crises, Carl argued, yet not all of them would be as cataclysmic as Sophie von Schwerin feared.[45]

Plagued by a series of mistakes and lack of resolve, Diebitsch's operation against the Polish rebels stalled. In February 1831 the Italian patriot and radical Ciro Menotti ignited an uprising in Modena with the declared goal of the unification of the Italian peninsula. The Duke of Modena, Francis IV, who had initially supported the rebellion (believing this would make him the king of Northern Italy), now turned against Menotti and sought the help of Austrian troops to quash the unrest. At least in the case of Belgium, the balance of power created by the Vienna Congress appeared to work as intended, in the form of an international conference in London. There, Leopold of Saxe-Coburg was chosen as the new monarch of the state, one acceptable to the Great Powers.

Nevertheless Carl saw potential for further trouble if Belgium also tried to claim the neighboring Grand Duchy of Luxembourg. Contested by both Prussia and the Netherlands, since 1815 the duchy had existed in an unusual legal situation. It was ruled by a personal union with King William I of the Netherlands while at the same time it was a member of the German Confederation. As a part of the compromise the Fortress of Luxembourg was occupied by Prussian troops, the outer line of defense in Berlin's security design against a possible French attack; to lose Luxembourg to Belgium would harm it significantly. Carl therefore asked Marie to research and write a report on the duchy's history and rulers and make a possible case for Belgium's claim. That he would even consider asking Marie to do such work highlights again the extraordinary nature of their partnership, something Carl himself acknowledged: "I ask: How many men could give a similar assignment to their wives?" When she sent Carl text from another author, he answered with disappointment that he would've preferred one compiled by Marie because it would have been "more thorough."[46]

For the most part, the Polish rebellion occupied their correspondence and thoughts throughout 1831. Despite the Clausewitz couple's convictions that the uprising was senseless and dangerous for Prussia and should be stopped, they still resented being outsiders in the reformers' circle. When in Berlin rumors spread that Carl had shouted anti-Polish statements in Posen, without even asking her husband about the truth, Marie vehemently denied the possibility that he would ever behave disrespectfully against anyone, no matter the cause. "That I, by the way, would never threaten Poles . . . with an expression of deep distrust or even offend their honor, belongs to my principles and philosophy," answered Carl.[47]

What made the couple's position particularly complex was the fact that they harbored few illusions about the Russian Empire. In shock, Marie reported to Carl in the summer of 1831 on seeing the Russian village Alexandrowka, the newest attraction in Potsdam, inhabited by members of a military choir given as "a present" by Tsar Alexander to Friedrich Wilhelm. "The thought that its inhabitants were <u>sent</u> to the king . . . makes it impossible for me to repress a shudder. . . . A situation that makes such presents possible is a horrible one." The harsh way the Russian troops treated the captured Polish rebels also deeply upset Marie: "I could almost accept the sentences to death although they go too far as well, but the forty floggings that every captured has to receive are truly outrageous and not much different, than the way Napoleon treated Schill's people. . . . It seems to me that such an ungracious behavior could only damage the Russian cause." Despite their realism when it came to Russia's brutality, Marie and Carl still supported the Empire. "I wish them a victory from all my heart," Marie wrote, even as she also wished that they would "show themselves worthy of it."[48]

The more tenuous and complex the situation in Europe turned during 1830–1831, the more anti-Revolutionary both Marie and Carl became. They belonged to the generation that fought against the French Revolution's most dangerous excesses, but had little to no real memory of the great hopes the Revolution had risen from. Then the tumultuous days and political violence of 1819 strengthen their reservations. Thus Marie and Carl observed every radical move or fiery oration with deep suspicion and fears of bloody chaos. "One thing remains true[,] that the conditions of all European states have been clouded by the fretful, barmy liberalism, and it is a great opportunity for France to fish in the murky waters," Carl bitterly commented.[49] Marie was likewise disheartened: "I admit that the thought of paying for better times again with all the atrocities of revolution is too abominable for me," she wrote to him a couple of weeks later.[50]

Despite the country's shortcomings and their own discontent, the couple still put all their trust in the Prussian state. Marie and Carl persisted in their patriotism to the point of dismissing or being outright hostile toward those who believed that a better government and society could be built outside of it. "The Germans are in this case more irritating than the Poles, because they imagine that in the thousand years *Reich* of New Poland everything would be truly democratic. Such betrayal of the Germans of their own peoples, what unfortunately is a real national defect, as we can see in [France's German-speaking province] Alsace and some other examples, appalls me more than all other wrongness," Carl wrote to Marie.[51] In this sentiment, they were far from alone—the historian Friedrich Christoph Dahlmann wrote in 1832 that Prussia had a historic mission, one it needed to embrace, by first reforming itself. A thinker along similar lines was the Würtemberger jurist and journalist Paul Pfizer, who caused a scandal when he published his book *Letters between Two Germans* in the spring of 1831. There he argued that the resolve and commitment Prussia had showed in defeating Napoleon gave it moral authority to become a protector and leader of all German territories. Just like the Clausewitz couple, these thinkers criticized sharply Prussia and its stalled reforms but still believed that it remained the best hope for the future of Germany.[52] The fiery dissidents of 1808–1809 were long gone, now replaced by true believers in the nonviolent means of evolution within the limits of state power.

If in the beginning the November Uprising only tested Marie's liberalism, the news in the summer of 1831 about cholera spreading throughout Central Europe with the advance of the Russian troops filled her with horror and an outright wish for the rebellion's suppression, at any cost. In June 1831, General Diebitsch died from the horrible illness. Carl denied Marie's pleas to come to Posen to care for him in case of need: "Here people think to send away their wives and children—and I should let you come in exactly this moment? Nursing by ladies is almost completely out of the questions in this brief illness, during which physicians and surgeons constantly attend one—and don't you believe that I am ten times more likely to fall victim to the disease when I am afraid of infecting you than when I have no need to worry for you?"[53]

In Berlin, Marie's mood swung between somberness and desperation. She wrote with deprecation about people's irrational fears, noting that the virulent scenes reminded her of those from the plague of 1630 described in Alessandro Manzoni's masterpiece *The Betrothed* (*I promessi sposi*).[54] Then again, Marie sent her husband and friends every wonder drug she could find promising to stop or heal cholera. Deeply worried, she contemplated writing a new last will and asked Carl, always too proud to discuss his wife's finances, for his opinion. In case of her early death, she wrote, he could use her money to buy a small estate, retire, and devote his time to his studies: "I beg you, do not take away from me this solace."[55]

The theory that germs caused illnesses was starting to gain more support and scientific attention during these years, but it would be two more decades before John Snow proved the link between cholera and contaminated water. The measures in 1831 thus mirrored the widespread lack of understanding as to what caused the disease. As the chief-of-staff of the army in the east, Clausewitz was tasked with organizing a sanitary cordon around the border and keeping Prussia safe. The personally invasive and widely unpopular measure blocked travel and trade, delayed mail, and forced people into involuntary twenty-day isolation periods. Sometimes soldiers even shot at peasants trying to cross the border. Carl insisted on these measures but did not fear the cholera, stating that "very seldom do people who live under good conditions become victims of this illness."[56] Marie believed that unhealthy humidity in a house bred sickness, and avoided it at any cost.[57] Hearing that unclean skin might impede the body's flushing out of bad fluids, she asked Jascha, who cared for and lived in close proximity with her beloved husband, to take more showers.[58]

On July 28, Carl informed Marie that his orderly Hensel had died. The servant, along with Gneisenau's groom Schulz and the horses, had not housed with his master but in Prince Radziwiłł's residence in Posen. As proprietor of the duchy, Radziwiłł had opened it for friends and people in need, some of them sick. Schulz first fell ill, probably infected Hensel, and soon after died too.[59] When despite the sanitary cordon, the cholera crossed into the old provinces of Prussia, Carl suggested to his wife and her mother that they leave Berlin and move into a small village in Silesia. Instead, Marie took Princess Louise's offer to move into the spacious Radziwiłł residence in Berlin, which could be easily quarantined from the outside world—evidence that despite the political differences, their friendship held strong.[60]

In the late summer of 1831 with the faltering Polish uprising and Belgium becoming an independent state—despite the Netherlands' refusal to recognize the fact and their last-ditch attempt to recover territory with a messy and unsuccessful military campaign in August—it appeared that the danger for another great European war was dying down. Yet for Marie every day that delayed the Polish defeat was too much to bear.[61]

On the morning of August 23, Carl sent a courier to his wife with the terrible news that Gneisenau had fallen ill. On the very same evening, he had to dispatch another one: "There is no hope anymore, dear Marie, and I probably will finish this letter with the news of his death."[62] Shortly before midnight Gneisenau died of cholera without regaining consciousness or saying goodbye to the gathered friends and family. Carl arranged his funeral, wrote an official report to the king, and prepared an obituary for the Posen newspaper.

After the initial shock and grief, Marie once again assumed an industrious role in the circle of the remaining reformers in Berlin. In informal meetings they discussed how to secure Gneisenau's legacy and move the king and the crown prince to pay generous pension to the family. There Marie presented her own views and ideas together with those of Carl. He was not only far away from the capital but also found himself, in the beginning of September, in involuntary isolation along with his staff in a country house outside of Posen.[63] "I am constantly disturbed by visits," Marie complained to Carl, just as he lamented his quarantine.[64]

After Gneisnau's death Carl had grown embittered and suspicious that Friedrich Wilhelm had not paid enough homage to his friend's death. His wife gently tried to dissuade him and reported on the king's open expression of feelings of loss and grief.[65] Friedrich Wilhelm might have often spurned the circle of moderate reformers and ignored their ideas because his nature was deeply conservative and indecisive. But in moments of great need, he had also found the courage to follow their advice and never completely divorced himself from the progressive faction. The king indeed felt great personal sympathy toward Gneisenau and, contrary to Carl's suspicions, later helped the field marshal's family by buying the estate Erdmannsdorf for a generous sum and thus allowed the heirs to cover their debts. In September Marie also had a long talk with the man who had sent her husband and his staff to the countryside—General Ludwig Gustav von Thile, the head of the interior ministry's special commission for cholera prevention. She tried to convince Carl that while harsh, Thile's order had good intentions and that Thile expressed deep sorrow for the inconveniences.[66]

Carl had hoped too that since the hostilities in Poland were winding down, he would be appointed to Gneisenau's position for the end of the operation. When he was finally released from his quarantine, however, another disappointment followed when General Karl Friedrich von dem Knesebeck, a renowned conservative, was appointed as the commander of the Army of Observation. Ever the skillful networker, Marie had managed to befriend Knesebeck's governess, who reported to her daily prior to his appointment and departure to the headquarters.[67] The reactionary faction's suspicion against Carl apparently concerned mostly his political views, not his expertise in military affairs—as both Knesebeck and his wife, another skilled operative behind the curtains, went to great lengths to befriend Marie and assure the chief-of-staff's support for his new commander.[68]

In early October 1831, the remaining Polish rebels crossed the Prussian border and surrendered. With the "last act of this great drama," in Marie's words, the uprising was over.[69] She sprang into action, starting to prepare to resume their life back in Breslau, paying outstanding bills, and hiring new servants.[70] Sophie von Brühl's health worried Marie, but she had come to believe her mother's repeated illnesses to be the product of anxiety rather than a real physical suffering.[71] Cholera had reached Berlin in September. Nonetheless the initially low number of sick and dying in the capital created the impression that the epidemic could be managed, and Marie didn't fear that her mother would contract the disease. So, once the headquarters were disbanded, and Carl had traveled back to Breslau, Marie followed him there on November 9, in a "jubilant" mood.[72]

"I was prepared to find him different because he wrote me about it many times," Marie stated in a letter to Elise von Bernstorff. Instead, she found that Carl was "truly rejuvenated and celestial, had become stronger, looked perfectly healthy." For Marie's arrival, he and the servants decorated the house with flowers and made a small arch. "Under these wreaths he embraced me; it was the most happiest reunion despite all preceding sadness," Marie continued her letter. It was only after this, when they remained alone, that Marie realized that in reality Carl was "horribly distressed and irritated" because of what had happened in the last few months. Nevertheless they spent "eight altogether very happy days" full of visits, business, and a few private moments.

On November 16, Carl felt under the weather but spent most of the day, as in previous times, writing in Marie's room. With Carl still feeling sick that evening she sent for the doctor, but mostly for precaution. Fritz von Brühl also came to their house. "Only around one o'clock in the morning certain symptoms of cholera revealed themselves, muscular cramps, vomiting and so on," Marie related afterward. She recalled them as a "few horrible hours but around four o'clock everything appeared going away; he was lying covered in sweat, had again his natural facial color and a very peaceful unchanging expression." Soon after, Carl suffered a second round of pain, even more severe than the first. By early morning, he had died.

"At nine o'clock he expired!" Marie described to Elise in agony. "The last moments were very peaceful compared to what went before, and made me quiet and hopeful that his suffering was not so horrible as it appeared to us standing around him." Carl was just fifty-one years old, had survived the terrible cholera epidemic in Posen, and was ready to embark upon a new position and finally complete his treatise *On War*. None expected this swift and surprising death, least of all Carl himself. It was a terrible blow to Marie, who had hardly been prepared for such a turn of events. She was now left behind, desperate, grieving, and overwhelmed by one task she had always tried to dismiss and turn down: making his writings posthumously public.

11

The Emergence of *On War*
(December 1831–January 1836)

The shock of Carl's sudden and painful death had barely passed when Marie began devoting all of her energy to securing and shaping his legacy. The unforeseen circumstances of her beloved husband's death forced upon her decisions she was not prepared for, and these choices would cast a long shadow over Clausewitz's biography, bibliography, and scholarship. In the centuries to come, the scarce knowledge about Marie's role and motivation would exacerbate the misunderstandings. In some cases, it would lead to outright mistakes in interpretations of his life and work.

Carl's funeral on November 18, 1831 was a sad and lonely affair. Due to the strict regulations put in place by the Prussian government to fight cholera, his body had to be buried in the night and no one was permitted to attend. "I did not dare to wish an exception, which would have surely made a malicious impression upon the public," Marie described the events in a letter to her friend Countess von Dernath, Elise von Bernstorff's mother. The only consolation, granted to the family thanks to new and relatively relaxed measures, was that they were able to bury the body at the military cemetery in Breslau rather than at grounds isolated for cholera victims. Still, Fritz von Brühl bribed the guards and was present at the funeral. Fritz placed a laurel wreath on Carl's chest. "On Sunday at noon there was a religious ceremony at the grave attended by the whole garrison. . . . I relish very much [that fact that] I could have been present at this service if it had been possible for me not to faint in front of everybody," Marie added.[1]

Despite the bottomless sorrow—or perhaps as a means of coping with it—the fifty-two-year-old Marie almost immediately committed her attention to Carl's legacy. While marked by an intimate tone, her prolific correspondence about Clausewitz's death had unmistakably been written

Hier ruht
in Gott
Carl Philipp Gottfried v. Clausewitz
(Königl. General-Major u. Inspecteur der Artillerie)
geb. d. 1. Juni
1780
gest. d. 16. Nov.
1831

Figure 11.1. The grave of Marie and Carl von Clausewitz in Burg bei Magdeburg. *Photo Vanya Eftimova Bellinger.*

with a broader society in mind as addressee. In the same letter to Countess von Dernath, devoted to Carl's funeral, Marie put a note about which parts should be not publicly shared (in this case, the mention of Fritz's bribe to attend the burial). Similarly, the letter to Elise von Bernstorff right after Clausewitz's death, quoted in the previous chapter, clearly bears the sign of sophisticated structure aimed at molding her husband's public image for posterity. Particularly because of the stature and influence of Countess von Bernstorff's salon in Berlin court and society, Marie hurried to present a narrative that could reverberate in the public memory. Indeed until this day, biographies and interpretations of the military theorist continue to echo the account, while mostly failing to recognize its context and intent.

As in a classic tragedy, Marie's letter to Elise von Bernstorff opened with the joyful description of the reunion with her husband only to dramatically stun the audience with the horrific turn of events days later. In describing Carl's last moments, Marie masterfully aimed at shaming those whose suspicions and negative attitudes cost him promotions and recognition throughout the decades. "The doctors believed that the state of his nerves had contributed much more than the cholera for his death. . . . It is a great comfort for me that at least his last moments were peaceful and painless but still there was something heart-breaking in the manner, in the tone with which he exhaled his last breath; because it was as if he had shuddered life away as a heavy burden. . . . Ach, life indeed consisted for him of an almost ceaseless row of laborious experiences, suffering and offenses."[2] Then Marie turned her attention to the less knowing public and, by mixing facts of Clausewitz's biography with comment, molded a favorable impression against any anticipated attacks or critical opinions. "Admittedly, he had accomplished in general more than he had expected in the beginning; he felt this deeply and acknowledged it with a thankful heart. But he never achieved the highest, and by every joy he was granted, there was always a thorn that darkened his mood. He lived through such great, glorious days but was never so fortunate to experience himself a victorious battle. The night of June of 18th to 19th [after Waterloo] that the Field Marshal [Gneisenau] spent pursuing Napoleon and cared to call the greatest of his life, was for [Clausewitz] after the Battle of Wawre the most horrible. He enjoyed in extraordinary degree the friendship of the noblest men of his time but not the recognition that would have offered opportunities to be truly useful for his home country."[3]

What Marie could not foresee is how these lines would turn into a noto-riously cartoonish image plaguing the perception of the military theorist's personality and lifework until this day. As Peter Paret observes, the letter to Elise von Bernstorff almost singlehandedly shaped the notion of Clausewitz as a depressed scholar, angry at the world that never recognized him.[4] In the text, Marie mixed in her own disappointment that Carl had not achieved the higher political post that she dearly desired but, as their correspondence in 1831 has revealed, he was less eager to assume this position. Marie, too, had seen his theoretical work not as a parallel intellectual endeavor but as a stepping-stone toward greater influence and an illustrious career. As she wrote in 1831, his country needed him for both *Rat und Tat* ("words and deeds").[5] Marie had also suggested, or maybe even gently pushed for, making *On War* public in his lifetime.[6] In his own correspondence, Carl remained rather realistic about his place in history and, more importantly, somber about the limits of political influence. Robbed of the opportunity one day to see her beloved husband in the midst of European affairs, Marie was the one truly depressed.

Yet just days after the initial shock, she embraced and started prolifer-ating a less emotionally heightened image of her husband than the one first presented in the letter to Elise von Bernstorff. The official obitu-ary in Berlin's *Staatszeitung* on November 22, anonymously published but in all probability written by their close friend Gröben, presented a long account of Clausewitz's achievements as the soldier's soldier fight-ing since boyhood and then participating "in that colossal battle at the gates of Moscow [Borodino]"; as a talented staff officer "at the side of greatest commanders"; and as an influential instructor in military theory for young officers. Marie must have been intimately involved in the cre-ation of this text not only because of her close relationship with Gröben but also because the last passage hinted toward the manuscript of *On War* and her intentions to publish it soon. "His understanding of the art of war merged deepest research and experiences. It was determined by higher purpose in the broadest sense, brilliant and therefore simple as well as practical. His remaining works will show this also to those who did not know [Clausewitz] personally. His noble, dolorous widow, may God console her, will not hold them back from the world."[7] This line of presentation—bringing forward his achievements and then emphasizing the groundbreaking character of his general theory on war—would be Marie's way of dealing with the challenges ahead.

In her own appendix to Clausewitz's essay on Scharnhorst a few months later, Marie even clarified the remarks about her husband's depression. As she wrote, the "great pain" of Gneisenau's death "profoundly shocked" Carl's nerves and, according to the medical knowledge of the day, weakened his body and made it susceptible to cholera. Marie even went so far as to communicate the hopes for Carl's career she had harbored in 1830–1831, and then saw crushed by his untimely death. The outpouring of public emotions after Gneisenau's death, Marie believed, would boost her husband's stature and advancement. Hence she wrote, for Clausewitz to die in such a moment, when he had a chance to make a greater mark on the Fatherland, "could only be called a bitter fate."[8]

Yet the cartoonish image of the Prussian scholar, "an "unpromoted" and "unhonoured" but self-seeking brown-noser (and simultaneously a traitorous dog who willfully disobeyed his rightful monarch), whose career was "blighted by his own extremism," in Christopher Bassford's colorful description, has been too useful for Clausewitz's detractors to ever surrender it. And the fact that Marie's writings and role have remained understudied only fed this, to use again Bassford's words, "grand tradition of trashing" Clausewitz in the nearly two centuries following his death.[9]

Just as the obituary indicated, almost immediately after Carl's death Marie started working on the manuscript of *On War*. In the last weeks of 1831 in the company of her brother Fritz von Brühl, she opened the papers left with her for safekeeping and started sifting through them. Despite the fact that for a mostly unfinished work the process of editing is usually considered crucial, in the case of *On War* it has remained, for the most part, an understudied subject. The main reason for this is that many of the original documents had been lost, but it is also undeniable that the editing process has been overlooked because the questions it raises are extremely difficult to answer.

When scholars have turned to Marie's role as editor, it has mostly been to criticize the choices she made. In 1935, Herbert Rosinski argued that Marie's failure to highlight the revisions Clausewitz made to his manuscript after 1827 complicated later understanding of the work.[10] In more recent decades, Azar Gat has suggested that Marie might have been mistaken in declaring the second undated note published in the preface of *On War* as being written after the one from July 10, 1827—thereby making it Clausewitz's final statement about the progress of his work. Since the second undated note assesses the draft much more harshly ("nothing but a collection of materials from which a theory of war was to have been distilled"),[11] this created, according to Gat, wrong impressions that the manuscript was left in a much more incomplete state than it was in reality. However, if the 1827 note was indeed the last report about *On War*'s progress, Gat argues, it would mean that by that time Clausewitz had more or less finished Books VII and VIII, revised Book I, and had left only incorporation of his idea about the two types of war—limited and unlimited—in the remaining parts. Hence by 1830, he probably fulfilled most of his plans and his seminal work was very close to completion.[12] After all, Marie herself had reinforced such a notion by writing in the "Preface" that Carl had hoped to complete the treatise "in the course of the winter" of 1831.[13]

The role of editor of her husband's posthumous works was not one Marie had ever envisioned for herself, but she strived to fulfill it in the best possible manner. By studying in depth the process and the motivations behind her decisions, one can gain valuable insight, if not quite exhaust all of the questions about *On War*'s state of completion. For her husband's posthumous works Marie turned to the publisher and bookseller Ferdinand Dümmler, another veteran of the Wars of Liberation. It remains unclear how it was decided which of Clausewitz's other studies would be printed next to his seminal treatise. The plan agreed upon with Dümmler envisioned the publishing of *Posthumous Works* in ten parts—*On War* would comprise the first three while the rest would be made up of other texts and studies. The inaugural part consisted of Books I through IV and Clausewitz's notes explaining the process of the creation of *On War*; the Second Part contained Books V and VI; and the Third Part consisted of Books VII and VIII. The remaining seven parts were made up of studies of various campaigns during the Napoleonic Wars, other military studies, and historical essays.

Despite relying on her brother Fritz in the beginning, and later involving in the process two close friends, Franz August O'Etzel and Carl von Gröben, Marie kept, as we shall see, tight control over the manuscript of *On War*. Fritz von Brühl helped her sort out the drafts of the first six books of the treatise, and O'Etzel drew the maps and proofread the whole manuscript afterward, but Marie ultimately presided over and carried out the editing process. Only when it came to the additional campaign studies did she transfer original papers and leave it to her friends, in this case O'Etzel and Gröben, to prepare the texts for publishing.

For her work as editor, as stated in the "Preface" in Part One from 1832, she formulated a simple principle: all manuscripts should be published as they were found, "without one word being added or deleted."[14] At first sight, the principle of minimal intervention might appear easy to employ or even inconsequential, but it actually led to profound outcomes. Despite her belief that the treatise was close to completion, Carl's unique working style forced Marie to face unexpected challenges. In the "Preface," she explained that he had "arranged his papers, sealed and labeled the individual packages."[15] This account would suggest that Carl had separated and put the different texts into envelopes, probably together with each text's notes, research, and envisioned corrections. In all likelihood the manuscript of *On War*, with all the variations and revisions from fifteen years of writing, comprised its own sizable bundle.

But despite the appearance of organization, Marie still complained that the "publication called for a good deal of work, arranging of material, and consultation." The revisions for Book I were discovered "in the course of careful checking and sorting the material," and then had to be inserted into "those places . . . for which they were intended."[16] Marie's account in the "Preface" would therefore suggest that Clausewitz had not rewritten the first six books in a clear copy but rather left instructions, revisions, and long amendments to be incorporated later; Books VII and VIII remained in their raw state. Hence the small team of proofreaders Marie gathered had to carefully sift through the papers, compare notes, and add to the text the intended revisions. In this regard, the modern criticism that she had failed to highlight the corrections after 1827, and thus impeded the understanding about how Clausewitz's thought process evolved, is understandable but rather insubstantial. Although Carl failed to add the revisions himself, Marie's duty was to present his work to the world just as he had envisioned it. Even while encountering and confronting controversies in her own lifetime, Marie could never have imagined the far-reaching popularity and influence of *On War* and all its conflicting interpretations yet to come.

Keeping the interventions minimal was not entirely clear-cut or easy to do in every circumstance, since the manuscripts included outdated information, inconsistencies, and arguments disavowing the prevailing attitudes of the day. After Marie's death her brother Fritz von Brühl, for instance, would be less resistant to the temptation to reedit *On War* and bring the text more in accordance with the military's growing emancipation from political leadership. As Werner Hahlweg has discovered, in the second edition of 1853 Brühl introduced several hundred changes, far beyond fixing grammatical and print errors or modernization of the language. He also altered

·the meaning of whole paragraphs, the most momentous and far-reaching being the reversal of the relationship between policy and the military. Where in Book VIII, Chapter VI B, Clausewitz emphasized that the political leadership, "the cabinet," should be involved in the major aspects of conduct of war, the revised text suggested the complete opposite: the military commander should be part of the cabinet, "so he could participate in the most important moments in its deliberations and decisions." The "Brühl's version," as Hahlweg calls the 1853 edition, therefore enhanced the military commander's authority and comfortably fit the general staff's desire for greater independence in the realm of the military while gaining influence over political decision-making. The revised text, rather than the original, would remain the standard until after World War II.[17]

Even in her own time, Marie's decision to leave the text exactly as it had been found was not free of controversy or easy to defend. As early as 1833, while reviewing the publication of *Posthumous Works*, the Austrian scholar Johann Baptist Schels criticized inaccuracies in the history of the Campaign of 1796.[18] As the editor of her husband's literary estate, Marie responded to this criticism in the "Preface for the Seventh Volume" from December 1834 by pointing out that Clausewitz never had the opportunity to revise his text before it appeared on paper. Yet she still defended the commitment to publish the draft in its original form by stating that, "To engage in significant editing was impossible without harming the peculiarity of the work."[19]

Facing just the beginning of the controversies in 1834, Marie indeed encouraged critical examination of the text, but she emphasized that such endeavors should not aim at a plain rejection but should search through vigorous debate to "convey the truth . . . that was the author's goal above all."[20] More intuitive than calculated, she therefore formulated and imposed her own interpretation upon *On War*. Just like the man she loved and supported for three decades, she embraced and upheld the descriptive character of his theory. But in doing so Marie actually went one step further than Carl. He argued that the treatise should help understand war but not prescribe how to win one. Still, Clausewitz had had in mind finishing his treatise and presenting to the public a complete text. Now Marie suggested that particularly the unfinished character of the work, with all its deficiencies and conflicting ideas, should provoke debate through which an understanding of the complex phenomenon of war would emerge.

Contrary to modern interpretations, which question Clausewitz's harsh assessment of the state of his own work, in the undated note, Marie herself accepted the criticism, or at least did not assess it as illogical in comparison to Clausewitz's relatively satisfactory tone in the earlier note from July 10, 1827. It should be reiterated that she herself never put an exact year on the undated note but added a remark that it appeared to have been written "in a very recent date." Only later scholars assigned the year 1830 to the note.[21] In her "Preface" for the publication of the Third Part of Carl's remaining works in 1834, Marie went to great lengths to explain that Books VII and VIII were "fleeting drafts and preliminary works," but "also in this incomplete state they [are] of interest, because at least they reveal the way the author was intending to take."[22] In light of what the newly found correspondence has revealed about the couple's intellectual interaction, however, Marie's remark should be read less as a statement about the actual qualities or state of completion of Books VII and VIII but rather as an expression of her own disappointment about what they could have been. As in case of the essay about Scharnhorst, the written pages could not compare to and did not include all of the ideas and arguments she once heard from or discussed with her husband.

While these circumstances do not put to rest all of the debates about the state of progress in which Clausewitz left *On War*, unraveling them clarifies Marie's tenets on the editing process. The only way to establish with certainty the evolution of Clausewitz's thought would be to study it throughout the original drafts. The surfacing of Marie and Carl's intimate correspondence in 2012, also thought to be long-lost, gives hope that *On War*'s manuscripts had not been destroyed and lost for posterity, but just forgotten and stored away in archives and private collections.

By the summer of 1832, the owner of the publishing house in Berlin, Ferdinand Dümmler, had already put out an announcement to interest potential readers in subscribing to the work about to be printed in installments.[23] In just a couple of months, Marie with the support of her brother Fritz had managed to transcribe and sort out the drafts and insert changes Carl initially intended for Books I through VI of *On War*, despite the excruciating personal pain and changing circumstances of her existence. Then she had to take a break, pack all her belongings, and leave Breslau to embark on a new life and duties back in Berlin. In early 1832, Marie assumed the position as *Oberhofmeisterin* or chief lady-in-waiting to Princess Augusta, the king's daughter-in-law. The new post guaranteed her financial security, enormous social visibility, and tasks she enjoyed but also put great strain on her time and energy. In the modern scholarship on Clausewitz, his widow's appointment at the court has received little attention and very often has even mistakenly been described as serving under her good friend Princess Marianne. In reality, Marie became *Oberhofmeisterin* of the future Empress Augusta, the wife of the younger Prince Wilhelm, Friedrich Wilhelm's son who would become later the first German Emperor Wilhelm I. The confusion has its roots in the fact that both Princess Marianne and Princess Augusta were named in public, after their husbands, "Princess Wilhelm." In the "Preface" of *On War* Marie actually drew attention to her position by describing the "new and valued task" of caring for and educating the little Prince Friedrich Wilhelm, Augusta's son and later Emperor Friedrich III.[24]

This statement not only mirrored Marie's pride in assuming the prestigious job but also had a deterring function against possible critics of what could be perceived in the Restoration era as her "unwomanly" role as editor and publisher of a treatise on military and political matters. In the very first sentence of the "Preface," Marie indeed acknowledged and addressed head-on the reactionary attitudes of "readers" who would be "rightly surprised that a woman should dare to write a preface for such a work as this."[25] Next to explaining the circumstances of her marriage, she also added her new career path. If subtle from a modern point of view, for the contemporaries, even those living outside the Berlin court, her post as Augusta's *Oberhofmeisterin* and governess for the young prince would have signaled unmistakably that Madam von Clausewitz's persona, knowledge, and virtues were beyond reproach. Only a lady of extraordinary qualities and life achievements could have been allowed to serve Prussia's future queen and entrusted with the care and education of a boy that one day would rule the state. Stating her new position thus guaranteed her the benefit of the doubt in a public sphere increasingly inhospitable to outspoken women.

An *Oberhofmeisterin* enjoyed her own independent rank at the court that was higher than all other ladies (ranked after the titles of either their husbands or fathers), and it put Marie right after the members of the princely family she served. Usually the widowed wife of a deserving public official, the chief lady-in-waiting was a companion and adviser to the royal princess, kept her social calendar in order, upheld the protocol, and presided over all other female courtiers.[26] In the 1830s, Princess Augusta was only the wife of the king's second son, but the complicated question of secession guaranteed her and her household's increasingly important role at the Prussian court. Since Crown Prince Friedrich Wilhelm and his wife Elisabeth Ludovika failed to produce an heir, his brother Wilhelm and then Wilhelm's son,

Figure 11.2. The Marmor Palace in Potsdam. Marie spent extended periods of time here as the chief lady-in-waiting for Princess Augusta and wrote the "Preface" for the first edition of *On War. Photo Vanya Eftimova Bellinger.*

born on October 18, 1831, were expected to follow on the throne. Trapped in a loveless marriage, Augusta took control over the life and education of little Prince Friedrich Wilhelm. While no details or accounts exist describing how and why the princess chose Marie as her *Oberhofmeisterin*, from the very beginning she was bestowed with the foremost duties of supervising nannies, tutors, and servants.[27] Without a doubt in such an important matter as the education of the future ruler, the king had also weighed and approved the appointment, a clear statement about Marie's standing at court and also probably, in Friedrich Wilhelm's usual belated manner, an acknowledgment of her husband's service to the country. With her duties of caring for the little heir of the mighty Hohenzollern dynasty, she now assumed one of the highest positions in the state open for women.

Augusta was a well-educated, energetic, and open-minded woman, interested in fine arts and most of all politics (during the tumultuous days of 1848, the liberal faction actually considered the possibility of installing her on the throne as her son's regent). Deeply unhappy in Berlin, wrote Caroline von Rochow, the princess developed "an urge to make a name for herself in the European world." Despite all her qualities, Rochow still noted that Augusta never grew really close to anyone in Prussia, an observation that probably included Rochow's old friend Marie von Clausewitz.[28] Between the new absorbing tasks, continuing to work on her husband's manuscript, and caring for the mentally deteriorating Sophie von Brühl, Marie saw less of her old friends. "Marie Clausewitz came as often as her duties allowed; on the March 24 [1834] she appeared with the future heir to the throne, the lovable three-year-old Friedrich Wilhelm," Elise von Bernstorff, in this period weakened and ill, wrote in her diary. "He then wished that Marie Clausewitz would play the piano for him, and then called at me: 'The other *Ralin* (he called the Madam General [*Generalin*] Clausewitz *Ralin*), should also play,' and did not want to understand why I didn't comply with his wishes."[29]

With her arrival at the court in the beginning of 1832, Marie already had with her clean copies of the first six books. Now without Fritz von Brühl at her side she had to "take care of everything else" in Berlin.[30] In her methodical way, Marie turned toward her two close family friends since the Coblenz period, O'Etzel and Gröben. The two military men's involvement must have contributed authority to the editing process, although neither O'Etzel nor Gröben questioned Marie's leadership and overarching supervision. "It had become my honorable task, given me by Madam von Clausewitz, to publish from the literary estate of her immortal husband some of his military works," Gröben stated in the opening sentence of Ninth Part, while in the Fifth Part of *Posthumous Works* O'Etzel vehemently denied being anything but a proofreader of Clausewitz's works.[31] Both men also painstakingly followed the policy set out by Marie to publish with minimal intervention. "The literary estate of the immortal and highly esteemed man ... is printed 'without one word being added or deleted,'" O'Etzel repeated in his note to the Fifth Part.[32]

Already realizing how much she was pushing the societal limits for women, Marie also delegated many of the more public tasks of publication to O'Etzel and Gröben. Yet when she could not rely on the two men, she did not shy away from directly asserting her role. In July 1832, O'Etzel's absence from Berlin prevented him from calling upon Ferdinand Dümmler concerning the print corrections for the first part. This prompted Marie to write to the owner of the publishing house herself. The letter discovered by

Hahlweg in the Dümmler archives discussed a rather minimal set of errors, but in this reveals how painstakingly she, at the last instance, read and reread the pages prepared for print. The printer (or maybe Dümmler himself) had slashed in her preface the adverb "profoundly" from the sentence, "From twenty-one years I was profoundly happy at the side of such man." Very politely but certainly firmly, Marie insisted that her text, "written with sincere feeling," would be published in full.[33]

In the months prior to the release of the first installments of *On War*, Marie also prepared Carl's essay on Scharnhorst for publication. For this, she chose the most ambitious venue of the day—Leopold von Ranke's first edition of his *Historisch-Politische Zeitschrift*. Ranke is known today as the father of modern source-based history, and his legendary journal sought to popularize his ideas of writing history as it happened, with the greatest possible objectivity, and in a highly literary language. Marie, an avid reader of Ranke's previous works, had met the historian in person the previous year at the house of her friend Luise von Voß. Right after the encounter she reported to Carl that Ranke was, quite contrary to his serious public image, "a short, chubby, jolly man" and she found talking to him a real pleasure.[34] In the published version of "On the Life and Character of Scharnhorst," the historian removed those parts too critical to institutions and prominent persons, and polished the language.[35] In this case, Marie had clearly lost editorial control over her husband's work, but still strived to keep that of the overall narrative. While Ranke did not name Madam von Clausewitz as the author, he nevertheless published as an annex her short essay about Clausewitz's own life and ideas.[36]

In the fall of 1832, the first part of *On War*, consisting of the first four books and Clausewitz's notes explaining his thinking and writing process, became public in only 1,500 copies. In the beginning of 1833, the Second Part (Books V and VI) came out as well, but because the Dümmler Publishing House relied mostly on readers who had already subscribed for all the series, it could break the logical order, and did so following the Second Part. The unfinished Books VII and VIII (Third Part) demanded more time for transcribing and sorting, so Dummler next published the already completed "Campaign of 1796" (Fourth Part) and "Campaigns of 1799 in Italy and Switzerland I" (Sixth Part) instead. Since O'Etzel supervised the publication process of the Fourth, Fifth, and Sixth Parts (the latter being "Campaigns in Italy and Switzerland II"), Marie used the time to prepare the two last books of *On War*.[37] In December 1833, she finally submitted the clean copies to Dümmler after O'Etzel proofread them as well.[38]

From the beginning Marie envisioned *On War* as a text to be read and debated well beyond the professional military audience. Already with the publication of *Scharnhorst* and her own essay about Clausewitz in Ranke's *Historisch-Politische Zeitschrift* she had aimed at drawing the curiosity of wider circles to Carl's work and ideas. Once the first edition of *On War* was out, Marie sent copies to members of the royal family, as her letter to Prince Wilhelm, the husband of her old friend Princess Marianne, attests.[39] The poet and saloniere Sophie von Schwerin received one and praised Clausewitz's clear language and ideas illuminating the complexities of war and politics.[40]

In 1835, when writing the preface for the Seventh Part, Marie finally dropped most of the pretense and openly discussed her role and the challenges she encountered as the editor of her husband's lifework. What had changed between the publication of the First Part and now was the fact that the public and especially the professional military audience had positively received *On War* and Clausewitz's historical writings and none had questioned his widow's role. Indeed some readers glanced over her editing and assumed that either O'Etzel or Fritz von Brühl had done the heavy lifting, which, while legitimizing the work done, left the two assisting men in a rather awkward position. In the Fifth Part O'Etzel addressed and tried to put "this misapprehension" to rest.[41] The presumed greater involvement of Fritz von Brühl led to controversies in Austria where military writers had already criticized the representation of the campaigns in 1796 and 1799. That an officer, for so long serving in Austrian uniform, would neglect to acknowledge the less controversial view of Archduke Carl's leadership skills appeared borderline scandalous. Marie therefore had to publicly address the issue and absolve her brother from any responsibilities for editing of any other parts but the first six books of *On War*.[42]

The Seventh Part also contained Clausewitz's essays on the campaigns in Russia (1812) and the anti-Napoleonic operations in 1813 and 1814. Hence, suspecting more controversies and criticism about the way the texts were put together, Marie addressed head-on the problems she had faced publishing unfinished texts. For the Russian campaign, for instance, she found three sections where the first and the third appeared as if intended for another work, while the second part sandwiched between them actually broke the narrative's logic. "However they were left in the order now shared with the reader and one did not feel justified in making any alterations," Marie wrote.[43] The Russian campaign constitutes an interesting case because, despite all her previous declarations about minimal intervention, she indeed edited it.[44] Some of introduced changes were simple fixes of numerical inaccuracies or typographical errors. Marie also omitted the most controversial and harsh remarks about the abilities and the actions of Friedrich Wilhelm, Tsar Alexander, and various Russian officers or fellow Prussians serving in the Russian army in 1812. Perhaps Marie believed that with the years Carl's opinion had changed (the text was originally written in 1823-25) but, again, he had failed to revise the manuscript. After the controversies the essay about 1796 Campaign created, in all probability Marie had also grown more cautious. In the published version, Carl's comments about Frederick Wilhelm's actions on the eve of the Napoleon's invasion and Tsar Alexander's unpreparedness for it were still in the text but the negative tone was significantly muffled.

The relentless pace of editing and publishing Carl's writings that Marie adopted came from a certain feeling of urgency. Already the cholera epidemic had made her realize her own mortality, and her husband's surprising death surely had exacerbated these thoughts. The period of the 1830s also appeared to be raising more questions about the future than giving possible answers. The liberal revolutions and violent uprisings, while confirming reactionary prejudices, brought fewer real changes to Europe. In the case of Poland, the movement actually caused a retreat of progress when Russia assumed an even more repressive regime in its territories, and the Polish elite either left for France or were sent to Siberia. The more liberal course in the Prussian-ruled Duchy of Posen was likewise abandoned and replaced by Germanizing policy.[45] With the reactionary faction in various German kingdoms and principalities emboldened, the Austrian foreign minister Metternich suggested once again relinquishing all constitutions. These most reactionary plans were forestalled, but the so-called Six Articles from 1832 subjugated the local Diets and laws in all member-states to those passed by the German Confederation. This meant that any attempts for more liberal policies or popular democracy in the various states had no chance to flourish or spread from country to country. Any progressive tendencies were to be suffocated by the reactionary climate ruling the Confederation.

The deaths of many prominent personalities also increased public anxiety. In the first half of the 1830s, the individuals who had shaped German political, military, and intellectual life throughout the past three decades suddenly and abruptly succumbed one after another: the poet Arnim, Baron vom Stein, Gneisenau, the salonier Rahel Levin Varnhagen, the philosopher G.W.F.Hegel, Prince Antoni Radziwiłł, the foreign minister Bernstorff. "And so it seems almost as if for all that is ahead of us, the providence does not want to use any component of the past, but leaves everything new, yet to mature, hands," bemoaned Caroline von Rochow right after Carl's death.[46] In this changing political and cultural environment Marie must have felt increasingly lonely and isolated. In 1835 after her own husband's death, Elise von Bernstorff left Berlin forever and sought a quieter and healthier refuge for her sickly daughter Marie. The other salon where Madam von Clausewitz had been a fixed presence for most of her adult life, that of the Radziwiłłs', closed its doors after the sudden death of Prince Antoni in 1833. The residence became a sad place where the gravely ill and immobilized Princess Louise was slipping away and her daughter Elise suffered incurably from tuberculosis.[47]

Under the pressure of her position at the court and the self-imposed urgency to publish her husband's works, Marie lived a hectic and irregular life. Throughout her life she had enjoyed robust health, but from at least the beginning of 1835 she started to complain of tightness in her chest, restlessness, and ringing ears.[48] By the summer of that year, when Marie accompanied Princess Augusta to Silesia for the yearly maneuvers of the Prussian army, it became obvious that the *Oberhofmeisterin* was not well. "You must have already noticed in Breslau that Marie was not in her usual state," Marie's cousin Carl von Brühl wrote to her sister-in-law Hedwig von Brühl. "When she came back to Berlin, it became worse. She complained about tightness [in the chest] and inconsistency. She could not find peace anywhere, often wandered in her room for a half hour and blamed herself for everything, above all about money matters. . . . She wrote long letters and essays; she let her friends know that she would be visiting them in the evening but then did not come without sending a word that she wouldn't make it, shortly the inconsistency soared to the highest level."[49]

Marie's physical and mental state seemed worrisome enough for her to seek a doctor's advice in December. Dr. Bremer, Prussia's premier high-society doctor, ordered onetime bloodletting and sodium sulfate capsules. When Marie continued to complain, her cousin Carl, an enthusiastic proponent of homeopathy, suggested an eight-day-long cure with strict diet and herbal medicine. Keeping her busy schedule as usual, she did not follow the prescribed treatment: "The mental state became more restless and more worrisome but I could not notice it because Marie went out a lot with her princess."[50] Soon after, Marie also suffered a psychological break-down after an intense fight with Sophie von Brühl.

Marie's powerful friends now became involved, and under pressure from Mademoiselle von Bischoffwerder the Crown Prince Friedrich Wilhelm's closest personal adviser, the royal physician, Dr. Rust, was called for con-sultations. With so much attention, Dr. Bremer probably felt the need to step up the treatment and ordered more bloodletting combined with both a laxative and nauseant. The prevailing medical doctrine of the day believed that bad body fluids made a patient sick, and therefore aimed at getting rid of them. In a state of severe physical weakness, Marie stopped sounding lucid. When the doctors decided to send her to a mental asylum, however, Carl von Brühl together with the royal family vocally opposed the plan.

Observing Marie's deterioration, Carl von Brühl correctly concluded that the heavy treatment was making her sicker. For the third bloodlet-ting in a row performed without the help of any anesthetics, she had to be held down by her servants, and when the opening of one blood vessel was unsuccessful, the surgeon tried a second. From this procedure Marie lost "four coffee cups" of blood, and to bring her back to a state of alert-ness, Bremer ordered another harsh measure—cold showers first once and then twice per day. When Luise Hensel, hired to nurse her, saw Marie again on January 21, she found her "mentally and physically very changed, for the worse."[51] To save Marie's dignity and reputation, her friends had already quartered her outside the royal palace, but Carl von Brühl decided to move her even further to the quieter and less exposed environment of Dresden. There, too, he could leave her under the supervision of the homeopathic doctor Paul Wolf. Carl still insisted on permission from Fritz von Brühl—who was himself gravely ill in Breslau and unable to take care of his sister—as the closest and most senior relative because the alternative treatment he wished to employ was seen as new and risky.[52]

Homeopathy, a system of alternative medicine, was the brainchild of the Saxon doctor Samuel Hahnemann. Hahnemann and his followers argued that the traditional approaches, especially bloodletting, did more harm than good to patients. Looking for an alternative, the new medical doctrine suggested that some drugs, which produced symptoms resem-bling those of a specific illness, would cure a person if used in small doses. From a modern perspective, this homeopathic medicine often delivered rather minuscule results or had no effect whatsoever but at least it spared its patients the horrendous pain and harm of bloodletting. In the case of

Marie, the opening of her arteries for bloodletting most likely caused her death. On the way to Dresden her nurse, Luise Hensel, noticed that Marie's right arm had become infected in the area where the surgeon had cut twice, and the wounds were now swollen and full of pus. These were clear signs of developing sepsis. Hensel's description of Marie's eyes as "yellow" also suggests that she may have contracted hepatitis from the bloodletting instruments.[53]

Employed after Luise von Voß's enthusiastic recommendation, Hensel could hardly be described as a medical expert or professional nurse, simply because in the early nineteenth century neither the term nor the line of work officially existed. By the time Carl von Brühl hired her to accompany and care for Marie in Dresden, she had gathered significant experience and informal medical knowledge.[54] Touched deeply by the suffering she observed, Luise Hensel wrote a posthumous report about Marie's last days for the Brühl family.

In Berlin, Dr. Bremer had not believed Madam von Clausewitz to be gravely ill, and even Hensel had questioned whether her mental state was so hopeless. The nurse actually attributed Marie's mood swings and vehement reactions to bitterness and fears that she had inherited her mother's mental illness, which would thrust upon her a sad and lonely life. When, however, Dr. Wolf saw Marie on January 23 after a prolonged and uncomfortable journey to Dresden, he informed Carl von Brühl that she was very close to death.[55] Without knowledge about germs and lacking antibiotics, the doctor could barely do anything for Marie except diagnose her with damaged nerves and stop the treatments Dr. Bremer had prescribed.

Away from heavy treatment, Marie regained her mental capacities and confessed to Hensel feeling embarrassed about her mood swings. She also shared her fears about looming poverty in old age without her position at the court, and swore her nurse not to leave her at the hands of men in an asylum. "All her expressions were full of love and all her being shined utmost graciousness," wrote Luise Hensel. But after moments of clarity and hope, the physical pain made Marie delirious: "She spoke often about herself in the third person: 'The poor, poor woman—how she has to suffer!' 'No, she won't bear it for too long!' "[56]

On January 28, 1836, Marie felt her life was coming to an end. "In the morning she said with fear: 'Ach! Only if I could pray—I would like to pray!' " the nurse wrote of her last hours. "Around 9 am came the cousin [Carl von Brühl] so much loved by her; when I announced him, a smile tried to come upon her lips. . . . Her struggle became more severe—around 11 o'clock at noon she passed away."[57]

Only fifty-six years old, Marie had lived to see most of her husband's work published and his name established among the leading lights of military theory. She had not, however, lived long enough to secure her own legacy nor to anchor her ideas firmly into the Clausewitz scholarship.

Postscript

The news about the sudden and painful death of Marie von Clausewitz, born Countess von Brühl, Princess Augusta's *Oberhofmeisterin* and responsible for the education of Prussia's heir to the throne, was a sensation in Berlin society. Her high-ranking position, the prominence of her family at the court, and Marie's own extensive network of powerful friends, together with the question if she had indeed been mentally ill, fueled the interest. "I left after the day of her funeral and arrived here, with sick body and soul and full of resentment, but I had to, as soon as possible, give an account to the princesses about their friend," Luise Hensel, wrote in a letter, "and even now I cannot come to peace with this sad story that interests all Berlin."[1] Carl von Brühl also informed the highest circles about his cousin's sad end: "The king uttered to me his condolence in a really earnest and affectionate way. But most of all, he keenly voiced his opinion that the doctors let Marie die. I am also satisfied from the way Prince and Princess Wilhelm received me and asked engagingly about every detail."[2] Adding to the public interest in her death were Carl von Brühl's very public accusations against the physicians, and especially Dr. Bremer, Berlin's most regarded doctor, for wrongly diagnosing Marie as mentally ill and ordering heavy treatment that ultimately led to her demise.[3]

In all of the accounts of Marie's death, especially striking from a modern perspective is the fact that they treated her as a prominent person in her own right. Luise Hensel did not even mention Carl or his work, but emphasized Marie's senior position at the court as the reason for the public interest. Carl von Brühl hardly doubted that his cousin occupied an important place in Berlin's society, and her sad end naturally deserved attention from the highest places. The need to protect Marie's qualities, many achievements, and the Brühl family status probably prompted his vehement reaction against Dr. Bremer as well. If a diagnosis of mental illness were allowed to stick to Marie's name, all of her great attainments would be undermined. For her contemporaries, Marie was defined less by Carl's legacy but rather as a courtier who served in the highest places, only to be cut down by a preposterous medical mistake.

After Marie's death on January 28 in Dresden, Carl von Brühl let the body be embalmed and took it to his estate nearby in Seifersdorf. Three days later, accompanied by his wife, Luise Hensel, Marie's maid Albertine, and all the remaining servants, he laid Marie to rest temporarily in his family crypt. Fritz von Brühl, still recovering from health problems in Breslau, now had the time to decide where his sister would rest forever. "Maybe you want to bury her next to her husband. I do believe she wanted it," suggested Carl von Brühl.[4] Fritz followed the advice, and Marie's corpse was later moved to the military cemetery in Breslau. Under the gray marble cross bearing the name of Carl, a stone marker was put up for her. To an inscription at the foot of the cross, "Amara mors amorem non separate," was added, "A bitter death cannot separate love."

Eventually in 1971 the government of the city, now called Wrocław and located within the borders of Poland, decided to level the cemetery and erect apartment buildings. Socialist East Germany, afraid that West Germany would contest its claims over Clausewitz's legacy, organized a hurried and highly secretive operation to move the remains and the tombstones to Burg.[5] Since then, the Clausewitzes' bodies have lain in the cemetery in his hometown. Marie's stone marker over the grave has not weathered the centuries and moves as well as Carl's cross and now is almost unreadable.

When she learned about her daughter's death, Sophie von Brühl kept her composure.[6] She survived her daughter by another two years, and died in 1837 in a state of complete mental deterioration. Just eighteen months later Marie's cousin Carl von Brühl passed away too. In 1837 the last two parts of Clausewitz's *Posthumous Works* (Ninth and Tenth, respectively military studies of the period 1600–1700s and various historic essays) appeared, proofread and edited by Carl von Gröben.

Despite the expressed wish in 1831 to leave some of her small estate to Carl's family, Marie never wrote a new will. Her financial assets were instead split in thirds between her brother, mother, and niece Fanny. After some of Marie's books and belongings were given to friends as memorabilia, Fritz von Brühl received the rest of her papers, furniture, and collection of paintings. They must have constituted a significant number because Carl von Brühl had to pay 50 thaler for their packing and transportation to Breslau, out of 171 thaler cash Fritz inherited from his sister.[7] At that time, however, Fritz was struggling with financial troubles and piling expenses for doctors and cures, and decided to sell some of the paintings. Already in late 1836 one of Carl's portraits was hanging at Berlin's foremost art dealers' store, the Gropius Brothers.[8] For the most part, the fate of Marie's paintings remains unclear. Her only work known today is the portrait of Gneisenau from 1816, now shown in the permanent exhibition of the German Historical Museum in Berlin.

The forty-five-year-old Fritz von Brühl recovered his health. After his first daughter Caroline Sophie was born in January 1835, he fathered three more. Fritz and Hedwig named their second child, born in July 1836, Marie. After her husband's death in 1856, Hedwig became one of the prominent ladies in Berlin and was immortalized in Adolph Menzel's sketch from 1875 of a soiree at the eminent salon of Mimi von Schleinitz. When Helmuth von Moltke, after his glorious victories in the German Unification Wars, famously named the Bible, Homer, and *On War* as his sources of wisdom and thus made the latter a bestseller, Hedwig was probably the first point of contact for those searching to know more about the man behind it.

Despite the fact that Karl Schwartz titled his 1878 Clausewitz biography *The Life of General Carl von Clausewitz and Madam Marie von Clausewitz, Born Countess von Brühl*, Marie's life was inevitably overshadowed by interest in the military theorist in the years following her death, and remains so up to the present day. In many ways, Marie was unlucky to have died relatively soon after her husband. Had she lived longer, she might have gained enough confidence to start writing and publishing her own texts. Her friend Bettina von Arnim, for instance, built a career as a successful and influential writer only after the death of her husband in 1831. In similar circumstances to Marie, Bettina first posthumously published Achim von Arnim's remaining works, and then with her newly gained credentials and autonomy wrote a series of compelling books that brought her fame and recognition as an author in her own right. Marie, in contrast, believed she did "not hav[e] the language of Goethe or Schiller under [her] sway."[9] It is true that her correspondence often suffered from lack of clarity and order. However, her mature and long contemplated texts, such as the prefaces to the various parts of Clausewitz's posthumous works, the essay for Ranke's *Historisch-Politische Zeitschrift*, and the letter to Elise von Bernstorff after Carl's death, reveal a thoughtful author. Had she lived longer, Marie might have even written and published hers and Carl's remarkable life story. After all, throughout the years she composed notes and meticulously preserved their correspondence, with that same idea in mind. Marie had envisioned Carl as the plausible author but at the end might have found the time and the tenacity to write the story on her own.

Alternatively she could have chosen to devote all her energy to her career as a courtier, and might have become one of the legendary women that from time to time dominated the court in Berlin. The most famous among them was Marie Sophie Countess von Voß, the *Oberhofmeisterin* of Queen Louise, who served as the closest confidante both to her mistress and to Friedrich Wilhelm III, and after the queen's death became a part of the king's notorious conservative camarilla deciding upon state matters.[10] In her position as *Oberhofmeisterin* of Princess Augusta and governess for the little prince Friedrich Wilhelm, the later Emperor Friedrich III, Marie had a chance to repeat this remarkable path. Being so close to the heart of state power, one could easily imagine that a smart and highly political woman, as she without a doubt was, would attempt to yield influence and actively intervene in future events.

Yet Marie's surprising death at the age of fifty-six robbed her of chances to assume a more visible role. She would remain, as she is today, known largely as her husband's intellectual partner and the publisher of his posthumous works. But even for a complicated woman who had to live within so many limitations, this is no small achievement.

In publishing *On War* as an unfinished text, Marie hoped to see the treatise widely debated—a desire that has become a reality, and even more so in our own times. In recent years, the distinguished Clausewitz scholar Hew Strachan argues, for instance, that the fact that *On War* had remained a "work in progress" is "the very source of its enduring strength." By not completing his treatise, Clausewitz left room for developments he just anticipated and for the evolution of military thought.[11] Yet the perception of *On War* as a fragmentary text has also led to countless manipulations and outright abuse. Where Marie sought to encourage rigorous, almost intimate interaction with Carl's clear prose, many instead found a way to reduce his original and complex thought to a minimalist collection of quotes. This only further spread the misconception that *On War*, in reality rewritten by Clausewitz over and over again in order to simplify the language and clarify complicated ideas, would be unreadable unless condensed and minimalized in this way.

Such manipulation of the text began in the decades after its publication, and ultimately influenced the way in which *On War* was understood and applied in the field. Helmuth von Moltke, the general who famously named Clausewitz's treatise as the inspiration for his victories in the Wars of German Unification and thus made it a bestseller, was a cousin of Marie and Carl's old friend Charlotte von Moltke and in 1822 actually served under her husband Marwitz.[12] The following year Moltke entered the War College, but as numerous historians have commented, there is not evidence that the future legendary field marshal and Clausewitz closely interacted. Although he incorporated and popularized only those ideas of Clausewitz's that happened to coincide with his own, as Michael Howard writes, *On War* and its author's image were transmitted to the world "through Moltke as totally as the image of Marx was transmitted to the Russian peoples through Lenin."[13] Clausewitz's main influence, as translated through Moltke, can be found in the proactive and bold manner the Prussian and German armies sought to destroy their enemies on the battlefield well into the twentieth century. The understanding of war as a complex phenomenon helped free their approach toward tactics and led to the creation of the *Auftragstaktic,* the principle of hammering away at overall strategy on the supreme-command level but leaving more room for flexibility and initiative for the commanders in the theater.[14]

What Moltke and his disciples subsequently ignored was Clausewitz's essential premise that war is a political act and thus political goals have precedence over military ones. Fritz von Brühl's edition of *On War* in 1853, which erroneously reversed the relationship between military and politics, did not appear in a vacuum but verbalized the Prusso-German general staff's growing emancipation and desire for independence. This development would come to a tragic end with World War I and the so-called Schieffen Plan, which sought a quick and decisive battle of annihilation first against France in the West before turning to Russia in the East. The massive preemptive mobilization of the German army, required by the plan, meant that in this pivotal moment, military means guided political considerations and the generals pressured diplomats and politicians into declaring war.

Ironically, after 1919 military thinkers like Basil Liddell Hart held Clausewitz's ideas on proactive and decisive leadership and his discussion of unrestrained violence responsible for the senseless carnage in World War I, famously slandering the Prussian philosopher as the "Mahdi of Mass." The insistence that *On War*'s powerful language deluded the pre-1914 generals into pursuing decisive battles presents an especially curious case, because in the period between two world wars Erich von Ludendorff, the former German chief of the general staff, found in Clausewitz's central concept of political supremacy the main obstacle to the German efforts at all-out warfare. It restricted war-making from achieving the totality that would have brought the enemies to their knees, Ludendorff argued, and concluded that in future total conflict, from the very beginning, "overall policy must serve the war."[15] These ideas, unsurprisingly, were later adopted by the general's onetime political ally, Adolf Hitler, and the Nazi war machine. Hitler, for his part, also happened to grasp better than anyone the powerful fusion between politics and war that Clausewitz had debated. As the Nazi rule in Germany demonstrated, not only could political polarization escalate the war effort, but also the preparation for war and the war effort itself could help in consolidating power and carrying out most radical policies.[16]

After 1945, *On War* slowly but surely started to dominate Anglo-Saxon strategic thought. Confronted with the utter destruction in Hiroshima and Nagasaki, the so-called nuclear strategists like Thomas Schelling and Bernard Brodie studied in depth Clausewitz's ideas of escalation of war toward its absolute form, since with the creation of nuclear bomb the latter appeared a very real possibility. Henry Kissinger, famously even called a "neo-Clausewitzian," based his understanding of diplomacy on the concept how state policy could use war as a tool. The Cold War's reality, when unrestrained military conflict between two superpowers, the United States and the USSR, promised to bring mutual destruction, also revived interest in the idea of limited war.[17]

Since the 1970s, *On War* has again been at the center of military studies and passionate strategy debates, primarily because the United States' debacle in Vietnam returned to the forefront the bitter revelation that without sound political strategy military gains are senseless. Paradoxically, formulating achievable political objectives to guide the conduct of war remains a challenge even in the twenty-first century, as the recent examples of the wars in Iraq and Afghanistan make clear. Clausewitz's famous phrase that war is a mere continuation of politics with other means is nowadays more widely quoted than ever, but translating it into realistic strategy remains as hard to master as it was in the nineteenth century.

Perhaps one of the reasons for the longstanding difficulty in the tangible application of Clausewitz's treatise is the fact that for almost 180 years Marie's voice and interpretation have been missing from the debate. Today professional service members, military historians, and foreign policy strategists comprise the limited circle studying and debating the treatise in depth. It is a logical development since many of its issues—assault, defense, counteroffensive—are written with practical military problems in mind. Yet it should be noted that many of these chapters, which cover topics including building fortresses, sieges, and the attack of fortified camps, are also of least relevance for modern warfare when the tactics and technology are so different than the early nineteenth century. Clausewitz's ageless contribution is not in giving prescriptions for winning wars but teaching his readers how to think about war.

Telling his life's story from Marie's perspective does more than shine light on the personal, political, and social environment from which *On War* has sprung. The newly discovered correspondence firmly places the emphasis on the essential understanding of war as a complex phenomenon central to the dealings of the state and the interests of its people—and by doing so it also reveals previously understudied aspects of Clausewitz's treatise.

Carl embraced more inclusive and dynamic notions of politics and, contrary to the prevailing attitudes of the day, he anticipated that even women, as subjects without actual rights or formal public standing in his time, could influence the processes. This reinforces the arguments that when writing on war as a continuation of politics with other means, Clausewitz was far from suggesting that it was always, as his detractors claimed, a cogent stately act (since women did not play a role in formal governance). The German word *Politik* he used, of course, could mean both "policy" (rational execution of power) or "politics" (the messy process of clashing with and carrying out certain interests). Indeed Clausewitz's famous phrase for the conduct of war also bears a certain dualism, as Christopher Bassford points out, because while accepting that there would always be complications and contradictions in the process (the irrational side), politicians should know what makes up and how to apply the limits of the instrument of war (the rational side).[18] This insight, together with Clausewitz's dynamic notion of politics, highlights once again that his theory is far more complex and forward-looking than his detractors have ever given him credit.

The newly discovered correspondence documents how Carl and Marie experienced and braved the enormous upheaval of the French Revolution and its aftershocks. One of the reasons for the continuing relevance of *On War* is that we still live in the same complex world created by the unleashed forces of nationalism and popular democracy and their ugliest militant outgrowths. In Carl and Marie's own time all of these phenomena were still new, never before experienced, and their understanding was unburdened by the patina of long historical precedents and haunting emotions. It is the couple's fresh perspective toward the burst of popular enthusiasm, people's participation in politics and war, political radicalism and militarism, and the granting of more rights to minorities and the societal backlash against them that brings further and deepens our understanding of modernity's challenges.

Throughout their lives Carl and Marie indeed found themselves over time on the reverse sides of the same phenomena. They opposed the revolutionary French army and its politics but welcomed social reforms; pinned their hopes on popular enthusiasm, only to be shocked later by its militant turn; verbally ostracized Jews but then came into close contact with them; saw women embrace a greater social role in the Napoleonic Wars only to experience hostility in peacetime; and supported freedom and independence for Germany but rejected the Polish aspirations in 1830s. Inevitably such widely differing and contradictory experiences created a complex worldview, clearly mirrored in Clausewitz's choice to write in realistic language free of righteous judgment. Later generations might have been shocked, for instance, by his proclamation that moral considerations of "kind-hearted people" should not play a role when military decisions are made, since war is such a dangerous business that it has to be conducted with utmost decisiveness.[19] But it came from complex and contradictory experiences and from a conviction that relating knowledge in the most realistic manner was the only way to truly understand the world.

Another even more significant revelation gained from studying *On War* through the prism of Marie's own ideas is the reversal of genuine perspective. Marie never envisioned Carl's influence, while he still was alive or posthumously, to be constrained to the battlefield but firmly believed it should spread into the wider political realm. Her principle of minimal intervention during the editing process, and the interpretation of *On War* as a book of perpetual discourse, likewise reinforced the perception of it as a text well beyond a utilitarian military application. Marie, in other words, presented and encouraged the viewpoint of proactive political subjects seeking to debate and understand the most powerful and devastating phenomena in world history. This is surely an interpretation that should resonate today more than ever.

We live in times when statistics describe a steady decrease in the number of world conflicts, and the professional military is gradually losing its influence and manpower while it is increasingly divorced from the civilian realm. Simultaneously, the feeling of insecurity and vexing global complexity is also growing, conceivably because so few common citizens understand the complicated interaction between militaries and governments, the way the escalation of violence can bring political gains, or the reality that seemingly irrational nonstate actors with relatively modest but brutal efforts can reshape the international stage. As much as these examples appear different and unrelated to the times and conflicts Carl and Marie faced, at their core they are a product of the same conditions. Although determined by the specifics of their time and societies, war and its application as an instrument are expressions of certain political realities and goals. Clausewitz provided the framework and the historical background, but it's up to us to understand our own challenges.

Until now Carl's life and viewpoint as a soldier have encouraged the notion that the professional military should learn about war's profoundly political character in order to wage a successful one. Marie's role as curator of *On War* advances the idea that the people as rational actors have to understand the most terrible political instrument of all, if there is ever a chance to avoid being enticed into costly and bloody mistakes. In those rare moments that require unleashing of violence, they must have this understanding in order to make the choice with clear knowledge of its limitations and possibilities of success.

Above of all, the newly discovered correspondence between Marie and Carl reveals what intellectual heights two independent but loving partners could achieve when they treat each other as equals and reciprocally nurture their aspirations. Contrary to the prevailing attitudes of the early nineteenth century and long after that, Marie came to play a role very few women historically had a chance to—not only of a loving wife and trusted companion, but also of a highly political individual. Carl recognized her political knowledge and talents and encouraged them to flourish. Marie, for her part, indulged his need as a thinker to test ideas against a worthy opponent and wholeheartedly supported his career and writing ambitions. Most significantly, she devoted her energies to publishing *On War* in a form closest to Carl's original idea. The Clausewitzes boldly broke the oppressive social mold and embraced an equal, savvy, and very modern intellectual partnership. And from it sprung a book that has continued to stand for centuries.

Notes

INTRODUCTION

1. Karl Schwartz, *Das Leben des Generals Carl von Clausewitz und der Frau Marie von Clausewitz geb. Gräfin von Brühl* (*The Life of General Carl von Clausewitz and Madam Marie von Clausewitz*).
2. The gap of knowledge, however, is rapidly closing. For instance, concerning the period of the Napoleonic Wars, several excellent studies have been published in the past decade. Among them: Karen Hagemann, *Mannlicher Muth und Teutsche Ehre: Nation, Militär und Geschlecht zur Zeit der Antinapoleonischen Kriege Preußens*; Hagemann, "Reconstructing 'Front' and 'Home': Gendered Experiences and Memories of the German Wars against Napoleon—A Case Study"; Hagemann, *Revisiting Prussia's Wars against Napoleon. History, Culture and Memory*; Waltraud Maierhofer, Gertrud M. Roesch, and Caroline Bland, *Women against Napoleon: Historical and Fictional Responses to His Rise and Legacy*.
3. Schwartz, *Das Leben von Carl und Marie von Clausewitz*, 1:7–14.
4. Karl und Marie von Clausewitz, *Ein Lebensbild in Briefen und Tagebuchblätter*, ed. Karl Linnebach; and Karl und Marie von Clausewitz, *Ein Leben im Kampf für Freiheit und Reich*, ed. Otto Heuschle. Marie's correspondences with August Neidhardt von Gneisenau was published in Pertz and Delbrueck, *Das Leben des Feldmarschalls Grafen Neidhardt von Gneisenau*. The two letters Marie wrote immediately after Carl's death were published in Bernstorff, *Ein Bild aus der Zeit 1789 bis 1835*: 2:225–28. Additional letters from Marie to her friend Elise von Bernstorff concerning the Radziwill family were published in Baer, *Prinzessin Elisa Radziwill*, 141–48. The published correspondence between Marie and Carl von Clausewitz is more widely accessible in Karl Linnebach's edition from 1925 (*Ein Lebensbild in Briefen und Tagebuchblätter*). Hence, it is used throughout this book as well and cited as *Correspondence*
5. Bernstorff, *Ein Bild aus der Zeit 1789 bis 1835*; and Rochow and Motte-Fouqué, *Vom Leben am preussischen Hofe, 1815–1852*.
6. Marwitz, *Ein märkischer Edelmann im Zeitalter der Befreiungskrieg*.
7. Gentzkow, *Liebe und Tapferkeit: Frauen um deutsche Soldaten* (*Love and Courage*).
8. Rother-Carlowitz, *Clausewitz und die vollkomenste der Frauen* (*Clausewitz and the Most Accomplished of All Women*).

9. "Die-Deutsche-Wochenschau-Nr.721," June 28, 1944. https://archive.org/details/1944-06-28-Die-Deutsche-Wochenschau-Nr.721.

10. Hahlweg, "Das Clausewitzbild einst und jetzt," in von Clausewitz, *Hinterlassene Werke* (1980), 37–38.

11. Gat, *Origins of Military Though*, 255–63.

CHAPTER 1

1. The term "Sturm und Drang" is commonly translated in English as "storm and stress," in my view a rather bleak term that fails to express all the passion and vigor the original one contains. Hence I have kept the German version.

2. The municipal center of the old duchy, Oświęcim or Auschwitz is nowadays tragically known because of the concentration camp in its vicinity. The information about Heinrich von Brühl comes from Walter Fellmann's exhaustive biography, *Heinrich Graf Brühl. Ein Lebens- und Zeitbild*.

3. Charles von Brühl's correspondence with Friedrich Wilhelm II was published in Seidel, "Karl Adolph Graf von Brühl," 199–202.

4. As quoted in Krosigk, *Karl Graf von Brühl*, 22 and 45.

5. The dates of promotion are taken from König, *Biographisches Lexikon*, 1:226.

6. Krosigk, *Karl Graf von Brühl*, 26.

7. Fellmann, *Brühl*, 386–87.

8. According to the memoirs of Fanny von Brühl's husband Friedrich August Ludwig von der Marwitz. Marwitz, *Gesammelte Schriften*, 1:175.

9. See, e.g., Boynton, "William and Richard Gomm," 359–402.

10. Kahan, *Plow, the Hammer, and the Knout*, 189.

11. Lebedev, "European Business Culture," 27.

12. For more about Gomm's activities in Russia, see Cross, *By the Banks of the Neva*, 74–79.

13. Unpublished document, "Death of William Gomm Esq."

14. Gomm, *Letters and Journals*, 27.

15. The essay was first published in Karl Schwartz's biography and named "Notes of Madam von Clausewitz about Her Early Life" (cited here for convenience "Jugendleben") Until now it has been undated but in a unpublished letter to Carl, 12 May 1812, Marie mentioned her work on it. Marie von Clausewitz, "Aufzeichnungen der Frau von Clausewitz über ihr Jugendleben," in Schwartz, *Das Leben*, 1:175–82.

16. Marie von Clausewitz, "Jugendleben," in Schwartz, *Das Leben*, 1: 176.

17. In an unpublished letter to Carl from 14 June 1815, Marie wrote about discovering with surprise that their friend Leopold von Gerlach did not speak "excellent" French. The signatures of all unpublished letters can be found in the bibliography at the end of the book.

18. Unpublished letter, Marie to Carl, 11 September 1813.

19. Geffarth, *Religion und arkane Hierarchie*, 67–68.

20. Seidel, "Karl Adolph Graf von Brühl," 199–202.
21. Paret, *Clausewitz and the State*, 101.
22. As quoted in Krosigk, *Karl Graf von Brühl*, 143.
23. Marie von Clausewitz, "Jugendleben," in Schwartz, *Das Leben*, 1: 176.
24. Delbrück, *Erziehungs-Geschichte*, , 81n.
25. Krosigk, *Karl Graf von Brühl* 147.
26. Luise Hensel to Christoph Berhnhard Schlüter, 8 March 1836, in Hensel and Schlüter, *Briefe*, 65.
27. Marwitz, *Gesammelte Schriften*, 1:175–76.
28. Staël, *Germany*, 1:111–12.
29. As quoted in Wehler, *Deutsche Gesellschaftsgeschichte*, 1:351.
30. About Clausewitz's birthday, see Paret, *Clausewitz and the State*, vii–viii; and Hilbert, "Ergänzungen zum Lebensbild," 208–11.
31. The published correspondence between Marie and Carl von Clausewitz is more widely accessible in the edition edited by Karl Linnebach from 1925, *Ein Lebensbild in Briefen und Tagebuchblätter*. Hence, it is used throughout this book as well and cited as *Correspondence* Carl to Marie, 13 December 1806, *Correspondence*, 73.
32. Paret, *Clausewitz and the State*, 14.
33. Carl to Marie, 13 December 1806, *Correspondence*, 74.
34. Unpublished letter, Marie to Carl, 13 December 1812.
35. While the essay was originally published anonymously, there is little doubt that Marie von Clausewitz was its author. Anonymous (Marie von Clausewitz), "General Clausewitz," 214.
36. Groehler, *Heerwesen*, 66.
37. Krosigk, *Karl Graf von Brühl*, 195.
38. The details about Charles von Brühl's travels are taken from Marie von Clausewitz, "Jugendleben," in Schwartz, *Das Leben*, 1:177.
39. Paret, *Clausewitz and the State*, 29.
40. Carl to Marie, 28 January 1807, *Correspondence*, 83.
41. Ibid.
42. Marie von Clausewitz, "Jugendleben," in Schwartz, *Das Leben*, 1:179.
43. Clark, *Iron Kingdom*, 292.
44. Marwitz, *Gesammelte Schriften*, 1:188.
45. Marie von Clausewitz, "Jugendleben," in Schwartz, *Das Leben*, 1:179.
46. Marwitz, *Ein märkischerGesammelte Schriften*, 1:188.
47. Delbrück, *Erziehungs-Geschichte*, 90.
48. Marwitz, *Gesammelte Schriften*, 1:176.
49. Gneisenau to Carl, 28 June 1819, in Pertz and Delbrueck, *Gneisenau*, 5:374.
50. Marwitz, *Gesammelte Schriften*, 1:180.
51. Ibid, 1:188.
52. Ibid.
53. Rochow, *Vom Leben*, 38.

54. Unpublished letter, Marie to Carl, 15 April 1813.

55. Unpublished letter, Carl von Brühl to Fritz von Brühl, 3 November 1836.

56. Carl to Marie, 22–23 March 1814, *Correspondence,* 367.

57. Unpublished letter, Marie to Carl, 16-17 March 1807.

58. Marwitz, *Gesammelte Schriften,* 1:180; Gneisenau to Marie, 15 August 1816, in Pertz and Delbrueck, *Gneisenau,* 5:139.

59. Carl to Marie, 28 January 1807, *Correspondence,* 83.

60. "Einlandung-Schrift," 25 January 1779, Burgische Französische Schule, Private Collection Bernd Domsgen/Olaf Thiel.

61. Paret, *Clausewitz and the State,* 41.

62. Ibid., 41–44.

63. Stoker, *Clausewitz,* 26.

64. Groehler, *Heerwesen,* 67.

65. Carl to Marie, 3 July 1807, *Correspondence,* 128.

66. Rochow, *Vom Leben,* 24–25.

67. Adams, *Traveled First Lady,* 47.

68. Unpublished letter, Fritz von Brühl to Marie, 3 December 1811.

69. Carl to Marie, 16 June 1831, *Correspondence,* 450.

70. Adams, *Traveled First Lady,* 52.

71. Ibid., 70–71.

72. Adams, *Berlin and the Prussian Court,* 12–14, 18–19, 26.

73. Carl to Marie, 3 July 1807, *Correspondence,* 128.

74. Anonymous (Marie von Clausewitz), "General Clausewitz," 214.

75. Carl to Marie, 28 January 1807, *Correspondence,* 128.

76. Unpublished letter, Marie to Carl, 15 August 1815.

77. About the influence of Scharnhorst over Clausewitz, see Paret, *Clausewitz and the State,* 65–77; about Montesquieu see Aron, *Clausewitz,* 51 and 225; Gat, *Origins of Military Thought,* 161–62.

78. Paret, *Clausewitz and the State,* 69, 161–62.

79. Unpublished letter, Marie to Carl, 26 February-11 March 1807.

80. Marie von Clausewitz, "Jugendleben," in Schwartz, *Das Leben,* 1:181.

81. Unpublished letter, Marie to Carl, 9–13 August 1807.

82. Wilhelmy, *Der Berliner Salon,* 50.

83. Staël, *Germany,* 113–14.

84. Unpublished letter, Karl Gustav von Brinckmann to Marie, 6 March 1803.

CHAPTER 2

1. Paret, *Clausewitz and the State,* 109.

2. Schwartz, *Das Leben,* 1:172.

3. Marie von Clausewitz, "Aufzeichnungen der Frau von Clausewitz über die Zeit der ersten Bekanntschaft mit ihrem Gatten," (shortened to "Erste Bekanntschaft") in Schwartz, *Das Leben,* 1:183–95.

4. Unpublished letter, Marie to Carl, 12-13 May 1812.

5. Unpublished part of letter, Carl to Marie, 25 March 1813.

6. Marwitz, *Gesammelte Schriften,* 1:174 and 178.

7. Ibid., 1:188

8. Ibid., 1:178

9. Ibid., 1:188

10. Unpublished letter, Marie to Carl, 15 May 1807.

11. Marie von Clausewitz, "Erste Bekanntschaft," in Schwartz, *Das Leben* I:183

12. In the other undated notes about her earlier life, Marie wrote that she came back to Berlin in December 1803. Marie von Clausewitz, "Jugendleben," in Schwartz, *Das Leben,* 1:181.

13. Unpublished letter, Marie to Carl, 8 April 1813.

14. Marie von Clausewitz, "Erste Bekanntschaft," in Schwartz, *Das Leben* I:182

15. Carl to Marie, 3 July 1807, *Correspondence,* 130.

16. Unpublished letter, Marie to Carl, 8-15 January 1807

17. Unpublished letter, Marie to Carl, 7 February 1807.

18. Marwitz to Marie, 3 April 1805 and 10 October 1807, in Marwitz, *Gesammelte Schriften,* III:530 and 540

19. Marwitz, *Gesammelte Schriften,* 1:188-189

20. It is very difficult to give a present-day value of these sums since there is a significant difference in the way people spent their money in the early nineteenth century. The prices of labor, for instance, were low while clothing was expensive.

21. Unpublished letter, Marie to Carl, 24 March 1831.

22. Unpublished letter, Marie to Carl, 8-15 January 1807.

23. Carl to Marie, 16–17 March 1807, *Correspondence,* 95–96.

24. Ibid., 97.

25. Hartl, *Carl von Clausewitz,* 26.

26. Marie von Clausewitz, "Erste Bekanntschaft," in Schwartz, *Das Leben* I:189.

27. Ibid., 1:190-91.

28. Ibid., 1:192.

29. Carl to Marie, 29 September 1806, *Correspondence,* 66.

30. Marie von Clausewitz, "Erste Bekanntschaft," in Schwartz, *Das Leben* I:193.

31. Ibid., I:194.

32. Paret, *Clausewitz and the State,* 102.

33. Carl to Marie, 13 December 1806, *Correspondence,* 74–75.

34. Unpublished letter, Carl to Carl Leopold von Clausewitz, 26 November 1826.

35. Heinrich, "Der Adel in Brandenburg-Preußen," 259–314.

36. Unpublished letter, Marie to Carl, 8 April 1813.

37. Unpublished letter, Marie to Carl, 27 April 1813.

38. Unpublished letter, Carl's letter to Carl Leopold von Clausewitz, 15 May 1829.

39. Marie von Clausewitz, "Erste Bekanntschaft," in Schwartz, *Das Leben* I:193-194.
40. In Carl's letter to Marie, 10 August 1808, he wrote that he feared losing half of his paycheck, 10 thaler, if he asked to be released from his duties as adjutant, i.e., his yearly income was 20 thaler. *Correspondence*, 164.
41. Groehler, *Das Heerwesen*, 58–62 and 23.
42. Marie reported these sums in an unpublished letter to Carl, 30 September-22 October 1807.
43. Diemel, *Adelige Frauen*, 120.
44. Carl to Marie, 11 September 1806, *Correspondence*, 56.
45. Clausewitz, "Strategie," in *Verstreute kleine Schriften*, 181.
46. Paret, *Clausewitz and the State*, 110–19; Gat, *Military Thought*, 174.
47. Unpublished letter, Marie to Carl, 18 July 1807.
48. The overlapping descriptions are from two unpublished letters, Marie to Carl, 20 May–4 June and 18 June 1807, emphasis is hers.

CHAPTER 3

1. Jackson, *Diaries and Letters*, 2.
2. Clausewitz, *Nachrichten*, 467.
3. Rochow, *Vom Leben*, 26.
4. Jackson, *Diaries and Letters*, 3.
5. Clausewitz, *Nachrichten*, 474.
6. Ibid., 465–66.
7. Ibid., 437.
8. Rochow, *Vom Leben*, 27–28.
9. Carl to Marie, 11 September 1806, *Correspondence*, 55.
10. Carl to Marie, 29 September 1806, *Correspondence*, 66.
11. Carl to Marie, 29 September 1806, *Correspondence*, 64.
12. Unpublished letter, Marie to Carl, 8-10 April 1807.
13. Carl to Marie, 12 October 1806, *Correspondence*, 67.
14. Carl to Marie, 30 August 1806, *Correspondence*, 52–53.
15. Carl to Marie, 11 September 1806, *Correspondence*, 56.
16. Carl to Marie, 20 September 1806, *Correspondence*, 62.
17. Ibid., 65–66.
18. Carl to Marie, 29 September 1806, *Correspondence*, 65.
19. Hans Rothfels first noted this interesting detail. Rothfels, *Clausewitz*, 90.
20. Carl to Marie, 12 October 1806, *Correspondence*, 67.
21. Ibid.
22. Paret, *Clausewitz and the State*, 125.
23. Unpublished letter, Carl to Marie, 28 April 1830.
24. Varnhagen, *Ausgewählte Schriften*, 1:364.

25. Ibid.

26. Unpublished letter, Marie to Carl, 18 October 1806.

27. Varnhagen, *Ausgewählte Schriften*, 1:364-65.

28. Parquin, *Napoleon's Army*, 46.

29. Cavan, "Der Einzug des Davoutschen Korps in Berlin am 25ten. October" in Schulze, *Die Franzosenzeit*, 1:76–77.

30. Clausewitz, *On War*, 592.

31. Rochow, *Vom Leben*, 28.

32. Clausewitz described these events as an appendix to Clausewitz, *Nachrichten*, 543–48.

33. Carl to Marie, 1 December 1806, *Lebensbild*, 69–70.

34. Clausewitz, *Nachrichten*, 547.

35. Hopkins, *Prisoners of War*, 78–79.

36. Carl to Marie, 13 December 1806, *Correspondence*, 71.

37. These notes again were without a title but clearly dated as composed in the beginning of 1813. Hence Schwartz named them "Madam von Clausewitz's recollections about her life in connection with the turn of the year's days." Marie von Clausewitz, "Erinnerungen der Frau von Clausewitz aus ihrem Leben, angeknüpft an die Tage des Jahreswechsels," (shortened to "Jahreswechsel") in Schwartz, *Das Leben*, 1:196–202.

38. Unpublished letter, Marie to Carl, 8-10 April 1807.

39. Beguelin, "Die finanzielle Lage des preußischen Staates nach der Katastrophe" in Schulze, *Die Franzosenzeit*, 176.

40. Unpublished letter, Marie to Carl, 8-15 January 1807.

41. Unpublished letter, Marie to Carl, 8-10 April 1807.

42. Unpublished letter, Marie to Carl, 8-15 January 1807.

43. Unpublished letter, Marie to Carl, 18 February 1807.

44. Unpublished letter, Marie to Carl, 26 February–11 March 1807.

45. Unpublished letter, Marie to Carl, 20 May-4 June 1807.

46. Unpublished letter, Marie to Carl, 18 June 1807.

47. Unpublished letters, Marie to Carl, 26 April and 15 May 1807.

48. Unpublished letter, Marie to Carl, 8–10 April 1807.

49. Unpublished letter, Marie to Carl, 20 May-4 June 1807.

50. Unpublished letter, Marie to Carl, 8-15 January 1807.

51. Unpublished letter, Marie to Carl, 18 February 1807.

52. Unpublished letter, Marie to Carl, 16-17 September 1807.

53. Carl to Marie, 28 January 1807, in *Correspondence*, 83.

54. The issue was debated in Marie's unpublished letters from 26 April and 15 May 1807; Carl's answers from 29 March, 8 April, and 28 April 1807, *Correspondence*, 102, 108–9, 113–14.

55. Unpublished letters, Marie to Carl, 18 February and 18 June 1807.

56. Unpublished letter, Marie to Carl, 26 April 1807.

57. Unpublished letters, Marie to Carl, 20 May-4 June 1807. Emphasis is hers.

58. Unpublished letter, Marie to Carl, 24 July 1807. Emphasis is hers.
59. Unpublished letter, Marie to Carl, 9–13 August 1807.
60. Unpublished letter, Marie to Carl, 24 July 1807.
61. Carl to Marie, 15 September 1807, *Correspondence,* 136.

CHAPTER 4

1. Unpublished letter, Marie to Carl, 29 July 1808.
2. Unpublished letter, Marie to Carl, 25 April 1808.
3. Carl to Marie, 5 August 1808, *Correspondence,* 160–61.
4. The issue rose once again with the marriage of her brother Fritz von Brühl, and Marie clarified the legal situation in a letter to Gneisenau. Gneisenau to Marie, 1 October 1827, and Marie to Gneisenau, 6 October 1827, in Pertz and Delbrück, *Gneisenau,* 5:537–38 and 540.
5. Paletschek, "Adelige und bürgerliche Frauen," 168.
6. Carl to Marie, 15 September 1807, *Correspondence,* 137.
7. Carl to Marie, n.d. April 1808, *Correspondence,* 152.
8. Carl to Marie, 17 August 1808, *Correspondence,* 166–67.
9. Carl to Marie, 5–10 August 1808, *Correspondence,* 165.
10. Unpublished letter, Marie to Carl, 16–17 September 1807.
11. Marie to Carl, 4 January 1809, *Correspondence,* 200.
12. Stein to his wife, 3 February 1813, in Stein, *Briefe und Amtliche Schriften,* 3: 29–30.
13. Unpublished letter, Marie to Fritz von Brühl, 12 June 1809.
14. Unpublished letter, Marie to Carl, 16–17 September 1807.
15. Clausewitz, "On the Life and Character of Scharnhorst," 103.
16. Carl to Marie, 28 December 1808, *Correspondence,* 198.
17. Clark, *Iron Kingdom,* 326.
18. Carl to Marie, 10–11 August 1808, *Correspondence,* 153–55.
19. Clark, *Iron Kingdom,* 319–20, 325–28.
20. Unpublished letter, Marie to Carl, 4 January 1809.
21. Unpublished letters, Marie to Carl, 4 October, 13 November, 18 December 1808 and 4 January 1809.
22. Carl to Marie, 20 October 1808, *Correspondence,* 175. Unpublished letter, Marie to Carl, 13 November 1808.
23. Unpublished letters, Marie to Carl, 11–12 September 1808.
24. Unpublished letter, Marie to Fritz von Brühl, 12 June 1809.
25. Marwitz, *Gesammelte Schriften,* 1:178–79.
26. Stein to Princess Louisa Radziwill, 8 July 1810, in Stein, *Briefe und Amtliche Schriften,* 3:330–31.
27. Unpublished letter, Marie to Carl, 9 July 1828.
28. Unpublished letter, Marie to Carl, 12–18 April 1808.
29. Marie to Carl, 4 October 1808, *Correspondence,* 171–72.

30. Carl to Marie, 13 October 1807, *Correspondence,* 173.
31. Carl to Marie, 20 October 1808, *Correspondence,* 175.
32. Unpublished letter, Marie to Carl, 22–23 October 1808.
33. Unpublished letter, Marie to Carl, 15 December 1808.
34. Unpublished letter, Marie to Carl, 11–14 April 1809.
35. Unpublished letter, Marie to Carl, 24–26 November 1808.
36. Princess Marianne to Marie, January 1809, quoted in Weppermann, *Prinzessin Marianne,* 133–34.
37. Carl to Marie, 5 August 1808, *Correspondence,* 160.
38. Carl to Marie, 31 March 1809, *Correspondence,* 221.
39. Unpublished letter, Marie to Carl, 29 March 1831.
40. Marie to Carl, 22 October 1808, *Correspondence,* 176.
41. Unpublished part of Marie's letter to Carl, 22–23 October 1808.
42. Unpublished letter, Marie to Carl, 24–26 November 1808.
43. Unpublished letter, Marie to Carl, 27 April 1813.
44. Carl to Marie, 23 May 1815, *Correspondence,* 378; the couple enjoyed the friendship and company of Gerlach even in the 1830s. Unpublished letter, Marie to Carl, 30 July 1831.
45. Gröben, "Vorrede zum Neunten Band," 15.
46. Unpublished letters, Marie to Carl, 22–23 October and 22 December 1808.
47. Unpublished letter, Marie to Carl, 26 November 1808.
48. Unpublished letter, Marie to Carl, 22–23 October 1808.
49. Unpublished letter, Marie to Carl, 25 April 1808.
50. Marie to Carl, 1 April 1808, *Correspondence,* 149–50.
51. Carl to Marie, 21 November 1808, *Correspondence,* 185-86.
52. The events were described in Weppermann, *Prinzessin Marianne,* 144–67.
53. Marie to Carl, 15 December 1808 and 7 January 1809, *Correspondence,* 207.
54. Stein's letters to Countess Werther, 30 January 1809, reveals that he stayed with Therese von Thun; Stein, *Briefe und Schriften,* 3:38.
55. Carl to Marie, 23 February 1809, *Correspondence,* 213–14.
56. Unpublished letter, Marie to Carl, 3 March 1809.
57. Hahlweg, *Schriften,* 90–208; Paret, *Clausewitz and the State,* 140–41 and 144–45.
58. Unpublished letter, Marie to Carl, 27 March 1809.
59. Carl to Marie, 7 January 1809, *Correspondence,* 202.
60. Carl to Marie, 23 April 1809, *Correspondence,* 223-24
61. Arendt, *Varnhagen,* 122–23.
62. Marie to Carl, 17 March 1809, *Correspondence,* 219–20.
63. Clausewitz, "Scharnhorst," 95–96.
64. Arendt, *Varnhagen,* 122.
65. Unpublished letter, Marie to Carl, 4 January 1809.
66. Ibid.
67. Unpublished letter, Marie to Carl, 11–14 April 1809.
68. Stein to his wife, 15 May 1808, Stein, *Briefe,* 2:733–34.

69. Marie to Carl, 29 April 1809, *Correspondence*, 227.
70. Ibid.
71. Carl to Marie, 20 July 1809, *Correspondence*, 253.
72. Unpublished letter, Marie to Carl, 31 July 1815; for more about Goethe's stand on the topic see Kohn, *Prelude to Nation-State*, 152–53.
73. Carl to Marie, 23 April 1809, *Correspondence,* 225–26.
74. Carl to Marie, 6 May 1809, *Correspondence*, 229.
75. Marie to Carl, 10 May 1809, *Correspondence*, 230.
76. Carl to Marie, 6 May 1809, *Correspondence,* 228.
77. Unpublished letter, Marie to Carl, 23 May 1809.
78. Ibid.
79. Carl to Marie, 21 May 1809, *Correspondence*, 234.
80. Carl to Marie, 28–29 May 1809, *Correspondence*, 237–38.
81. Marie to Carl, 2 June 1809, *Correspondence*, 241.
82. Marie to Carl, 8 June 1809, *Correspondence*, 243.
83. Clausewitz, *On War,* 100 and 106; emphasis is his.
84. Carl to Marie, 15–19 and 26 June 1809, *Correspondence*, 246 and 249.
85. Unpublished letter, Marie to Carl, 18–20 July 1809.
86. Marie to Carl, 20 June 1809, *Correspondence*, 250–51.
87. Clausewitz, *On War*, 89.

CHAPTER 5

1. Marie von Clausewitz, "Jahreswechsel," in Schwartz, *Das Leben*, 198.
2. Ibid., 198–99.
3. Alexandra to Marie, January 1826, in Bernstorff, *Ein Bild.* 2: 54.
4. Stein to Princess Louise, 8 July 1810; Princess Louise Radziwill to Stein, 29 June 1810 and 27 December 1810, in Stein, *Briefe und Amtliche Schriften* 3: 330–31, 327–28, 444–45.
5. Unpublished letter, Marie to Carl, 17 December 1812.
6. Evangelisches Landeskirchliches Archiv in Berlin (ELAB); Kirchenbuchstelle Berlin-Brandenburg, microfiches 5749, p. 99, nr. 239.
7. Marie von Clausewitz, "Jahreswechsel," in Schwartz, *Das* Leben, 198.
8. The poems are published in *Correspondence,* 267–70.
9. Rochow, *Vom Leben*, 40–41.
10. Paret, *Clausewitz and the State*, 211. In his letter to Marie from 20–21 April 1812 Carl named 1,300 thaler as the wage he expected to be paid, *Correspondence,* 279.
11. Paletschek, *Frauen*, 169.
12. Unpublished letter, Marie to Carl, 11–14 April 1809.
13. Unpublished letters, Marie to Carl, 28 August and 29 September–8 October 1809.
14. Unpublished letter, Marie to Carl, 18 June 1807.

15. Carl to Marie, 5 November 1808, *Correspondence*, 180.
16. Unpublished letters, Marie to Carl, 28 August and 29 September 1809.
17. Carl von Clausewitz, "The Necklace on Marie," *Correspondence*, 106; Marie von Clausewitz, "Jahreswechsels," in Schwartz, *Das Leben*, 198.
18. Unpublished letter, Marie to Carl, 20–21 May 1812.
19. Unpublished letters, Marie to Carl, 20 –21 May and 3 December 1812.
20. Unpublished letter, Marie to Carl, 31 July 1815.
21. Unpublished part of a letter, Carl to Marie, 23–25 May 1815.
22. Marie von Clausewitz, "Jahreswechsel," in Schwartz, *Das* Leben, 198.
23. Berg, *Louise Königin von Preußen*.
24. Carl to Marie, 4 December 1808, *Correspondence*, 188; unpublished letter, Marie to Carl, 15 December 1808.
25. Bernstorff, *Ein Bild.* 2: 5 and 49.
26. Kohn, *Prelude to Nation-States*, 269
27. Unpublished letter, Marie to Carl, 28 July 1807; Carl to Marie, 3 October 1807, *Correspondence,* 139.
28. Unpublished letter, Marie to Carl, 25 April 1808.
29. Steffens, *Was ich erlebte*, 51.
30. Miller, "Literarisches Leben," 31.
31. Oesterle, "Juden, Philister und romantische Intellektuelle," 69–70 and 72.
32. Carl to Marie, 15 May 1812, *Correspondence*, 287.
33. Paret, *Clausewitz and the State*, 212–13.
34. Carl to Marie, 11 April 1814, *Correspondence*, 371.
35. Hagemann, *Revising Prussia's Wars against Napoleon,* 116.
36. Carl von Clausewitz, "Scharnhorst," 96.
37. Paret, *Clausewitz and the State*, 214.
38. For more on the subject see Paret, *Clausewitz and the State*, 215–19.
39. Just as for the quote, the colorful details are taken out of Princess Louise von Prussia, *Forty-Five Years*, 333–34.
40. Ibid., 335.
41. Carl to Marie, 2 April 1812, *Correspondence*, 270.

CHAPTER 6

1. Hahlweg, *Clausewitz. Soldat-Poltiker-Denker*, 35.
2. Paret, *Clausewitz and the State*, 103.
3. More about Clausewitz's letter of resignation see ibid., 220.
4. Most clearly, Marie expressed these views when suggesting that theirs would be the lost generation in the fight against Napoleon. Still, she would not "give up to despair," Marie wrote to Carl, but believe "in the spirit of the nation and in a better future." Unpublished letter, Marie to Carl, 16–17 September 1807.
5. Unpublished letters, Marie to Carl, 12–13 May and 1–7 June 1812.
6. Unpublished letter, Marie to Carl, 15 December 1808.

7. Carl to Marie, 20–21 April 1812, *Lebensbild*, 279.

8. The details and the quote are from Princess Louise, 336–37.

9. Unpublished letter, Marie to Carl, 29 June 1812.

10. Carl to Marie, 18 April 1812, *Correspondence*, 276.

11. Ibid.

12. Carl to Marie, 5 May and 8 May 1812, *Correspondence*, 283–84.

13. Carl to Marie, 8 May 1812, *Correspondence*, 285.

14. Unpublished letter, Marie to Carl, 28 May 1812.

15. Ibid.

16. Carl wrote to Marie about even meeting his brothers in person in Tauroggen, at the end of the campaign. Carl to Marie, 18/30 December 1812, *Correspondence*, 306

17. Unpublished letter, Marie to Carl, 12–13 May 1812.

18. Unpublished letters, Marie to Carl, 12–13 May 1812.

19. Unpublished letter, Marie to Carl, 1–7 and 17 June 1812.

20. Unpublished letter, Marie to Carl, 17 June 1812.

21. Unpublished letter, Marie to Carl, 29 June 1812.

22. Caroline "Mademoiselle" von Bischoffwerder was an influential lady-in-waiting at the court. Aunt Heinrich is the widow of Marie's uncle Heinrich, Laura von Brühl. Anton Wilhelm von L'Estocq was a famous Prussian general who, among others, commanded the Prussian troops in the Battle of Eylau in 1807. Unpublished letter, Marie to Carl, 29 June 1812.

23. Unpublished letter, Marie to Carl, 10 September 1812.

24. Unpublished letter, , Marie to Carl, 13 December 1812.

25. Unpublished letter, Marie to Carl, 30 July 1812.

26. Czygan, *Zur Geschichte*, 60.

27. See for instance Paret, *Clausewitz and the State*, 220; Aschmann, *Preußens Ruhm*, 200.

28. Unpublished letter, Marie to Carl, 13 December 1812.

29. Ibid.

30. Unpublished letter, Marie to Carl, 19 October 1812.

31. Unpublished letter, Marie to Carl, 27 August 1812.

32. Ibid.

33. Unpublished letter, Marie to Carl, 13 December 1812.

34. Carl to Marie, 6 June 1812, *Correspondence*, 290.

35. The remarks about Jascha are found in unpublished letters, Marie to Carl, 8 and 13 April 1813, and 21 July and 9 August 1831.

36. Carl to Marie, 6 July 1812, *Correspondence*, 291–92.

37. Carl to Marie, 12 August 1812, *Correspondence*, 294–95.

38. See Clausewitz's vivid account of his observations and experience at the Russian headquarters in 1812: Clausewitz, "Campaign of 1812," 110–204.

39. Carl to Marie, 18/30 September 1812, *Correspondence*, 297.

40. Carl to Marie, 15/27 October 1812, *Correspondence*, 298.

41. Unpublished letter, Marie to Carl, 1 October 1812.

42. Carl to Marie, 23 October/4 November 1818, *Correspondence,* 299–302.

43. Paret, *Clausewitz and the State,* 232.

44. Kohn, *Prelude to Nation-States,* 253 and 262.

45. Unpublished letter, Marie to Carl, 13 December 1812.

46. Carl to Marie, 29 October/10 November 1812, *Correspondence,* 302.

47. Carl to Marie, 17/29 November 1812, *Correspondence,* 305.

48. Carl to Marie, 18/30 December 1812, *Correspondence,* 305–6.

49. Paret, *Clausewitz and the State,* 230.

50. Clark, *Iron Kingdom,* 360-62.

51. Unpublished letter, Marie to Carl, 19 January 1813.

52. Rochow, *Vom Leben,* 50.

CHAPTER 7

1. Unpublished letter, Marie to Carl, 13 April 1813.

2. Baur, *Prinzess Wilhelm von Preussen,* 152.

3. Rochow, *Vom Leben,* 51.

4. Princess Louise, *Forty-Five Years,* 348–49.

5. Paret, *Clausewitz and the State,* 235.

6. Unpublished letter, Marie to Carl, 23 and 27 March 1813.

7. Unpublished letter, Marie to Carl, 8 and 13 April 1813.

8. Unpublished letter, Marie to Carl, 1 December 1812, emphasis is hers.

9. According to the memoirs of Hauptmann Steinmann von Friederici in Schwartz, *Das Leben,* 2:248.

10. Carl to Marie, 1 September 1813, *Correspondence,* 349.

11. Unpublished letter, Marie to Carl, 15 April 1813.

12. Carl to Marie, 25 April 1813, *Correspondence,* 330.

13. Unpublished letter, Marie to Carl, 13 April 1813.

14. Unpublished part of letter, Carl to Marie, 26–28 March 1813.

15. Carl to Marie, 4 April 1813, *Correspondence,* 325.

16. Unpublished letter, Marie to Carl, 27 March 1813. The two letters copied were attached to it. Friedrich Wilhelm's is from 19 March and Scharnhorst is from 21 March 1813.

17. Carl to Marie, 22 April 1813, *Correspondence,* 328

18. Unpublished letter, Marie to Carl, 18 April 1813.

19. Unpublished letter, Marie to Carl, 13 April 1813.

20. Carl to Marie, 22 April 1813, *Correspondence,* 328.

21. Carl to Marie, 9 April 1813, *Correspondence,* 326.

22. Carl to Marie, 18 April 1813, *Correspondence,* 327.

23. Carl to Marie, 2 June 1813, *Correspondence,* 339.

24. Unpublished letter, Marie to Carl, 18 April 1813.

25. Unpublished part of letter, Carl to Marie, 22 April 1813.

26. Unpublished part of letter, Carl to Marie, 1 May 1813.

27. Carl to Marie, 1 April 1813, *Correspondence,* 322–23.

28. Unpublished letter, Marie to Carl, 8 April 1813,emphasis is hers.

29. Unpublished letter, Marie to Carl, 13 April 1813, emphasis is hers.

30. Unpublished letter, Marie to Carl, 18 April 1813.

31. Carl to Marie, 22 April 1813, *Correspondence,* 328.

32. Unpublished letter, Marie to Carl, 11 April 1813.

33. Unpublished letter, Marie to Carl, 27 April 1813.

34. Unpublished letter, Marie to Carl, 22 April 1813.

35. Unpublished letter, Marie to Carl, 22 and 27 April 1813.

36. Unpublished letter, Marie to Carl, 27 April 1813.

37. Princess Louise, *Forty-Five Years,* 351.

38. Rochow, *Vom Lebem,* 52.

39. Roesch, "Liberation from Napoleon, 115–16; Varnhagen, *Gesammelte Werke,* 5:33.

40. Huber-Sperl, "Organized Women," 86–87.

41. Unpublished letter, Marie to Carl, 29 April 1813.

42. Rahel Levin to Varnhagen, 10 July 1813, in Varnhagen, *Briefwechsel,* 3:128.

43. Marie von Clausewitz, *Aufzeichnungen: Abschriften von Zitaten, Gedichten, Grabinschriften und Briefen/*Marie von Clausewitz o.O. [nach 1831].

44. Carl to Marie, 3 May 1813, *Correspondence,* 331.

45. Leggiere, *Napoleon and Berlin,* 53–54.

46. Princess Louise, *Forty-Five Years,* 357.

47. Leggiere, *Napoleon and Berlin,* 60 and 65.

48. Princess Louise, *Forty-Five Years,* 359.

49. Rochow, *Vom Lebem,* 53.

50. Unpublished letter, Marie to Carl, 19 May 1813.

51. Leggiere, *Napoleon and Berlin,* 67.

52. All the details are from unpublished letter, Marie to Carl, 22 May 1813.

53. Unpublished letter, Marie to Carl, 26 May 1813.

54. Carl to Marie, 31 May 1813, *Correspondence,* 337–38.

55. Unpublished letter, Marie to Carl, 26 May 1813.

56. Pertz and Delbrueck, *Gneisenau,* 3:44; Unpublished letter, Marie to Carl, 2 June 1813.

57. Pertz and Delbrueck, *Gneisenau,* 1:52–53.

58. Unpublished letter, Marie to Carl, 31 May 1813.

59. Unpublished letter, Marie to Carl, 7 June 1813.

60. Unpublished letter, Marie to Carl, 8 June 1813.

61. Carl to Marie, 4 June 1813, *Correspondence,* 340.

62. Carl to Marie, 10 June 1813, *Correspondence,* 340; Paret, *Clausewitz and the State,* 238–39.

63. Unpublished letter, Marie to Carl, 13 July 1813.

64. All the details and quotes are from unpublished letter, Marie to Carl, 2 July 1813.

65. Schultze, *Standhaft und Treu*, 123.
66. Roesch, "Self-Liberation," 119–20.
67. Unpublished letter, Marie to Carl, 2 July 1813.
68. Carl to Marie, 14 August 1813, *Correspondence*, 345.
69. Unpublished letter, Marie to Carl, 23 August 1813.
70. Carl to Marie, 14 August 1813, *Correspondence*, 345.
71. Unpublished letter, Marie to Carl, 27 April 1813.
72. Unpublished letter, Marie to Carl, 28 August 1813.
73. Unpublished letter, Marie to Carl, 9 September 1813.
74. Carl to Marie, 1 September 1813, *Correspondence,* 349.
75. Unpublished letter, Marie to Carl, 30 September 1813.
76. Unpublished letter, Marie to Carl, 21 October 1813.
77. Carl to Marie, 3 July 1815, *Correspondence,* 389.
78. Gneisenau to Marie, 16 October 1813, Pertz and Delbrueck, *Gneisenau,* 3:459–60.
79. Gneisenau to Marie from 24 October 1813, Pertz and Delbrueck, *Gneisenau,* 474–75.
80. Marie von Clausewitz, Tagebuchblätter 17.08.1813–30.11.1813.
81. Unpublished letter, Marie to Carl, 4 March 1814.
82. Carl to Marie, 16 November 1813, *Correspondence,* 357.
83. Carl wrote later how much he longed seeing her again paint in his presence, Carl to Marie, 23 May 1815, *Correspondence,* 379.
84. Unpublished letter, Marie to Carl, 4 March 1814.
85. Unpublished letter, Marie to Carl, 7 March 1814.
86. Unpublished letters, Marie to Carl, 7, 15, and 19 March 1814.
87. Unpublished letter, Marie to Carl, 15 March 1814.
88. Marie to Gneisenau, 20 April 1814, in Pertz and Delbrueck, *Gneisenau,* 4:248–541.
89. Unpublished letter, Marie to Carl, 13–17 April 1814.
90. Unpublished letter, Marie to Carl, 7 March 1814.
91. Unpublished letter, Marie to Carl, 13–17 April 1814.
92. Paret, *Clausewitz and the State,* 244.
93. Carl to Marie, 22 April 1813, *Correspondence,* 328.
94. Unpublished letter, Marie to Carl, 26 April 1814.
95. Paret, *Clausewitz and the State,* 244–46.
96. Carl to Marie, 19 April 1814, *Correspondence,* 374.
97. Gneisenau to Carl, 12 December 1814, Pertz and Delbrueck, *Gneisenau,* 4:301.
98. Unpublished letter, Marie to Carl, 16 May 1815.
99. Carl's letter to Gneisenau, 9 February 1815, mentions their plans for the vacation, Pertz and Delbrueck, *Gneisenau,* 4:317.
100. Carl to Marie, 11 April 1814, *Correspondence,* 317.
101. Paret, *Clausewitz and the State,* 247.
102. Unpublished letter, Marie to Carl, 14 May 1815.

103. Unpublished letters, Marie to Carl, 16 and 20 May 1815.
104. Unpublished letter, Marie to Carl, 20 May 1815.
105. Unpublished letter, Marie to Carl, 12 June 1815.
106. Unpublished part of letter, Carl to Marie, 6 June 1815.
107. See the newly published Clausewitz and Wellesley, *On Waterloo.*
108. Unpublished letter, Marie to Carl, 27 June 1815.
109. Gneisenau to Marie and Julie von Dohna, 24 June 1815; Marie to Gneisenau, 27 June 1815, Pertz and Delbrueck, *Gneisenau,* 4: 535–39 and 565–66.
110. Unpublished letter, Marie to Carl, 27 June 1815; Marie to Gneisenau, 6 June 1815, Pertz and Delbrueck, *Gneisenau,* 4:566.
111. Unpublished letter, Marie to Carl, 27 June 1815.
112. Unpublished letter, Marie to Carl, 4 July 1815.
113. Chézy, *Unvergessenes,* 125–27.
114. Unpublished letter, Marie to Carl, 10 July 1815.
115. Ibid.
116. Carl to Marie, 7 July 1815, *Correspondence,* 391.
117. Clausewitz, *On War,* 633.
118. Unpublished part of letter, Carl to Marie, 13 July 1815.
119. Unpublished part of letter, Carl to Marie, 14 July 1815.
120. Unpublished letter, Marie to Carl, 20 July 1815.
121. Unpublished letter, Marie to Carl, 31 July 1815.

CHAPTER 8

1. Unpublished letter, Marie to Carl, 14 July, 5 August, and 4 July 1815.
2. Carl to Gneisenau, 18 August 1815, Pertz and Delbrueck, *Gneisenau,* 4:608.
3. Carl to Marie, 12 July 1815, *Correspondence,* 339–41.
4. According to the account of Ferdinand von Stosch, a staff officer at the command, published in Pertz and Delbrueck, *Gneisenau,* 5:119.
5. Carl's entrance in his travel journal from 6 January 1807, in *Correspondence,* 77.
6. Unpublished letter, Marie to Carl, 8–15 January 1807.
7. Unpublished letter, Marie to Carl, 22–23 October 1808.
8. For more on the subject see Beate Engelen's excellent study: Engelen, *Soldatenfrauen.*
9. Carl to Marie, 19 April 1814, *Correspondence,* 374.
10. Lehnsdorff, *Die Tagebücher,* 337.
11. Hagemann, "Female Patriots," 408.
12. These details come again from Stosch's account in Pertz and Delbrueck, *Gneisenau,* 5:120.
13. Unpublished letter, Marie to Carl, 30 June 1816.

14. Karl von Meusebach's poem after her husband's death leaves such impression, Schwartz, *Das Leben*, 2:192–93.

15. Unpublished letters, Marie to Carl, 22 April and 14–15 May 1830.

16. When Marie left for Berlin in the summer of 1816, she advised Carl, if bored or lonely, to seek the company of Emma, unpublished letter, Marie to Carl, 18 July 1816.

17. Stosch in Pertz and Delbrueck, *Gneisenau*, 5:120.

18. Gneisenau to Gibsone, 12 August 1816, Pertz and Delbrueck, *Gneisenau*, 5:135.

19. Gneisenau to Boyen, 5 August 1816, Pertz and Delbrueck, *Gneisenau*, 5:132–33.

20. Princess Louise, *Forty-Five Years*, 394.

21. Kissinger, "The Congress of Vienna: A Reappraisal".

22. Unpublished letter, Marie to Carl, 20 August 1816.

23. Marie to Gneisenau, 23 July 1816, Pertz and Delbrueck, *Gneisenau*, 5:127.

24. Clark, *Iron Kingdom*, 402–3.

25. Paret, *Clausewitz and the State*, 266.

26. Marie to Gneisenau, 30 August 1816, Pertz and Delbrueck, *Gneisenau*, 5:145.

27. Unpublished letter, Marie to Carl, 25 July 1816.

28. Marie to Gneisenau, 23 July 1816, Pertz and Delbrueck, *Gneisenau*, 5:127.

29. Gneisenau to Carl, 19 September 1816, Pertz and Delbrueck, *Gneisenau*, 5:147.

30. Carl to Gneisenau, 11 December 1816, Pertz and Delbrueck, *Gneisenau*, 5:271–72.

31. Carl to Gneisenau, 17 August 1816, Pertz and Delbrueck, *Gneisenau*, 5:141–42.

32. Marie to Gneisenau, 30 August 1816, Pertz and Delbrueck, *Gneisenau*, 5:145.

33. Carl's letter has been lost but the content could be reconstructed through unpublished letter, Marie to Carl, 3 August 1816.

34. Adams, *Traveled First Lady*, 200.

35. Rochow, *Vom Leben*, 87–88.

36. Unpublished letters, Marie to Carl, 25 July and 3 August 1816.

37. Unpublished letter, Marie to Carl, 25 July 1816.

38. The quote and the following detail are taken out of Carl to Gneisenau, 12 October 1816, Pertz and Delbrueck, *Gneisenau*, 5:152–53.

39. Carl to Gneisenau, 12 November 1816, Pertz and Delbrueck, *Gneisenau*, 5:163.

40. According to excerpts of Meusebach's diary, published in Schwartz, *Das Leben*, 2:195–96.

41. Carl to Gneisenau, 27 December 1816, Pertz and Delbrueck, *Gneisenau*, 5:178.

42. Marie von Clausewitz, "Preface," 66.

43. Clausewitz, "Note from 1818," 63.

44. Clausewitz, "Agitation," 364–65.

45. Meusebach, "Carolinchen an die schöne Dame," published in Schwartz, *Das Leben*, 2:193–94.

46. Gneisenau to Carl, 29 September 1817, Pertz and Delbrueck, *Gneisenau*, 5:243–44.

47. Gneisenau to Carl, 23 February 1818, Pertz and Delbrueck, *Gneisenau*, 5:292.

48. Gneisenau to Carl, 23 December 1817, Pertz and Delbrueck, *Gneisenau*, 5:276–78.

49. Gneisenau to Carl, 7 May 1818, Pertz and Delbrueck, *Gneisenau*, 5:312–13.

CHAPTER 9

1. Carl to Gneisenau, 1 October 1818, Pertz and Delbrueck, *Gneisenau*, 5:342–43.
2. Carl to Gneisenau, 7 November 1818, Pertz and Delbrueck, *Gneisenau*, 5:358.
3. Bernstoff, *Ein Bild*, 1:235.
4. See, e.g., Paret, *Clausewitz and the State*, 318.
5. Bernstorff, *Ein Bild*, 1:3-6.
6. Bernstorff, *Ein Bild*, I,:235; also Paret, *Clausewitz and the State*, 318 and 318n.
7. Unpublished letter, Carl to Marie, 25–26 May 1830.
8. Bernstorff, *Ein Bild*, 2:47.
9. Carl to Gneisenau, 25 October 1818, Pertz and Delbrueck, *Gneisenau*, 5:351.
10. Recently Kotzebue's personality and ideas have been a subject of revision. Karen Hagemann argues that the diplomat possessed "a firmly independent and undogmatic early-liberal mindset." Kotzebue criticized, according to Hagemann, the rising Germanomania and advocated complete equality between the nobility and the middle classes and absolute freedom of opinion. See Hagemann, *Revisiting Prussia's Wars*, 117.
11. Carl to Gneisenau, 25 October 1818, Pertz and Delbrueck, *Gneisenau*, 5:Pertz-Delbrueck, V, 351.
12. Clausewitz, "Agitation," 349-51.
13. Levinger, *Enlightened Nationalism*, 146.
14. Clark, *Iron Kingdom*, 401.
15. Bernstorff, *Ein Bild*, 1:264.
16. Gneisenau to Princess Louise, 22 October 1819, Pertz and Delbrueck, *Gneisenau*, 5:380–81.
17. Carl to Gneisenau, undated 1819, Pertz and Delbrueck, *Gneisenau*, 5:378.
18. Gneisenau to Princess Louise, 20 November 1819; and to Carl, 10 January 1820, Pertz and Delbrueck, *Gneisenau*, 5:384 and 412.
19. Unpublished letter, Marie to Carl, 30 September—22 October 1807.
20. Unpublished letter, Marie to Carl, 30 May 1809.
21. Unpublished letters, Marie to Carl, 16–17 September 1807 and 13–16 April 1814.
22. Bernstorff, *Ein Bild*, 2:23–24.
23. Clausewitz, "Prussian *Landwehr*," 329–34.
24. Gneisenau to Gröben, 18 November 1819, Pertz and Delbrueck, *Gneisenau*, 5:388.
25. More details are provided in Paret, *Clausewitz and the State*, 320–23.
26. Rochow, *Vom Leben*, 128–29.
27. Marwitz to Marie, 15 February 1820, in Marwitz, *Gesammelte Schriften*, 3:300.

28. Rochow, *Vom Leben*, 116.

29. Ibid., 167.

30. Marie von Clausewitz, Tagebuchblätter 17.08.1813–30.11.1813.

31. Carl to Gneisenau, 21 August 1820, Pertz and Delbrueck, *Gneisenau*, 5:439.

32. In 1818 Elise von Bernstorff reported that Sophie von Brühl suffering from serious complications of a broken arm, Bernstorff, *Ein Bild*, 1:251.

33. Unpublished letter, Marie to Carl, 25 June 1831.

34. Paret, *Clausewitz and the State*, 322–23.

35. Gneisenau to Princess Louise, 20 November 1819, Pertz and Delbrueck, *Gneisenau*, 5:385–86.

36. Clausewitz, "Agitation," 351.

37. Paret, *Clausewitz and the State*, 302–3; Levinger, *Nationalism*, 147–48; Clark, *Iron Kingdom*, 404.

38. Levinger, *Nationalism*, 152.

39. Carl to Gneisenau, 31 January 1820, Pertz and Delbrueck, *Gneisenau*, 5:421.

40. Carl to Gneisenau, 23 October 1820, Pertz and Delbrueck, *Gneisenau*, 5:444.

41. Ibid.

42. Carl to Gneisenau, 18 July 1821, Pertz and Delbrueck, *Gneisenau*, 5:461.

43. Gneisenau to Marie, 8 July 1822, Pertz and Delbrueck, *Gneisenau*, 5:470.

44. Unpublished letter, Marie to Carl, undated 1830; Rochow, *Vom Leben,* 80.

45. According to unpublished letters, Marie to Carl, 22 April 1830 and 10 and 30 June, 1831.

46. Bettina von Arnim to Amalie von Helvig, two undated letters from the spring and summer 1818, in Bissing, *Amalie von Helvig*, 399 and 394.

47. Bernstorff, *Ein Bild*, 1:249.

48. Bettina von Arnim to Amalie von Helvig, summer 1818, in Bissing, *Amalie von Helvig*, 399.

49. Bettina to Achim von Arnim, 3 June 1822, in Arnim, *Briefe*, 375.

50. Elisa von Radziwill to a friend, 30 August 1825, in Radziwill, *Ein Leben*, 128.

51. Rochow, *Vom Leben*, 101; about Bernstorff's salon, see Diemel, *Adelige Frauen*, 172–73.

52. Diemel, *Adelige Frauen*, 185.

53. Bernstorff, *Ein Bild*, 2:102.

54. Marie wrote to Carl in the summer of 1831 that she would like to extensively question and discuss with Minister Bernstorff the Belgium Revolution, but "I have not gathered enough courage to ask for it." Unpublished letter, Marie to Carl, 28 July 1831.

55. Bernstorff, *Ein Bild,*, 2:23–24.

56. Gneisenau to Stein, 1 June 1829, discussed theirs and Marie's involvement, Pertz and Delbrueck, *Gneisenau*, 5:560–61.

57. Unpublished letter, Marie to Carl, 13 April 1813.

58. Diemel, *Adelige Frauen*, 128.

59. Princess Louise's adopted daughter Blanche expressed her mistrust against Marie, Carl to Marie, 14 June 1831, *Correspondence*, 450.

60. As quoted in Paret, *Clausewitz and the State*, 324–25.

61. Hagemann, "Female Patriots," 409; Huber-Sperl, "Organized Women," 88.

62. Albertine to Wilhelmine von Boguslawska, 22 January 1826, in Boguslawski, *Aus dem preussischen*, 114–15.

63. Dudink and Hagemann, "Masculinity in Politics," 3–5.

64. Carl to Marie, 2 June 1807, *Correspondence*, 118–19; unpublished letters, Marie to Carl, 18 June 1807, 14 October 1813, and 28 July 1831.

65. Clausewitz, "War of the Spanish Succession," 15–18.

66. Carl to Marie, 5 August 1815, *Correspondence*, 408.

67. Carl to Marie, 28 May 1831, *Correspondence*, 441.

68. Clausewitz, On War, 86.

69. Marie to Gneisenau, 26 October 1822, Pertz and Delbrueck, *Gneisenau*, 5:476.

70. Carl to Gneisenau, 26 July 1823, Pertz and Delbrueck, *Gneisenau*, 5:489; Paret, 316.

71. Gneisenau to Marie, 8–9 July 1822, Pertz and Delbrueck, *Gneisenau*, 5:472.

72. The exact time when the essays "About the Art and Art Theory," "About the Concept of Physical Beauty," "Architectural Rhapsodies," and "Character of Private Houses" were created remains a subject of debate. Paret argues that it was during the Reform era while Rothfels and Schering assume a later period of his life. See Paret, *Clausewitz*, 162–63; Schering's introduction note in *Geist und Tat*, 153; Rothfels, "Ein kunsttheoretisches Fragment des Generals von Clausewitz,"375n1. The essays are published under the chapter "Kunstbetrachtungen" in Clausewitz, *Geist und Tat*, 153–78.

73. Unpublished letters, Marie to Carl, 11 March 1831.

74. Clausewitz, On War, 136.

75. Ibid., 581.

76. Hauptmann Steinmann von Friederici in Schwartz, *Das Leben*, 2:248–52.

77. From one of these annual maneuvers is his preserved letter from 1821: Carl to Marie, 18 May 1821, *Correspondence*, 261–62.

78. Bernstorff, *Ein Bild*, 1:326.

79. Ibid., 2:87.

80. Marie von Clausewitz, "Preface," 65–66.

81. Hahlweg, "Das Clausewitzbild," 37.

82. There are many examples for this throughout the correspondence. For instance, unpublished letters, Marie to Carl, 27 March, 8 April 1813 and 19 August 1831.

83. Unpublished letter, Marie to Carl, 16 May 1815.

84. Unpublished letter, Marie to Carl, 2 August 1831. The article in question was *Anonymous Letter on the Polish Insurrection*.

85. The manuscripts are kept at Wehrtechnische Studiensammlung in Coblenz, 900205, Pz/3.

86. Carl von Clausewitz, Manuskript. 18 Bogen: Vom Kriege, undatiert, 1.Buch1-2 Kapitel, nach 1817. Pz/3 CD 136.
87. At the time of publication of this book, Paul Donker's and Andreas Herberg-Rothe's studies of the remaining drafts of *On War* are yet to be revealed.
88. Carl von Clausewitz, "Note of 10 July 1827," in *On War*, 69.

CHAPTER 10

1. Paret, *Clausewitz and the State*, 325.
2. Caemmerer, *Clausewitz*, 70.
3. Erman, *Ein Berliner*, 209–10.
4. Unpublished letter, Carl to Carl Leopold, 28 March 1827.
5. All quotes are from Gneisenau to Carl, 18 August 1830, Pertz and Delbrueck, *Das Leben*, 5:603.
6. Carl von Clausewitz, "Tagebuch vom 7 September 1830 bis 9.März 1831," in Schwartz, *Das Leben*, 2:299.
7. Marie von Clausewitz, "Preface," 66.
8. Bernstorff, *Ein Bild*, 2:183.
9. All details are taken out of two unpublished letters, Carl to Marie, 23–25 and 28 September 1830.
10. These letters, however, have not been preserved. Carl's correspondence suggests that Marie extensively wrote to him on the subject. Unpublished letter, Carl to Marie, on 23-25 September 1830.
11. Bernstorff, *Ein Bild*, 2:179–80.
12. Unpublished letter, Carl to Marie, 23 September 1830.
13. Carl von Clausewitz, "Tagebuch 1830–31," Schwartz, *Das Leben*, 2:300.
14. Unpublished letter, Carl to Marie, 27–28 September 1830.
15. Unpublished letter, Marie to Carl, 30 May 1831.
16. Unpublished letter, Carl to Marie, 27–28 September 1830.
17. Ibid.
18. Unpublished letter, Carl to Marie, 28 September 1830.
19. Unpublished letter, Carl to Marie, 21–24 October 1830.
20. Bernstorff, *Ein Bild*, 2:184.
21. Carl von Clausewitz, "Tagebuch 1830–31," in Schwartz, *Das Leben*, 2:300.
22. In October 1831, Marie wrote the following to Carl: "Your campaign studies (or what else should I call them) are in Breslau, I have here only [the pages] part of your work [*deinem Werk*]." Unpublished letter, Marie to Carl, 8 October 1831.
23. Bernstorff, *Ein Bild*, 2:185.
24. Bernstorff, *Ein Bild*, 2:184.
25. Brudzynska-Nemec, "Polenbegeisterung in Deutschland nach 1830": 3–4.
26. Unpublished letter, Marie to Carl, 4 October 1831.

27. Clausewitz, "Europe since the Polish Partitions," 372–76. See also Paret and Moran's analysis, ibid., 369–72.
28. Bernstorff, *Ein Bild*, 2:184.
29. Ibid., 2:195
30. Parkinson, *Clausewitz*, 324–25.
31. Unpublished letter, Marie to Carl, 17 November and 13 December 1812.
32. Carl to Marie, 15 May 1812, *Correspondence*, 287.
33. Unpublished letter, Marie to Carl, 14 March 1831.
34. The original name is "Zurückführung der vielen politischen Fragen, welche Deutschland beschäftigen, auf die unsere Gesamtexistenz," in Schwarz, *Das Leben*, 2:408–17.
35. Unpublished letter, Marie to Carl, 2 and 9 April 1831; for more about the article see Paret, *Clausewitz and the State*, 406.
36. Carl to Marie, 10, 12, and 17 March 1831, *Correspondence*, 411, 414, and 417.
37. Carl to Marie, 16 June 1831, *Correspondence*, 452.
38. Unpublished letter, Marie to Carl, 28 April 1831.
39. Carl to Marie, 28 May 1831, *Lebensbild*, 439.
40. Unpublished letter, Marie to Carl, 22 March 1831.
41. Unpublished letter, Marie to Carl, 4 August 1831.
42. Carl to Marie, 6 August 1831, *Correspondence*, 474.
43. Unpublished letter, Marie to Carl, 22 March 1831.
44. Unpublished letter, Marie to Carl, 20 and 24 March 1831.
45. Unpublished letter, Marie to Carl, 29 March 1831; Carl to Marie, 31 March 1831, *Correspondence*, 424–25.
46. Carl to Marie, 23 and 27 June 1831, *Correspondence*, 454–55 and 459.
47. Unpublished letter, Marie to Carl, 14 April 1831; Carl to Marie, 16 April 1831, *Correspondence*, 431.
48. Unpublished letter, Marie to Carl, 24 May 1831.
49. Carl to Marie, 4 June 1831, *Correspondence*, 445.
50. Unpublished letter, Marie to Carl, 11 August 1831.
51. Carl to Marie, July 24, 1831, *Correspondence*, 468.
52. Koch, *History of Prussia*, 221.
53. Carl to Marie, 16 June 1831, *Correspondence*, 450–52.
54. Unpublished letter, Marie to Carl, 2 August 1831.
55. Unpublished letter, Marie to Carl, 23 July 1831.
56. Carl to Marie, 27 June 1831, *Correspondence*, 459.
57. Unpublished letter, Marie to Carl, 13 October 1831.
58. Unpublished letter, Marie to Carl, 21 July 1831.
59. Unpublished parts of letters, Carl to Marie, 28 July and 4 August 1831.
60. Unpublished letters, Marie to Carl, 6 August and 1 September 1831.
61. Unpublished letter, Marie to Carl, 6 August 1831.
62. Carl to Marie, 23 August 1831, *Correspondence*, 484–85.
63. Carl to Marie, 5 September 1831, *Correspondence,* 488.

64. Unpublished letter, Marie to Carl, 15 September 1831.
65. Unpublished letter, Marie to Carl, 3, 16 and 22 September 1831.
66. Unpublished letter, Marie to Carl, 10 September 1831.
67. Unpublished letter, Marie to Carl, 13 September 1831.
68. Unpublished letter, Marie to Carl, 15 and 18–20 September 1831.
69. Unpublished letter, Marie to Carl, 1 October 1831.
70. Unpublished letter, Marie to Carl, 2 and 6 October 1831.
71. Unpublished letter, Marie to Carl, 15 September 1831.
72. Marie to Elise von Bernstorff, November 1831, Bernstorff, *Ein Bild*, 2:442–43.

CHAPTER 11

1. Marie to Countess von Dernath, November 1831, Bernstorff, *Ein Bild*, 2:228–29.
2. Marie to Elise von Bernstorff, November 1831, Bernstorff, *Ein Bild*, 2:227.
3. Ibid., 227-28.
4. Paret, *Clausewitz and the State*, 431.
5. Unpublished letter, Marie to Carl, 4 August 1831.
6. Marie von Clausewitz, "Preface," 65.
7. Anonymous, "Nekrolog von Carl von Clausewitz," *Staatszeitung* on 22 November 1831, in Schwartz, *Das Leben*, 2:443–44. Schwartz suggests Gröben as author based on both the highly personal style and a conversation with his biographer Richard von Meerheimb.
8. Anonymous (Marie von Clausewitz), "General Clausewitz," 221.
9. Bassford, "John Keegan," http://www.clausewitz.com/readings/Bassford/Keegan/.
10. Rosinski, "Die Entwicklung von Clausewitz' Werk "Vom Kriege," 292.
11. Clausewitz, *On War,* 70.
12. Gat, *Origins*, 255–63.
13. Marie von Clausewitz, "Preface," 67.
14. Marie von Clausewitz, "Preface," 66.
15. Ibid., 67.
16. Ibid.
17. Hahlweg, "Das Clausewitzbild," 64–73 and 168–71.
18. As quoted in Schwartz, *Das Leben*, 2:54.
19. Marie von Clausewitz, "Vorrede zum Siebten Band," 9.
20. Ibid., 7.
21. See the first edition of *On War* in Clausewitz, *Hinterlassene Werke* (1832), 19.
22. Marie von Clausewitz, "Vorrede zum Dritten Teil," 865–66. This preface is not published in the Howard and Paret edition in English.
23. A copy of the announcement is published in Clausewitz, *Hinterlassene Werke* (1980), 1246–50.
24. Most visibly, in Paret's biography, Paret, *Clausewitz and the State*, 105. Paradoxically, together with Michael Howard, he also translated Marie's

"Preface" in *On War*, 65–67. In recent texts about Empress Augusta, Emperor Friedrich III, or nineteenth-century women's history in Prussia, Marie von Clausewitz has been correctly named as *Oberhofmeisterin* at the court of Prince Wilhelm-son during 1832–1835. See Krauze, *Vom letzten Preussen*, 48; Neumann, *Friedrich III*, 13.

25. Marie von Clausewitz, "Preface," 65.

26. Diemel, *Adelige Frauen*, 73 and 111–12.

27. Krauze, *Vom letzten Preussen*, 48; Rochow, *Vom Leben*, 205.

28. Rochow, *Vom Leben*, 204–6.

29. Bernstoff, *Ein Bild*, 2:284.

30. Marie von Clausewitz, "Vorrede zum Siebten Band," 9.

31. Gröben, "Vorrede zum Neunten Band," 8; Franz August O'Etzel, "Berichtigungen," 8.

32. O'Etzel, "Berichtigungen," 8.

33. Marie to Ferdinand Dümmler, 28 July 1832, in Clausewitz, *Hinterlassene Werke* (1980), 1245–46.

34. Unpublished letter, Marie to Carl, 14 April 1831.

35. In their English translation Paret and Moran published the full version of Clausewitz's manuscript and clearly marked Ranke's changes to the text in Clausewitz, *Historical and Political Writings*, 86–88. Marie's annex was not included.

36. Anonymous (Marie von Clausewitz), "General Clausewitz," 220–23.

37. In his description of proofreading the print copies of the Fourth and Fifth Parts, O'Etzel did not mention direct involvement on Marie's side except the general guidance. O'Etzel, "Berichtigungen," 8.

38. Marie von Clausewitz, "Vorrede zum Dritten Teil," 865.

39. Unpublished letter, Marie to Prince Wilhelm, 22 August 1831.

40. Marie wrote down in her journal from 1832–1836 Sophie von Schwerin's opinion. Marie von Clausewitz, *Aufzeichnungen: Abschriften von Zitaten, Gedichten, Grabinschriften und Briefen*/Marie von Clausewitz o.O. [nach 1831].

41. O'Etzel, "Berichtigungen," 8.

42. Marie von Clausewitz, "Vorrede zum Siebten Band," 9.

43. Ibid., 5–7.

44. In their English translation of "The Campaign of 1812" Peter Paret and Daniel Moran highlight the introduced changes. See Carl von Clausewitz, "The Campaign of 1812 in Russia," 110–219.

45. Koch, *Prussia*, 220; Clark, *Iron Kingdom*, 411.

46. Rochow, *Vom Leben*, 234.

47. Marie to Elise von Bernstorff, 9 April 1833, in Baer, *Prinzess Elisa Radziwill*, 142–43.

48. Unpublished letter, Carl von Brühl to Marie, originally undated; in all probability written on 31 January 1835.

49. Unpublished letter, Carl von Brühl to Hedwig von Brühl, 27 January 1836. The information about the following events is also taken from it.

50. Unpublished letter, Carl von Brühl to Hedwig von Brühl, 27 January 1836.
51. The quotes and the details about the bloodletting are from Hensel, *Tagebuch*.
52. Unpublished letters, Carl von Brühl to Fritz von Brühl, 24 January 1836; Carl von Brühl to Hedwig von Brühl, 27 January 1836.
53. Hensel, *Tagebuch*.
54. Luise Hensel was the sister of the artist Wilhelm Hensel and sister-in-law of the composer Fanny Mendelsson-Hensel. In her youth Luise was a celebrated beauty adored by the romantic poets Clemens Brentano and Wilhelm Müller and a talented poet in her own right.
55. Unpublished letter, Carl von Brühl to Hedwig von Brühl, 27 January 1836.
56. Hensel, *Tagebuch*.
57. Ibid.

POSTSCRIPT

1. Hensel to Christoph Berhnhard Schlüter, 8 March 1836, in Hensel, *Briefe*, 64–65.
2. Unpublished letter, Carl von Brühl to Fritz von Brühl, 16 February 1836. It is unclear which Prince and Princess Wilhelm he meant here—Marianne and her husband or Augusta and hers.
3. Unpublished letter, Carl von Brühl to Fritz von Brühl, 16 February 1836.
4. Unpublished letter, Carl von Brühl to Fritz von Brühl, 31 January 1836.
5. According to the research of Bernd Domsgen and Olaf Thiel. See the following newspaper articles: Bettina Schütze, "Neue Informationen zur Exhumierung," *Volksstimme Burg*, 08 September, 2014; Bettina Schütze, "Reise nach Wroslaw gibt Aufschuss über den Friedhof," *Volksstimme Burg*, 30 October 2014.
6. Unpublished letter, Carl von Brühl to Fritz von Brühl, 31 January 1836.
7. Unpublished letter, Carl von Brühl to Fritz von Brühl, 4–5 February 1837.
8. These details are taken out of unpublished letter, Carl von Brühl to Fritz von Brühl, 23 December 1836.
9. Unpublished letter, Marie to Carl, 9 October 1831.
10. Diemel, *Adelige Frauen*, 131–33; Clark, *Iron Kingdom*, 402.
11. Strachan, *Clausewitz's On War*, 26.
12. Jessen, *Die Moltkes*, 54-56.
13. Howard, *Clausewitz*, 60.
14. For more about this issue see Paret, "Clausewitz": 212–13.
15. Wallach, *The Dogma of the Battle of Annihilation*, 242.
16. Baldwin, "Clausewitz in Nazi Germany": 11.
17. For more about Clausewitz's influence over modern British and American strategic thought after 1945 see Bassford, *Clausewitz in English*, 195–223.
18. Bassford, "Grand Tradition of Trashing Clausewitz," http://www.clausewitz.com/readings/Bassford/Keegan/delenda.htm.
19. Clausewitz, *On War*, 75.

Bibliography

I. LIST OF UNPUBLISHED DOCUMENTS

Geheimes Staatsarchiv/Preußischer Kulturbesitz (Prussian Privy State Archives/Prussian Cultural Heritage Foundation)
VI.HA Familienarchive und Nachlässe, FA Buttlar-Venedien, v. (Dep.)

Marie to Carl von Clausewitz
8–15 January 1807   Nr.42
7 February 1807   Nr.43
18 February 1807   Nr.44
26 February–11 March 1807   Nr.45
17 March 1807   Nr.46
8–10 April 1807   Nr.48
26 April 1807   Nr.49
15 May 1807   Nr.50
20 May–4 June 1807   Nr.51
18 June 1807   Nr.52
28 June 1807   Nr.53
24 July 1808   Nr.54
9–13 August 1807   Nr.55
16–17 September 1807   Nr.56
30 September–22 October 1807   Nr.57
12–18 April 1808   Nr.58
25 April 1808   Nr.61
29 July 1808   Nr.62
11–12 September 1808   Nr.66
4 October 1808   Nr.67
22–23 October 1808   Nr.69
13 November 1808   Nr.73
24–26 November 1808   Nr.75
15 December 1808   Nr.79
18 December 1808   Nr.80
22 December 1808   Nr.81
4 January 1809   Nr.83
3 March 1809   Nr.88

27 March 1809   Nr.90

11–14 April 1809   Nr.92

23 May 1809   Nr.99

30 May 1809   Nr.100

18–20 July 1809   Nr.106

28 August 1809   Nr.110

29 September–8 October 1809   Nr.111

12–13 May 1812   Nr.115

20–21 May 1812   Nr.116

28 May 1812   Nr.117

1–7 June 1812   Nr.118

17 June 1812   Nr.119

29 June 1812   Nr.120

30 July 1812   Nr.122

27 August 1812   Nr.123

10 September 1812   Nr.124

1 October 1812   Nr.125

19 October 1812   Nr.126

17 November 1812   Nr.127

1 December 1812   Nr.128

3 December 1812   Nr.129

13 December 1812   Nr.131

17 December 1812   Nr.132

19 January 1813   Nr.138

23 March 1813   Nr.139

27 March 1813   Nr.140

4 April 1813   Nr.142

8 April 1813   Nr.143

11 April 1813   Nr.144

13 April 1813   Nr.145

15 April 1813   Nr.146

18 April 1813   Nr.147

22 April 1813   Nr.148

27 April 1813   Nr.149

29 April 1813   Nr.150

19 May 1813   Nr.151

22 May 1813   Nr.152

26 May 1813   Nr.153

31 May 1813   Nr.155

2 June 1813   Nr.156

7 June 1813   Nr.157

8 June 1813   Nr.158

2 July 1813   Nr.163

13 July 1813   Nr.166
23 August 1813   Nr.173
28 August 1813   Nr.175
9 September 1813   Nr.178
11 September 1813   Nr.179
30 September–2 October 1813   Nr.185
14 October 1813   Nr.188
21 October 1813   Nr.189
4 March 1814   Nr.190
7 March 1814   Nr.191
15 March 1814   Nr.192
19 March 1814   Nr.193
13–17 April 1814   Nr.196
26 April 1814   Nr.197
14 May 1815   Nr.199
16 May 1815   Nr.200
20 May 1815   Nr.201
12 June 1815   Nr.202
14 June 1815   Nr.203
27 June 1815   Nr.204
4 July 1815   Nr.205
10 July 1815   Nr.206
14 July 1815   Nr.207
20 July 1815   Nr.208
31 July 1815   Nr.211
5 August 1815   Nr.212
18 July 1816   Nr.207
30 June 1816   Nr.210
25 July 1816   Nr.209
3 August 1816   Nr.214
20 August 1816   Nr.215
9 July 1828   Nr.368
undated 1830   Nr.41
22 April 1830   Nr.369
14–15 May 1830   Nr.375
11 March 1831   Nr.381
14–15 March 1831   Nr.382
20 March 1831   Nr.384
22 March 1831   Nr.385
24 March 1831   Nr.384
29 March 1831   Nr.388
2 April 1831   Nr.392
9 April 1831   Nr.395

14 April 1831　　Nr.398
28 April 1831　　Nr.340
24 May 1831　　Nr.344
10 June 1831　　Nr.352
25 June 1831　　Nr.357
21 July 1831　　Nr.367
23 July 1831　　Nr.293
28 July 1831　　Nr.295
30 July 1831　　Nr.296
31 July 1815　　Nr.297
2 August 1831　　Nr.298
4 August 1831　　Nr.299
6 August 1831　　Nr.300
9 August 1831　　Nr.301
11 August 1831　　Nr.302
19 August 1831　　Nr.305
1 September 1831　　Nr.309
3 September 1831　　Nr.310
10 September 1831　　Nr.313
13 September 1831　　Nr.314
15 September 1831　　Nr.315
16 September 1831　　Nr.316
18-20 September 1831　　Nr.317
22 September 1831　　Nr.318
1 October 1831　　Nr.322
2 October 1831　　Nr.323
4 October 1831　　Nr.324
6 October 1831　　Nr.325
9 October 1831　　Nr.327
13 October 1831　　Nr.328

Carl to Marie von Clausewitz

25 March 1813　　Nr.507
26–28 March 1813　　Nr.508
22 April 1813　　Nr.513
1 May 1813　　Nr.515
23–25 May 1815　　Nr.564
6 June 1815　　Nr.566
13 July 1815　　Nr.576
14 July 1815　　Nr.577
28 April 1830　　Nr.217
25–26 May 1830　　Nr.221
23–25 September 1830　　Nr.223
27–28 September 1830　　Nr.224

28 September 1830   Nr.255
21–24 October 1830   Nr.226
28 July 1831   Nr.267
4 August 1831   Nr.270

Marie to Fritz von Brühl, 12 June 1809 Nr.1
Fritz von Brühl to Marie, 3 December 1811 Nr.1
"Death of William Gomm Esq." Nr.1

Luise Hensel, Tagebuch für den Arzt während der Krankheit der Frau Generalin
    von Clausewitz, geboren Gräfin von Brühl, Oberhofmeisterin Ihrer
    Königlichen Hoheit, die Prinzessin Wilhelm von Preussen

Private Collection Bernd Domsgen/Olaf Thiel, Clausewitz Society
(*Freundeskreis Clausewitz*), in Burg bei Magdeburg
Marie to Carl von Clausewitz, 18 October 1806
Carl to Carl Leopold von Clausewitz, 26 November 1826
Carl to Carl Leopold von Clausewitz, 28 March 1827
Carl to Carl Leopold von Clausewitz, 15 May 1829
"Einlandung-Schrift," 25 January 1779, Burgische Französische Schule

Universitäts- und Landesbibliothek Münster (University and State Library
in Münster)
Marie von Clausewitz, Aufzeichnungen: Abschriften von Zitaten, Gedichten,
    Grabinschriften und Briefen/Marie von Clausewitz o.O. [nach 1831].
    N. Clausewitz 5,022
Marie von Clausewitz, Tagebuchblätter 17.08.1813-30.11.1813. N. Clausewitz 5,021

Sächsische Staats- und Universitätsbibliothek Dresden (Saxon State and
University Library)
Carl von Brühl to Marie von Clausewitz, u.d. but probably 31 January 1835 Mscr.
    Dresd.App.514, A, 556
Carl von Brühl to Friedrich von Brühl, 24 January 1836 Mscr.Dresd.
    App.514,A, 514
Carl von Brühl to Hedwig von Brühl (wrongly attributed in the archive to
    Friedrich), 27 January 1836 Mscr.Dresd.App.514,A, 515
Carl von Brühl to Friedrich von Brühl, 31 January 1836 Mscr.Dresd.App.514,A, 517
Carl von Brühl to Friedrich von Brühl, 16 February 1836 Mscr.Dresd.
    App.514,A, 518
Carl von Brühl to Friedrich von Brühl, 3 November 1836 Mscr.Dresd.
    App.514,A, 524
Carl von Brühl to Friedrich von Brühl, 23 December 1836 Mscr.Dresd.
    App.514,A, 525

Carl von Brühl to Friedrich von Brühl, 4–5 February 1837 Mscr.Dresd. App.514,A, 526

Wehrtechnische Sammlung Koblenz (Military History Museum in Coblenz)

Carl von Clausewitz, Manuskript. 18 Bogen: Vom Kriege, undatiert, 1.Buch1-2 Kapitel, nach 1817. Pz/3 CD 136.

Klassik Stiftung Weimar/Goethe- und Schiller-Archiv (Goethe and Schiller Literary Archive in Weimar)

Karl Gustav von Brinckmann to Marie von Brühl, 6 March 1803, Bestand 5/ Berg-Voß GSA 5/50

Evangelisches Landeskirchliches Archiv in Berlin (ELAB) (Evangelical Church Archive in Berlin)

Kirchenbuchstelle Berlin-Brandenburg, microfiches 5749, p. 99, nr. 239

Hessisches Staatsarchiv Darmstadt (Hessian State Archive in Darmstadt)

Fischbacher Archiv, Nachlässe Prinz Wilhelm von Preussen und Prinzessin Marianne geb. von Hessen-Homburg (Abt. D 22) : 1792-1849

Marie von Clausewitz to Prince Wilhelm, 22 August 1832

II. PUBLISHED CLAUSEWITZ WORKS AND CORRESPONDENCE

Clausewitz, Karl, and Marie von. *Ein Lebensbild in Briefen und Tagebuchblätter (Correspondence).* Ed. and pub. Karl Linnebach. Berlin: Volksverband der Bücherfreunde Wegweiser-Verlag, 1925.

Clausewitz, Karl, and Marie von. *Ein Leben im Kampf für Freiheit und Reich.* Ed. and pub. Otto Heuschele. Leipzig: H. Schaufuß Verlag, 1935.

Pertz, Heinrich, and Hans Delbrueck, ed. *Das Leben des Feldmarschalls Grafen Neidhardt von Gneisenau.* Vols. 3, 4, and 5. Berlin: Georg Reimer Verlag, 1869–1880.

Schwartz, Karl. Das Leben des Generals Carl von Clausewitz und der Frau Marie von Clausewitz geb. Gräfin von Brühl, in Briefen, Tagebüchern, Aufsätzen und anderen Schriftstücken (The Life of General Carl von Clausewitz and Madam Marie von Clausewitz, born Countess von Brühl). 2 vols. Berlin: F. Dümmler, 1878.

Anonymous (Marie von Clausewitz). "Erinnerung an den General Clausewitz und sein Verhältnis zu Scharnhorst" ("General Clausewitz"). *Historisch-Politische Zeitschrift* 1 (1832): 220–23.

Clausewitz, Carl von. "Agitation." In Carl von Clausewitz, *Historical and Political Writings,* ed. and trans. Peter Paret and Daniel Moran, 335–68. Princeton: Princeton University Press, 1992.

Clausewitz, Carl von. "Europe since the Polish Partition." In Carl von Clausewitz, *Historical and Political Writings,* ed. and trans. Peter Paret and Daniel Moran, 369–76. Princeton: Princeton University Press, 1992.

Clausewitz, Carl von. "From *The Campaign of 1812 in Russia* (1823-1825). In Carl von Clausewitz, *Historical and Political Writings,* ed. and trans. Peter Paret and Daniel Moran, 110-204. Princeton: Princeton University Press, 1992.

Clausewitz, Carl von. *Geist und Tat. Das Vermächtnis des Soldaten und Denkers.* Ed. W. M. Schering. Stuttgart: Alfred Kröner Verlag, 1941.

Clausewitz, Carl von. *Hinterlassene Werke des Generals Carl von Clausewitz über Krieg und Kriegsführung.* Part One. Berlin: Ferdinand Dümmler, 1832.

Clausewitz, Carl von. *Nachrichten über Preussen in seiner grossen Katastrophe.* N.p.: Ernst Siegfried Mittler und Sohn, 1888.

Clausewitz, Carl von. "On the Basic Questions of Germany's Existence." In Carl von Clausewitz, *Historical and Political Writings*, ed. and trans. Peter Paret and Daniel Moran, 377–84. Princeton: Princeton University Press, 1992.

Clausewitz, Carl von. "On the Life and Character of Scharnhorst." In Carl von Clausewitz, *Historical and Political Writings*, ed. and trans. Peter Paret and Daniel Moran, 85–108. Princeton: Princeton University Press, 1992.

Clausewitz, Carl von. "On the Political Advantages and Disadvantages of the Prussian *Landwehr* (1819)." In Carl von Clausewitz, *Historical and Political Writings*, ed. and trans. Peter Paret and Daniel Moran, 329-334. Princeton: Princeton University Press, 1992.

Clausewitz, Carl von. *On War.* Ed. and trans. Michael Howard and Peter Paret. Princeton: Princeton University Press, 1984.

Clausewitz, Carl von. "Some Comments on the War of the Spanish Succession after Reading the Letters of Madame de Maintenon to the Princess des Ursins." In Carl von Clausewitz, *Historical and Political Writings*, ed. and trans. Peter Paret and Daniel Moran, 15–18. Princeton: Princeton University Press, 1992

Clausewitz, Carl von. *Verstreute kleine Schriften*, ed. Werner Hahlweg. Osnabrück: Biblio-Verlag, 1979.

Clausewitz, Carl von, and Arthur Wellesley [1st Duke of Wellington]. *On Waterloo: Clausewitz, Wellington, and the Campaign of 1815.* Ed. and trans. Christopher Bassford, Daniel Moran, and Gregorz W. Pedlow. Charleston, SC: Clausewitz.com, 2010.

Clausewitz, Marie von. "Vorrede zum Dritten Teil." In *Hinterlassene Werke. Vom Kriege. Neunzehnte Auflage* by Carl von Clausewitz, ed. Werner Hahlweg, 865–66. Bonn: Dümmler Verlag, 1980.

Clausewitz, Marie von. "Vorrede zum Siebten Band." In *Hinterlassene Werke: Siebter Band* by Carl von Clausewitz. Vols. 5–10. Berlin: Ferdinand Dümmler, 1835.

III. OTHER PRIMARY SOURCES

Adams, Louisa Catherine. *A Traveled First Lady: Writings of Louisa Catherine Adams.* Ed. Margaret A. Hogan and C. James Taylor. Cambridge, MA: Belknap Press of Harvard University Press, 2014.

Adams, Thomas Boylston. *Berlin and the Prussian Court in 1798. Journal of Thomas Boylston Adams.* Ed. Victor Hugo Paltsits. New York: New York Public Library, 1916.

Arnim. *Arnim Achim und Bettina in ihren Briefen.* Ed. Werner Vortriede. Frankfurt am Main: Insel Verlag, 1988.

Baer, Oswald. *Prinzessin Elisa Radziwill.* Berlin: Mittler und Sohn Königliche Hofbuchhandlung, 1908.

Bernstorff, Elise von, geborene Gräfin von Dernath. *Ein Bild aus der Zeit 1789 bis 1835. Aus Ihren Aufzeichnungen.* 2 vols. Berlin: Ernst Siegfried Mittler und Sohn Verlag, 1899.

Boguslawski, Albert von. *Aus dem preussischen Hof- und diplomatischen Gesellschaft.* Stuttgart and Berlin: J. G. Cotta'sche Buchhandlung, 1903.

Beguelin, Heinrich von. "Die finanzielle Lage des preußischen Staates nach der Katastrophe." In *Die Franzosenzeit in deutschen Landen 1806-1812. In Wort und Bild der Mitlebenden.* Vols. 1. Ed. Friedrich Schultze, 175-178. Leipzig: R Voigtländer, 1908.

Cavan, George. "Der Einzug des Davoutschen Korps in Berlin am 25ten. October." In *Die Franzosenzeit in deutschen Landen 1806-1812. In Wort und Bild der Mitlebenden.* Vols. 1. Ed. Friedrich Schultze, 76-78. Leipzig: R.Voigtländer, 1908.

Chézy, Helmina von. *Unvergessenes: Denkwürdigkeiten aus dem Leben.* Vol. 2. Leipzig: F. A. Brockhaus, 1858.

Czygan, Paul. *Zur Geschichte der Tagesliteratur während der Freiheitskriege.* Vol. 2. Leipzig: Duncker & Humblot, 1909–1911.

Delbrück, Johann Friedrich Gottfried. *Zur Jugend- und Erziehungs-Geschichte des Königs Friedrich Wilhelm IV. Von Preussen und des Kaisers und Königs Wilhelm I.* Ed. Georg Schuster. Berlin: Hoffmann & Com, 1904.

"Die-Deutsche-Wochenschau-Nr.721." June 28, 1944. https://archive.org/details /1944-06-28-Die-Deutsche-Wochenschau-Nr.721.

Erman, Paul. *Ein Berliner Gelehrtenleben 1764–1851.* Berlin: Mittler und Sohn, 1927.

Gomm, William Maynard. *Letters and Journals of Field-Marshal Sir William Maynard Gomm, G.C.B., Commander-in-Chief of India, Constable of the Tower of London: from 1799 to Waterloo, 1815.* Ed. Francis Culling Carr-Gomm. London: John Murray, 1881.

Gröben, Carl Graf von der. "Vorrede zum Neunten Band." In *Hinterlassene Werke: Neunter Band* by Carl von Clausewitz. Vols. 5–16. Berlin: Ferdinand Dümmler, 1837.

Hensel, Luise, and Christoph Berhnhard Schlüter. *Briefe aus dem deutschen Biedermeier, 1832–1876.* Ed. Josefine Nettesgeim. Münster: Regensberg Verlag, 1962.

Jackson, George. *The Diaries and Letters of Sir George Jackson K. C. H.: From the Peace of Amien to the Battle of Talavera.* Vol. 2. London: Richard Bentley and Son, 1872.

Lehnsdorff, Ernst Ahasverus Heinrich von. *Die Tagebücher des Grafen Lehnsdorf: Die geheimen Aufzeichnungen des Kammerherrn der Königin Elisabeth Christine.* Ed. Wieland Giebel. Berlin: Berlin Story Verlag, 2007.

Marwitz, Friedrich August Ludwig von der. *Ein märkischer Edelmann im Zeitalter der Befreiungskriege, Gesammelte Schriften.* Vols. 1 and 3. Ed. Friedrich Meusel. Berlin: Ernst Mittler und Sohn, 1908–1913.

O'Etzel, Franz August. "Berichtigungen." In *Hinterlassene Werke: Funfter Band* by Carl von Clausewitz. Vol. 8. Berlin: Ferdinand Dümmler, 1833.

Parquin, Denis-Charles. *Napoleon's Army*. Ed. and trans. Brian Thomas Jones. North Haven, CT: Archon, 1969.

Princess von Prussia, Louise. *Forty-Five Years of My Life* (1770–1815). Ed. Princess Radziwiłł, nee Castellane and trans. A. R. Allinson. London: Eveleigh Nash, 1912.

Radziwiłł, Elisa. *Ein Leben in Liebe und Leid: Unveröffentlichte Briefe aus der Jahre 1820–1834*. Ed. Bruno Hennig. Berlin: Mittler und Sohn, 1922.

Rochow, Caroline Louise Albertine von, Marie de La Motte-Fouqué. *Vom Leben am preussischen Hofe, 1815–1852*. Ed. Luise v. d. Marwitz. Berlin: Ernst Siegfried Mittler und Sohn, 1908.

Seidel, Paul. "Karl Adolph Graf von Brühl." *Hohenzollern-Jahrbuch* (1897): 199–202.

Steffens, Heinrich. *Was ich erlebte: aus der Erinnerung niedergeschrieben von Heinrich Steffens*. Vol. 7. Breslau: Josef Max und Komp, 1843.

Stein, Freiherr vom. *Briefe und Amtliche Schriften*. Vol. 2, *Das Reformministerium 1807–08. Bearbeitet von Erich Botzenhart und Walter Hubatsch*. Stuttgart: W. Kohlhammer Verlag, 1960.

Stein, Freiherr vom. *Briefe und Amtliche Schriften*. Vol. 3, *1809–12. Bearbeitet von Erich Botzenhart und Walter Hubatsch*. Stuttgart: W. Kohlhammer Verlag, 1961.

Varnhagen von Ense, Karl August. *Ausgewählte Schriften*. Vol. 1. Leipzig: F. A. Brockhaus, 1871.

Varnhagen von Ense, Rahel. *Briefwechsel zwische Varnhagen und Rahel*. Vol. 3. Leipzig: F. A. Brockhaus, 1875.

Varnhagen von Ense, Rahel. *Gesammelte Werke*. Vol. 5. Ed. Bearbeitet Konrad Feilhenfeldt, Uwe Schweinkert, and Rahel E.Steiner. München: Mathes und Seitz, 1983.

IV. SECONDARY SOURCES

Arendt, Hannah. *Rahel Varnhagen: The Life of a Jewish Woman*. New York and London: Harcourt Brace Jovanovich, 1974.

Aron, Raymond. *Clausewitz: Philosopher of War*. New York: Simon & Schuster, 1983.

Aschmann, Birgit. *Preußens Ruhm und Deutschlands Ehre: Zum nationalen Ehrdiskurs im Vorfeld der preußisch-französischen Kriege des 19. Jahrhunderts*. München: Wissenschaftsverlag, 2013.
der preußisch-französischen Kriege des 19. Jahrhunderts

Baldwin, P. M. "Clausewitz in Nazi Germany." *Journal of Contemporary History* 16, no. 1 (January., 1981): 5-26.

Bassford, Christopher. *Clausewitz. in English. The Reception of Clausewitz In Britain and America, 1815-1945*. New York: Oxford University Press, 1994.

Bassford, Christopher. "John Keegan and the Grand Tradition of Trashing Clausewitz." *War and Histor*, 1, no. 3 (November 1994): 319–336, http://www.clausewitz.com/readings/Bassford/Keegan/.

Baur, Wilhelm. *Prinzess Wilhelm von Preussen, geborne Prinzess Marianne von Hessen-Homburg: Ein Lebensbild aus den Tagenbüchern und Briefen der Prinzess.* Hamburg: Agentur des Rauhen Hauses, 1886.

Berg, Caroline von. *Louise Königin von Preußen.* Leipzig: Breitkopf und Härtel, 1814.

Boynton, Lindsay. "William and Richard Gomm." *Burlington Magazine* 122, no. 927 (1980): 359–402.

Brudzynska-Nemec, Gabriela. "Polenbegeisterung in Deutschland nach 1830." *Europäische Geschichte Online/Institut für Europäische Geschichte Mainz* (2010): 1–14. http://ieg-ego.eu/de/threads/euro-paeische-medien/europaeische-medienereignisse/1830er-revolution/gabriela-brudzynska-nemec-polenbegeisterung-in-deutschland-nach-1830.

Caemmerer, Rudolf von. *Clausewitz.* Berlin: B. Behr, 1905.

Clark, Christopher. *Iron Kingdom: The Rise and Downfall of Prussia, 1600–1947.* London: Penguin, 2007.

Cross, Anthony. *By the Banks of the Neva: Chapters from the Lives and Careers of the British in Eighteenth-Century Russia.* Cambridge: Cambridge University Press, 2007.

Diemel, Christa. *Adelige Frauen im bürgerlichen Jahrhundert: Hofdamen, Stiftsdamen, Salondamen, 1800–1870.* Frankfurt am Main: Fischer Taschenbuchverlag, 1998.

Dudink, Stefan, and Karen Hagemann. "Masculinity in Politics and War in the Age of Democratic Revolutions, 1750–1850." In *Masculinities in Politics and War. Gendering Modern History,* ed. Stefan Dudink, Karen Hagemann, and John Tosh. Manchester: Manchester University Press, 2004.

Engelen, Beate. *Soldatenfrauen in Preussen: eine Strukturanalyse der Garnisonsgesellschaft im späten 17.und im 18ten Jahrhundert.* Münster: Lit Verlag, 2005.

Fellmann, Walter. *Heinrich Graf Brühl. Ein Lebens- und Zeitbild.* Leipzig: Koehler & Amelang, 1989.

Gat, Azar. *The Origins of Military Thought from the Enlightenment to Clausewitz.* New York: Oxford University Press, 1989.

Geffarth, Renko D. *Religion und arkane Hierarchie: Der Orden der Gold- und Rosenkreuzer als Geheime Kirche im 18.Jahrhundert.* Leiden: Koninklijke Brill, 2007.

Geiger, Ludwig. *Berlin 1688–1840. Geschichte des geistigen Lebens der preussischen Hauptstadt.* Vol. 2. Berlin: Gebrüder Paetel, 1895.

Gentzkow, Liane von. *Liebe und Tapferkeit: Frauen um deutsche Soldaten* (Love and Courage). Dritte Auflage. Berlin: Fels-Verlag Dr.Wilhelm Spael KG, 1941.

Groehler, Olaf. *Das Heerwesen in Brandenburg und Preußen von 1640 bis 1806.* Berlin: Brandenburgisches Verlagshaus, 1993.

Jessen, Olaf. *Die Moltkes: Biographie einer Familie.* München: C.H.Beck, 2010.

Hagemann, Karen. "Female Patriots: Women, War and the Nation in the Period of the Prussian-German Anti-Napoleonic Wars." *Gender and History* 16, no. 2 (2004): 397–424.

Hagemann, Karen. 'Mannlicher Muth und Teutsche Ehre': Nation, Militar und Geschlecht zur Zeit der Antinapoleonischen Kriege Preußiens. Padeborn: Schoeningh Ferdinand, 2002.

Hagemann, Karen. Revisiting Prussia's Wars Against Napoleon. History, Culture and Memory. New York: Cambridge University Press, 2015.

Hahlweg, Werner. "Das Clausewitzbild einst und jetzt." In Carl von Clausewitz, Hinterlassene Werke. Vom Kriege. Neunzehnte Auflage, ed. Werner Hahlweg. Bonn: Dümmler Verlag, 1980.

Hahlweg, Werner. Clausewitz. Soldat-Poltiker-Denker. Göttingen: Musterschmidt Verlag, 1957.

Hartl, Maria. Carl von Clausewitz. Persönlichkeit und Stil. Emden: Verlag Kunst und Leben, 1956.

Heinrich, Gerd. "Der Adel in Brandenburg-Preußen." In Deutscher Adel 1555–1740, ed. Hellmuth Rossler, 259–314. Darmstadt: Wissenschaftliche Buchgesellschaft, 1965.

Hilbert, Klaus. "Ergänzungen zum Lebensbild des Generals Carl von Clausewitz." Zeitschrift für Militärgeschichte 20, no. 2 (1981): 208–11.

Hopkins, Tighe. Prisoners of War. London: Simpkin, Marshall, Hamilton, Kent, 1914.

Howard, Michael. Clausewitz. New York: Oxford University Press, 1983.

Huber-Sperl, Ritta. "Organized Women and the Strong State: The Beginnings of Female Activity in Germany, 1810–1840." Journal of Women's History 13, no. 4 (2002): 81–105.

Kahan, Arcadius. The Plow, the Hammer, and the Knout: An Economic History of Eighteenth Century Russia. Chicago: University of Chicago Press, 1985.

Kissinger, Henry. "The Congress of Vienna: A Reappraisal." World Politics, Vol. 8, No. 2 (Jan., 1956): 264-280.

Koch, H. W. A History of Prussia. New York: Longman, 1978.

Kohn, Hans. Prelude to Nation-States: The French and German Experience, 1789–1815. Princeton: D. Van Nostrand, 1967.

König, Anton Balthasar. Biographisches Lexikon aller Helden und Militärpersonen. Vol. 1. Berlin: A. Wever, 1788.

Krauze, Justyna M. Vom letzten Preussen zum deutschen Kaiser: das Bild der Hohenzollernkaiser in Tagebüchern und Berichten ihrer Zeitgenossen. Hamburg: Kovac Verlag, 2004.

Krohn von Bissing, Henriette. Das Leben der Dichterin Amalie von Helvig, geb. Freiin von Imhoff. Berlin: W. Hertz, 1889.

Krosigk, Hans von. Karl Graf von Brühl und seine Eltern. Lebensbild auf Grund der Handschriften des Archivs zu Seifersdorf. Berlin: Mittler und Sohn, Königliche Hofbuchhandlung, 1910.

Lebedev, Sergei K. "European Business Culture and St. Petersburg Banks." In Commerce in Russian Urban Culture, 1861–1914, ed. William Craft Brumfield, Boris V. Ananich, and Yuri A.Petrov, 21–38. Baltimore: Johns Hopkins University Press, 2002.

Leggiere, Michael V. *Napoleon and Berlin: The Franco-Prussian War in North Germany, 1813.* Norman: University of Oklahoma Press, 2002.

Levinger, Matthew. *Enlightened Nationalism: The Transformation of Prussian Political Culture, 1806–1848.* New York: Oxford University Press, 2000.

Miller, Norbert. "Literarisches Leben im Anfang des 19. Jahrhunderts. Aspekte einer Preußischen Salon-Kultur." *Kleist-Jahrbuch* (1981/82): 13–32.

Neumann, Hans-Joachim. *Friedrich III.: Der 99-Tage-Kaiser.* Berlin: Be.Bra Verlag, 2006.

Oesterle, Günter. "Juden, Philister und romantische Intellektuelle. Überlegungen zum Antisemitismus in der Romantik." *Athenäum* 2 (1992), http://edoc.hu-berlin.de/hostings/athenaeum/documents/athenaeum/1992-2/.oesterle-guenter-55/PDF/oesterle.pdf

Paletschek, Sylvia. "Adelige und bürgerliche Frauen (1770–1870)." In *Adel und Bürgertum in Deutschland 1770–1848*, ed. Elisabeth Fehrenbach, 159–85. Oldenbourg: Historisches Kolleg, 1994.

Paret, Peter. *Clausewitz and the State: The Man, His Theories, and His Times.* Princeton, NJ: Princeton University Press, 1985.

Paret, Peter. "Clausewitz." In *Makers of Modern Strategy:. From Machiavelli to the Nuclear Age*, ed. Peter Paret, 186–213.

Parkinson, Roger. *Clausewitz: A Biography.* New York: Stein and Day, 1970.

Roesch, Gertrud M. "The Liberation from Napoleon as Self-Liberation: The Year 1813 in the Letters of Rahel Varnhagen." In *Women against Napoleon: Historical and Fictional Responses to His Rise and Legacy*, ed. Waltraud Maierhofer, Gertrud M. Roesch, and Caroline Bland, 109–36. Frankfurt am Main: Campus Verlag, 2007.

Rosinski, Herbert. "Die Entwicklung von Clausewitz' Werk "Vom Kriege" im Lichte seiner "Vorreden" und "Nachrichten." *Historische Zeitschrift* 151, Vol.2 (1935): 278–93.

Rother-Carlowitz, Alfred. Clausewitz und die vollkomenste der Frauen (Clausewitz and the Most Accomplished of All Women). Burg: Schildhorn Verlag, 1940.

Rothfels, Hans. *Carl von Clausewitz: Politik und Krieg.* Berlin: F. Dümmler, 1920.

Rothfels, Hans. "Ein kunsttheoretisches Fragment des Generals von Clausewitz." *Deutsche Rundschau* 172 (December 1917): 373–82.

Schultze, Maximilian. *Standhaft und Treu. Carl von Röder und seine Brüder in Preussens Kämpfen von 1806–1815.* Berlin: Ernst Siegfried Mittler und Sohn, 1912.

Schütze, Bettina. "Neue Informationen zur Exhumierung." *Volksstimme Burg*, 08 September, 2014.

Schütze, Bettina. "Reise nach Wroslaw gibt Aufschuss über den Friedhof." *Volksstimme Burg*, 30 October 2014.

Staël-Holstein, Anne Louise Germaine de. *Germany.* Vol 1. New York: Derby & Jackson, 1859.

Stoker, Donald. *Clausewitz. His Life and Work*. New York: Oxford University Press, 2014.

Strachan, Hew. *Clausewitz's On War. A Biography*. New York: Atlantic Monthly Press, 2007.

Wallach, Yehuda L. *The Dogma of the Battle of Annihilation: Theories of Clausewitz and Schlieffen and Their Iimpact on the German Conduct of Two World Wars*. Westport, CT: Greenwood Publishing, 1986.

Wehler, Hans-Ulrich. *Deutsche Gesellschaftsgeschichte*. Vol. 1. Munich: C. H. Beck Verlag, 1987.

Weppermann, Leonie. *Prinzessin Marianne von Preußen, geborene Prinzessin von Hessen-Homburg in den Jahren 1804–1808: Beiträge zu ihrer Lebensgeschichte mit besonderer Berücksichtigung ihrer politischen Stellungnahme*. Bonn: Anton Brand, 1942.

Wilhelmy, Petra. *Der Berliner Salon im 19. Jahhundert: 1780–1914*. Berlin: De Gruyter, 1989.

Index